RESPONDIN

Dispossession, Colonial Violence, and Resistance
among Indigenous and Racialized Women

Responding to Human Trafficking is the first book to critically examine responses to the growing issue of human trafficking in Canada. Julie Kaye challenges the separation of trafficking debates into international versus domestic emphases and explores the tangled ways in which anti-trafficking policies reflect and reinforce the settler-colonial nation-building project of Canada. By placing existing discussions of human trafficking in Canada under scrutiny, including representations of trafficked persons from the perspective of frontline workers, government officials, law enforcement, and formerly trafficked persons, Kaye reveals how some anti-trafficking measures in fact create additional harms for the individuals they are trying to protect, particularly migrant and Indigenous women.

Drawing on theories of post- and settler-colonialism and Indigenous feminist thought, as well as data gathered from fifty-six one-on-one interviews with people in counter-trafficking employment across Western Canada, the book provides a new framework for critical analyses of anti-trafficking and other rights-based and anti-violence interventions. Kaye disrupts measures that contribute to the insecurity experienced by trafficked women and individuals affected by anti-trafficking responses by pointing to anti-colonial organizing and the possibilities of reciprocity in relationships of care.

JULIE KAYE is an assistant professor in the Department of Sociology at the University of Saskatchewan.

JULIE KAYE

Responding to Human Trafficking

Dispossession, Colonial Violence, and Resistance among Indigenous and Racialized Women

UNIVERSITY OF TORONTO PRESS
Toronto Buffalo London

© University of Toronto Press 2017
Toronto Buffalo London
www.utppublishing.com
Printed in Canada

ISBN 978-1-4875-0174-7 (cloth)   ISBN 978-1-4875-2161-5 (paper)

Library and Archives Canada Cataloguing in Publication

Kaye, Julie, 1980–, author
Responding to human trafficking : dispossession, colonial violence,
and resistance among Indigenous and racialized women / Julie Kaye.

Includes bibliographical references and index.
ISBN 978-1-4875-0174-7 (hardcover). – ISBN 978-1-4875-2161-5 (softcover)

1. Human trafficking – Canada.   2. Human trafficking – Law and
legislation – Canada.   3. Human trafficking victims – Canada – Social
conditions.   4. Human trafficking – Social aspects – Canada.   5. Human
trafficking – Canada – Prevention.   6. Colonization – Social
aspects.   7. Postcolonialism – Social aspects.   I. Title.

HQ281.K39 2017   364.15′510971   C2017-902109-5

This book has been published with the help of a grant from the Federation
for the Humanities and Social Sciences, through the Awards to Scholarly
Publications Program, using funds provided by the Social Sciences and
Humanities Research Council of Canada.

University of Toronto Press acknowledges the financial assistance to its
publishing program of the Canada Council for the Arts and the Ontario
Arts Council, an agency of the Government of Ontario.

Canada Council for the Arts   Conseil des Arts du Canada

ONTARIO ARTS COUNCIL
CONSEIL DES ARTS DE L'ONTARIO
an Ontario government agency
un organisme du gouvernement de l'Ontario

Funded by the Government of Canada   Financé par le gouvernement du Canada

Dedicated to Aywahande, the one who starts things with words.

Contents

Foreword

SARAH HUNT

As the 150th anniversary of Canada led to a resurgence of nationalistic pride, I found myself reflecting on the networks of resistance that have ensured Indigenous peoples survival in the face of fifteen decades of settler colonial expansion. While some might think of large-scale struggles over Indigenous lands, waters, and resources, what comes to mind for me are the more intimate struggles for self-determination, which have unfolded within and among the bodies and homes of our loved ones. My generation of Indigenous activists have benefited from the genealogies of resistance our ancestors have passed on to us, as they fought to retain sovereignty over the care and education of their children; the well-being, safety, and sacredness of their own bodies; and the deep and longstanding relationships they held with the land, water, animals, and ancestors that comprise our culturally distinct ways of being. Indeed, self-determination over our bodies and lands has always been interconnected, as it is through embodied land-based practices that we define ourselves as peoples. As Kwakwaka'wakw and Tlingit, I aim to navigate my relationship with the Canadian state in ways that honour my ancestors before me – people whose very being was defined by relations of reciprocity that have been nurtured within our territories since time immemorial. In the face of government efforts to criminalize the potlatch, steal our sacred cultural belongings, uproot us onto reserves, and institutionalize our children in a variety of ways, I have no doubt about the strength of my ancestors' resolve. If they weren't strong people, I wouldn't be here today.

Yet this strength, sense of survival, and insistence on self-determination over our bodies and lands are rarely reflected in the predominant stories we hear about Indigenous peoples, particularly women.

Beyond the walls of our homes, our ceremonial spaces, and our sites of governance and cultural practice, the stories Canadians hear about Indigenous lives are defined not by our strength but by our vulnerability. The term "at risk" is so readily applied to Indigenous peoples – especially children, youth, women, and Two-Spirit people – it has become a common-sense phrase to signal the natural conditions of contemporary Indigenous life in Canada. These narratives of risk have overwhelmingly provided the foundational terms in which violence against our loved ones has been addressed in this country, particularly over the past several decades as the murders of hundreds of Indigenous women and girls (and Two-Spirit people, though these stories have only received marginal attention) have come into public consciousness.

In the pages that follow, Julie Kaye powerfully traces diverse ways in which anti-trafficking discourses are materialized in frontline work, public policy, and individual treatment of people deemed to have been "trafficked" but I want to preface this important intervention by highlighting the contentious, diverse, and often adversarial relationships Indigenous peoples have with both "whitestream" (Grande 2003) feminism and Canadian legal approaches to ending violence. The analysis in this book invites conversation about both the possibilities and the harms of anti-violence strategies, as we seek respite from the ongoing, everyday, embodied violence of settler colonialism. Yet, as the interviews in this book demonstrate, anti-violence efforts often constitute a site of harm through Indigenous peoples' pathologization, incarceration, criminalization, and apprehension into state regimes of child "welfare." Thus, it is important to ask how violence is defined, how justice is envisioned, and who gets to define the two within the current dynamics of replicating and resisting settler colonialism in Canada.

Among the Indigenous anti-violence advocates I have worked with, the mobilization of human trafficking discourses has emerged within the desperate circumstances of trying to make Indigenous lives matter to settler colonial systems predicated on our dehumanization. For decades, Indigenous people in diverse places and circumstances have been working to address conditions of exploitation, coercion, abuse, and violation. Yet in the face of ongoing systemic and societal indifference to Indigenous suffering, the laws, policies, and funding associated with the state's increased investment in anti-trafficking have been taken up in the hopes that this new strategy will lead to the kinds of swift and widespread justice that have failed to otherwise materialize.

Indeed, long before government representatives, feminist advocates, or scholars recognized the phenomenon of "missing and murdered Indigenous women," and long before it became a site of national and international concern, the family members and friends of women who had been killed or disappeared struggled to make violence against Indigenous women matter enough to trigger a widespread response. On the ground, diverse tactics such as protests, marches, memorials, petitions, fliers, community reports and lobbying were used in an effort to make Indigenous lives visible in terms that "mattered" to state systems of justice. It is within this context that the discourse of human trafficking has come into popular use in Canada.

My own introduction to anti-trafficking discourses and initiatives was through the work of Global Alliance Against Traffic in Women (GAATW)–Canada, which was founded in the late 1990s. At the early international meetings I attended, the trafficking of Indigenous girls and women within or from Canada was rarely mentioned. Indeed, in trainings we organized for police, border guards, immigration specialists, and frontline workers at that time, trafficking of Indigenous girls was simply not a consideration. As I have observed elsewhere (Hunt 2010, 2016), it was in the wake of increasing awareness about missing and murdered women due the trial of mass-murderer Robert Pickton that trafficking came to be conflated with trading and selling sex, as well as with murder, disappearance, and violence against Indigenous women in general.

The increased use of anti-trafficking approaches have gone hand-in-hand with condemnation of Indigenous women's involvement in sex work, with the Pickton case held up as proof that trading and selling sex is inherently violent. This narrative has pushed out of view the fact that sex workers in Vancouver's Downtown Eastside, both Indigenous and non-Indigenous, were integral to the advocacy efforts that resulted in Pickton's conviction as well as efforts to reform negligent police practices that allowed this violence to be overlooked for more than a decade. Further, the conflation of sex work with human trafficking has reproduced racialized and gendered notions of "good" and "bad" women, as sex workers' voices have been pushed to the margins of national anti-violence efforts. As discussed in Kaye's research, these divisive dynamics have resulted in services and resources being provided for those women (and, to a lesser extent, men, trans, and Two-Spirit people) who want to be "rescued" from the sex trade by identifying with the trafficking narrative. I am well aware that coercion, force, and violence have long been a reality for some of our relations who trade and sell sex—it is these very realities that have driven my anti-violence work. But these same conditions were resisted for decades before the framework of human trafficking was introduced, so we must consider whether anti-trafficking efforts actually result in decreased violence or whether they inadvertently lead to additional kinds of harm.

As recognition of this violence has grown among state actors and the Canadian public, stories of violence against Indigenous women have been repeated in media reports, scholarly books, movies, and art, which have collectively brought the most extreme forms of sexual and physical violence to light in a sustained way. While we are more able to name this violence today than we were twenty years ago, increased visibility has failed to stop the violence itself. Moreover, the story of "the missing and murdered" is often told through a singular narrative in which Indigenous women are defined solely by their victimization. Evidence of this can be seen in the 2014 Royal Canadian Mounted Police (RCMP) report, which made public, for the first time, the cases of 1,181 Indigenous women who disappeared or were killed over a thirty-year timeframe. Although popularly referred to as "missing and murdered Indigenous women," the statistics clearly show that the majority of these women (1,017) were in fact murdered, while a much smaller number (164) had disappeared. Pinpointing sources of risk, the RCMP identified the women's own "risky behaviour" (drug and alcohol use, sex work involvement, and unemployment) rather than locating the source of risk within the behaviours and trends of those who killed or abducted them. Also out of view in this report were systemic risk factors, such as involvement in child welfare, attendance in residential school, previous incarceration, or displacement from home community due to resource extraction, urbanization, or development. This story of "missing women," told by the RCMP and echoed by many First Nations and Canadian leaders, as well as women's rights advocates internationally, has indeed brought attention to issues of violence against Native women, but, in the process, has reproduced the foundational myths upon which this country was founded. A key feature of this national myth is the portrayal of state actors and well-meaning Canadian citizens stepping in to save and protect vulnerable Indigenous women.

Indigenous women have long known that the myth of the colonial state as benevolent, as good, as neutral, as "caring" is just that – a myth. Moreover, we have known this narrative to be a lie. Residential schools were established in the name of "saving" Indigenous children, and were run by teachers, missionaries, and administrators, many of whom believed in the altruism of their civilizing mission. In the lands now called British Columbia, where my ancestors have lived since time immemorial, Indian reserves were set up to civilize Indigenous communities "for our own good." We know that these stories of so-called benevolence, alongside other colonial narratives of native savagery and white civility, have been established to hide the true motivation for these and other state interventions into our lives: the imposition and maintenance of Canadian claims to Indigenous territories. Yet in the absence of alternative mechanisms of justice through which to end the onslaught of brutality against our loved ones, engagement with the state is often strategically sought in order to try to address our most immediate needs.

I worked for many years in this capacity, as a contractor with provincial and federal agencies, thinking that if only I could reform these state systems, if I could make them work more effectively for Indigenous families and communities, I might be able to help improve the quality of life of our loved ones. And, indeed, many Indigenous people continue to work strategically within state agencies in order to lessen the harm, to try to change the systems and put their resources to work more effectively. We often do this work out of desperation, as, despite the unfolding efforts of the national inquiry into missing and murdered Indigenous women, stories of disappearance and death are a weekly, if not daily, reality. Yet working within state systems has also reaffirmed for me the harms caused by state surveillance of, and intervention into, our homes and families, as following the mundane everyday practices of upholding Canadian law can simultaneously be precisely how justice and rights are denied for Native people. As you will see in Kaye's rigorous analysis, far from upholding the self-determination of Indigenous people, anti-trafficking frameworks have the effect of deepening the "snare" (Christie 2007) that is our relationship with Canadian law, which overwhelmingly criminalizes us rather than seeks justice on our behalf.

In efforts to decolonize our lives and relations, we must accept that decolonization is not about saving anyone. Ultimately, Indigenous women, girls, and Two-Spirit people – indeed, our relations of all genders – don't need saving or healing. We need the dismantling of oppressive systems that create conditions from which we need to heal. We need to be recognized and affirmed as the subjects of our own long-standing relations, as having authority over our bodies, our lives, our lands, and our legacies. Unravelling the logics of settler colonialism is ultimately a project in redefining whose lives and deaths matter, and on whose terms. Efforts to end violence can be characterized as decolonizing only when our lives and lands come to matter in terms we deem recognizable to our ancestors.

It is my hope that *Responding to Human Trafficking: Dispossession, Decolonial Violence, and Resistance among Indigenous and Racialized Women* strengthens solidarities between Indigenous movements for sexual and reproductive justice and movements for the freedom and safety of migrants the world over – many of whom are themselves Indigenous people who have been violently displaced by imperial expansion. In Canada, these solidarities are vital for resisting hetero-patriarchal and racist violence that continues to shape everyday lives in Canada as a continuation of the colonial narratives through which Canada was founded. Kaye's research helps us to see that rather than upholding the humanity and dignity of Indigenous and racialized peoples, anti-trafficking discourses often contribute to the network of strategies that strengthen state sovereignty, closing down borders to people deemed unworthy or unwanted in Canada and solidifying its claim to Indigenous lands, resources, and lives. In particular, this book demonstrates that without the voices of those people in whose name we seek to end human trafficking – migrant workers, exotic dancers, people who trade and sell sex, live-in caregivers – efforts to end violence will fail. As Indigenous people who trade and sell sex have consistently and clearly stated (INCITE! 2011; JJ 2013; Indigenous Sex Sovereignty Collective 2015), affirming their self-determination means putting their voices at the centre, asking what support or help looks like for them, and affirming their rights to mobility – to use their bodies however they choose and to name their experiences. Pushing past divisive arguments about the legal status of sex work, efforts to address violence and exploitation should instead focus on the personal well-being of sex workers and others whose lives are put at risk by state-created precarity in the current context of settler colonialism. Only then can we uphold the genealogies of resistance passed on to us by our ancestors.

References

Christie, Gordon. 2007. Culture, Self-Determination and Colonialism: Issues around the revitalization of Indigenous legal traditions. Indigenous Law Journal 6 (1): 13–29.

Grande, Sandy. 2003. Whitestream Feminism and the Colonialist Project: A Review of Contemporary Feminist Pedagogy and Praxis. Educational Theory 53 (3): 329–46.

Hunt, Sarah. 2010. Colonial Roots, Contemporary Risk Factors: A Cautionary Exploration of the Domestic Trafficking of Aboriginal Women and Girls in British Columbia, Canada. Alliance News 33: 27–31.

Hunt, Sarah. 2016. Representing Colonial Violence: Trafficking, Sex Work, and the Violence of Law. Atlantis 37.2 (1): 25–39.

INCITE! 2011. "Indigenous Peoples in the Sex Trade: Speaking for Ourselves," blog entry by the National Youth Sexual Health Network, July 15. http://inciteblog.wordpress.com/2011/07/15/indigenous-peoples-in-the-sex-trade-%E2%80%93-speaking-for-ourselves.

Indigenous Sex Sovereignty Collective. 2015. "Centering the Voices of People Who Trade or Sell Sex in Indigenous Anti-violence Organizing," blog entry by the Indigenous Sex Sovereignty Collective, February 26. http://indigenoussexsovereignty.tumblr.com.

JJ. 2013. "We Speak For Ourselves: Anti-Colonial and Self-Determined Responses to Young People Involved in the Sex Trade." In Selling Sex: Experience, Advocacy and Research on Sex Work in Canada, ed. Emily van der Meulen, Elya M. Durisin, and Victoria Love, 74–81. Vancouver: UBC Press.

Royal Canadian Mounted Police (RCMP). 2014. Missing and Murdered Aboriginal Women: An Operational Overview. Ottawa, ON: RCMP. http://www.rcmp-grc.gc.ca/en/missing-and-murdered-aboriginal-women-national-operational-overview

Preface and Acknowledgments

Drawing on some early formative training in qualitative research, each semester I explain to my students that good research and writing must have the ability to fail. While I will leave it to the reader to decide whether this book is well written, I do know that this manuscript went through many revisions as the process unfolded, some of which – by my estimation – failed. Through these failures, and through the ongoing effort to question anti-trafficking response in light of settler colonialism in Canada, this research was able to take shape. Because of these continuous changes, the writing comes to you in a markedly different form than its initial conception. I am deeply thankful to my editor, Douglas Hildebrand at University of Toronto Press, who believed in this project and provided innumerable support throughout the publication process. I am also thankful to the anonymous peer reviewers for their enthusiasm and constructive critique. Their insights enabled me to bring the central arguments of this work into focus, especially the tangled ways in which anti-trafficking provides a site from which to examine the settler-colonial nation-building project of Canada.

This book is informed by years of work in social service agencies, directly and indirectly in critical response to human trafficking. My involvement in community-based research with individuals connected to the sex industry, and my time spent studying critical feminist sociology of development, policy, and criminology also helped shape the narrative. Such perspectives, including the ones inherent to me as an academic and as a settler, helped me to recognize that colonialism in Canada and efforts of dispossession extend beyond legacies, necessitating explicit engagement with ongoing processes of settler colonialism.

By referring to myself as settler, I do not simply mean non-Indigenous. To the best of my family's knowledge, my own ancestry is Scottish and British.[1] My ancestors settled in Canada during a time of rapid colonial expansion in the early twentieth century. With the exception of my paternal grandmother, who was born in Edinburgh, my grandparents were all born in Canada. Two of my grandparents were born in Toronto, Ontario, and one was born in Radville, Saskatchewan. Both my parents were born in Toronto, where many of my relations continue to reside. However, my parents eventually settled in Calgary – on the territory of the Niitsitapi, Nakoda and Tsuut'ina (Treaty 7 Territory) – in 1976, where I was born and raised. Like many non-Indigenous people living in a settler colonial nation like Canada, my life is interwoven with the first people of this land. I married into family who resisted and were displaced by colonial policies aimed at assimilation and eradication, I have also given birth to children, born in Misâskwatôminih, Kisiskâciwan (Saskatoon, Saskatchewan, situated on Treaty 6 territory and the homeland of the Métis), whose relations survived colonial dispossession. In this, my spirit is intertwined with my life partner's Cree, Métis, and Chinese families, including his Chinese grandfather and a grandmother born to Cree (paternal) and Métis (maternal) parents who married with his Norwegian ancestors. Narratives of colonial domination and colonial resistance are embodied in our relations. In this, we are particularly thankful to our Cree and Métis family and friends that embrace us – both individually and together – and teach us in spite of years of familial and colonial dislocation.

As a settler, I am also someone who benefits from the privileges of colonial dispossession, necessitating continuous reflection of how I benefit from ongoing settler colonial relations even while critiquing and working towards anticolonial and transformative change. Here, I am particularly grateful to my former mentor and friend, Trisha Monture. The enormous spaces left in the fields of sociology, Indigenous studies, Indigenous feminist theory, and law by the loss of Professor Monture have been felt at every turn of this project. This work began in conversation with her and I cannot count the times I wished I could sit with her again and work through these ideas. I am honoured to have sat with her at all, and I am thankful my conversations with her continue in her physical absence. Her arm of resistance will not be put down and her thundering voice will continue to echo through generations of research and resistance. I am also indebted to postcolonial mentors and friends, especially the kind support of Patience Elabor-Idemudia.

I have been challenged by many incredible writers and thinkers, and I am especially indebted to Sarah Hunt whose work ethic inspires and encourages me on a continual basis. Decolonial love rages with kindness. I am also thankful to many other critical thinkers who paved the way for this conversation, including, but not limited to, Leslie Ann Jeffrey, Gayle MacDonald, Emily van der Meulen, Deborah Brock, and others. I know and work with many incredible colleagues and friends in the community who, perhaps unknowingly, encouraged this project to completion.

Critical approaches such as these are central to the examination of human trafficking undertaken in this book. By providing an academic contribution to settler colonial theorizing on ongoing colonial gender violence, the book aims to provide a productive space to question the way settler colonialism operates and reproduces itself through rights-based endeavours. In this, I begin from the premise that rights-based interventions are simultaneously a source of resistance and oppression; of help and hindrance; with the capacity to draw attention to the necessity of social change, while also reproducing the ongoing conditions of colonial dispossession and restricting efforts to dismantle settler colonialism. As Jodi Byrd (2011: xvii) identifies, a "cacophony of competing struggles" and rights-based claims provide important challenges to the nation-building project of settler colonialism, while also serving to "misdirect and cloud attention from the underlying structures of settler colonialism" that reproduce the conditions in which varying forms of violence, including human trafficking, emerge. It is my hope this critical intervention will serve as a valuable theoretical and empirical resource for students, researchers, policymakers, and advocates working in areas that intersect with human trafficking, sex work, migration, social boundaries, development, securitization, policy, and critical criminology, gender studies, and anticolonial thought. My gratitude also extends to Jill Hanley, Daniel Béland, Pamela Downe, Jen Budney, Andrea Burkhart, and Lara Quarterman who all read and provided feedback on previous iterations of this work.

This book was written while I transitioned across three institutions to my academic home at the University of Saskatchewan. I am thankful to Ambrose University, King's University, and the University of Saskatchewan for the kind support and space that enabled me to bring this project to completion. The research informing this book was supported by the Social Science and Humanities Research Council of Canada and this book has been published with the help of a grant from the Federation for the Humanities and Social Sciences, through the Awards to Scholarly Publications Program, using funds provided by the Social Sciences and Humanities Research Council of Canada.

To my children: I am in no position to determine whether this book and the words therein are worth the absences from you they required. I will leave that to time and to your good judgment to assess. But know that you entered the world gently because incredible women empowered me to root what I do – birth, mother, play, love, work, teach, research, and write – in loving accountability, and because your dad, my incredible life partner, also learned from these women how to support me in all my labours. We do things together, this book included. I am thankful for the network of familial love and friendship that cares for and upholds us; for grandparents who stepped in and grounded us in love when we were apart. This book would never have reached completion without them. My gratitude extends to your Great-Aunties who risked imprisonment to pass knowledge on to their daughters, our Aunties. Like so many keepers of Indigenous knowledges, their resistance paved the way for your existence and allows us to have the many conversations we have today. You and the wide circle of children in our lives restore my hope for transformative change. With you, I hope and work for different ways of knowing and being.

Acronyms

ACT	Action Coalition on Human Trafficking
BCOCTIP	British Columbia Office to Combat Trafficking In Persons
CATW	Coalition Against Trafficking in Women
CBC	Canadian Broadcasting Corporation
CBSA	Canada Border Services Agency
CCJR	Centre for Criminology and Justice Research
CEDAW	Convention on the Elimination of All Forms of Discrimination Against Women
CIC	Citizenship and Immigration Canada
CIDA	Canadian International Development Agency
CNOP	Calgary Network on Prostitution
CTV	Canadian Television
DFAIT	Department of Foreign Affairs and International Trade
GAATW	Global Alliance Against Traffic in Women
HRC	Human Rights Caucus
ILO	International Labour Organization
IOM	International Organization on Migration
IRPA	Immigration and Refugee Protection Act
IWGTIP	Interdepartmental Working Group on Trafficking in Persons
LCP	Live-in Caregiver Program
LTTE	Liberation of Tamil Eelam (Tamil Tigers)
NAPCHT	National Action Plan to Combat Human Trafficking in Canada
NGO	Nongovernment Organization
NSWP	Network of Sex Work Projects
NWAC	Native Women's Association of Canada
OAS	Organization of American States

PRRA   Pre-removal Risk Assessment
RCMP   Royal Canadian Mounted Police
SAWP   Seasonal Agricultural Worker Program
SWC   Status of Women Canada
TFW   Temporary Foreign Worker
TIP   Trafficking in Persons
TRP   Temporary Resident Permit
UNDESA   United Nations Department of Economic and Social
           Affairs
UNDP   United Nations Development Program
UNHCR   United Nations High Commissioner for Refugees
UNODC   United Nations Office on Drug and Crime

RESPONDING TO HUMAN TRAFFICKING

Dispossession, Colonial Violence, and Resistance
among Indigenous and Racialized Women

Introduction

Once upon a time there was a child who was willful, and would not do as her mother wished.

> – Grimm and Grimm 1884: 125, as cited in Ahmed 2014: 1

Responses to human trafficking have steadily increased since the mid-1990s; over the past decade, Canada has allocated resources for developing national anti-trafficking strategies. In 2012, the Government of Canada, under the leadership of Steven Harper, former prime minister of Canada, dedicated $25 million to the National Action Plan to Combat Human Trafficking (NAPCHT), a significant portion of which is directed towards criminal justice–based initiatives.[1] The Canadian Women's Foundation (CWF), which claims to take "a lead on ending the trafficking of girls and women for the purpose of sexual exploitation," invested $2 million in 2012–2013 towards anti-trafficking grants and a National Task Force on Sex Trafficking of Women and Girls in Canada (CWF 2013). Other national anti-trafficking initiatives have been developed by groups as diverse as the Evangelical Fellowship of Canada (EFC), the Canadian Council of Refugees (CCR), the Global Alliance Against Trafficking in Women (GAATW) Canada, the Chrysalis Anti-Human Trafficking Network, Defend Dignity, the Salvation Army, and others.

Clearly, human trafficking has become an important political priority for lobbyists and special interest groups from a variety of perspectives. Yet, as Sanghera (2005: 21) highlights, "overenthusiastic responses" to human trafficking generally neglect the highly politicized nature of anti-trafficking discourses. As this book will demonstrate, in a context of settler colonialism, Canadian anti-trafficking responses and other anti-violence initiatives reproduce structures of domination more often than addressing ongoing forms of dispossession that continue to naturalize inequalities and produce contexts in which trafficking and varying forms of violence occur.

The concept of settler colonialism remains debated in the literature, and the characteristics shaping the hierarchy of settler colonial domination are contested. Some argue that settler colonial relations are structured by race (Razack 2002), while others focus on economic, political, or gendered forms of domination. Glen Coulthard (2014: 6–7), member of the Yellowknives Dene First Nation, specifically defines settler colonialism as "structured dispossession" whereby domination stems from each of these interrelated forms of power:

> A settler colonial relationship is one characterized by a particular form of *domination*; that is, it is a relationship where power – in this case, interrelated discursive and nondiscursive facets of economic, gendered, racial, and state power – has been structured into a relatively secure or sedimented set of hierarchical social relations that continue to facilitate the *dispossession* of Indigenous peoples of their lands and self-determining authority. In this respect, Canada is no different from most other settler colonial powers: in the Canadian context, colonial domination continues to be structurally committed to maintain – through force, fraud, and more recently, so-called "negotiations" – ongoing state access to the land and resources that contradictorily provide the material and spiritual sustenance of Indigenous societies on the on hand, and the foundation of colonial state-formation, settlement, and capitalist development on the other.

Significant for the aims of this book, the nation-building project of Canada was premised on "force," "fraud," and manipulation (sometimes resembling "negotiations") – precisely the activities underpinning human trafficking.[2] In the words of Kwakwaka'wakw scholar, Sarah Hunt (2008: 1), "Aboriginal people's relation to trafficking is as long as our history of colonial contact." While anti-trafficking advocacy is quick to condemn state complicity in countries *over there*, there is little contextual understanding of the role Canada plays in shaping and reproducing the conditions in which trafficking experiences and anti-trafficking responses are negotiated.

This book specifically problematizes discourses of human trafficking in Canada by challenging the separation of trafficking debates into *international* versus *domestic* spheres. Government and nongovernment anti-trafficking awareness materials characterize internal or domestic trafficking as that which occurs within the borders of Canada; international trafficking is defined by the crossing of borders into the Canadian nation-state. Despite early emphasis on international responses to human trafficking, the Government of Canada suggests that 90 per cent of cases of trafficking are domestic. But in a context of settler colonialism, what are the implications of representing specific subjects as internal or domestic as opposed to international or global? Indigenous[3] women, in particular, are frequently represented as being at risk for domestic trafficking – what does it mean to specifically portray Indigenous women as *at risk* and as *domestic*? What does it mean to be internationally trafficked? What are the implications of categorizing certain bodies, especially racialized women, as international in a settler colonial context?

Beyond formulating a mere corrective to anti-trafficking representations, this book draws on critical development perspectives to question the frameworks that enable anti-trafficking responses to provide "recognition and aid" even as they "also inflict their own forms of violence" (Hua 2011: viii). As Coulthard (2014) noted while discussing his book *Red Skin, White Masks*,[4] violence against Indigenous women informs many claims for recognition in Canada that, in turn, reinforce the power of the settler colonial state, reify the state as saviour, and undermine alternatives to state mechanisms of justice.[5] However, as Sarah Hunt (2014) corrects, "although we might agree with the rejection of recognition politics ... the lives of many Indigenous people remain bound up in state systems, both ideologically and material, [and as] such they cannot just simply turn away from them." In doing so, Hunt reinforces the need to strategically navigate state systems towards recognition of ongoing forms of dispossession – "the invasion of Indigenous women's bodies, the theft of [Indigenous] children, and locking [Indigenous women] up in prisons" – while also working and imagining alternative models of justice. It is in this context that solidarities among those affected by structural violence exist; however, far from enabling the mobilization of such supports, anti-trafficking and other anti-violence organizing often continues to reproduce systems of structural and material domination that impede the ongoing resistance of marginalized communities.

Situating human trafficking in the context of settler colonial domination, this book examines representations of trafficked persons, especially women,[6] in anti-trafficking discourses. Because anti-trafficking discourses form the subject of this critical analysis and such discourses are dominated by conversations about violence against women, the book prioritizes women in its analysis. However, this emphasis should be read within the broader structural context of heteropatriarchy that conceals multidimensional conceptions of gender and troubles gender binaries. In particular, erased almost entirely from anti-trafficking discourses are the experiences of Two-Spirit, trans, and male sex workers and migrants, as well as other individuals who disrupt colonial-imposed gender binaries. Despite discursive erasure, individuals facing gendered and racialized forms of oppression are directly affected by the implications of anti-trafficking. Thus, the focus on women in this analysis is not intended to participate in the complicity of this erasure; rather, the aim of this emphasis is to redirect "the immense attention that human trafficking has received" away from "defining and deciphering the proper individual victim" towards the conditions in which such identification reproduces structural and material forms of inequality and ongoing oppression (Suchland 2015: 5). This includes an examination of the perceptions and experiences of individuals who work directly with trafficked individuals as well as trafficked persons[7] and individuals affected by Canadian anti-trafficking responses. By problematizing the discursive practices that isolate trafficking discussions into categories of international versus internal, this book aims to disrupt the dialogue about human trafficking in the country and critically examine government and nongovernment policies and strategies designed to respond to the rights of trafficked persons while reproducing the structural and material context in which trafficking emerges. By disrupting such discursive practices, the book in no way aims to erase the very real violences experienced on a day-to-day basis; rather, the goal is to situate such violence within the ongoing conditions that facilitate its reproduction.

These questions and arguments are primarily informed by an analysis of fifty-six one-on-one conversational interviews, three group interviews, and two focus groups in which I engaged people who were directly involved in anti-trafficking work or in areas affected by anti-trafficking discourses and responses. This includes frontline workers, some formerly trafficked persons, individuals working in sex industries, government officials, nongovernment representatives, and law enforcement representatives in Vancouver, Calgary, and Winnipeg. By engaging and critically analysing responses to human trafficking, this work unsettles anti-trafficking, anti-violence, and other rights-based discourses with the aim of spurring alternate possibilities that disrupt the continuation of violence in spite of ongoing interventions. Because I am not a dispassionate observer of anti-trafficking work, my own experiences with anti-trafficking responses, in addition to formal field research, inform the structure and audience of this work. My experiences in this area are varied, as I have both participated in and critically questioned the role of anti-trafficking and related rights-based and social justice efforts. This positioning necessitates that I hold an empathetic and compassionate understanding of violences experienced on a daily basis without collapsing such experiences into my own or simplifying complex histories (Dean 2015), while also grappling with how such compassion and associated responses can co-exist with, and reinforce, the ongoing oppressions of settler colonial gender violence.[8] This affects my relationships with people who have experienced human trafficking and my efforts to provide critical services in response to their experiences, and encourages me to reflexively consider the many ways anti-trafficking and other rights-based interventions uphold and create continued harms. These experiences then also include hearing and seeing the fear of frontline workers and peer support providers who stand up to dominant viewpoints to provide services to people the law wishes to vanish, such as safe spaces for Indigenous and Two-Spirit persons involved in sex industries, undocumented or precarious status migrants, and harm reduction. In these spaces, I repeatedly heard the expressed fear that even articulating dissent would lead to the removal of funding, livelihoods, and the ability to provide alternate service models. I would then visit abolition-awareness venues – where trafficking is typically conflated with sexualized forms of labour – only to hear funders gloat, "we're so lucky, we don't have to deal with *such debates*. If someone tries to rise up [with opposing views], we just pull their funding." "Such debates" centre on polarized divisions between those who call for abolishing sex work and those who advance the rights of individuals in sex industries to safety, security, and self-determination. Although both standpoints consider themselves marginalized in the wider context of neoliberal Canadian discourse, the abolitionist perspective remains dominant within anti-trafficking discourse and has actively shaped the settler colonial nation-building project. Certain of the dominant abolitionist stance, funders can crassly discuss the overt disciplining and silencing of alternate perceptions. Beyond funding, this silencing occurs too when response strategies are formed with a refusal to consider trafficked persons as anything other than victims of crime. As a result, law enforcement measures are employed while systemic and sociological factors are ignored.

This book is also informed by the reality that even when awareness efforts move beyond the sensational and provide an education, such education too often stops short of acknowledging ongoing resistance or imagining transformation. Individuals in positions of power come to understand the limits and harms of a criminalization-centred model, only to state, "that makes a lot of sense, but there's no way my board/funders/constituents will go for that." In spite of positions of relative privilege, the default stance of these individuals falls short of resisting dominant structures that perpetuate harm. Similarly, policymakers charged with establishing anti-trafficking responses demonstrate an inability to reflexively consider the politicized nature of trafficking discussions, expressing surprise and disdain towards advocates that politicize efforts framed – and perhaps intended – as humanitarian assistance. When interveners come to see the limits of rights-based frameworks in contexts of systemic inequality, many continue to reproduce such frameworks in the name of neutrality: "we don't take a stance." Although I have great respect for those who aim to build inclusive spaces so that conversation and mutual understanding can occur, in a context of structural and material violence and inequality, there are limited possibilities for apolitical responses and efforts to depoliticize too frequently reinforce conditions of colonial dispossession.

I have received numerous requests from social justice, faith-based, and church groups that want to raise awareness about human trafficking, but that qualify their endeavours with unreflexive disclaimers that such a popular and important issue will re-legitimize their role in the eyes of *civil* society precisely because it can bring so many traditionally opposed agendas together. Human trafficking, in this space, serves as an opportunity for social conservatives and progressives to share the pews: A space "where right-wing religious men have joined the radical feminist campaign" (Jeffrey 2005: 40; Bernstein 2010) alongside liberal and progressive Canadians to hear the voices of Victor Malarek, Nickolas Kristof, and Benjamin Perrin, among others, proclaim a unifying mission of rescuing the enslaved (in the dark world over there) and abolishing sex industries (in our own backyard).

Doezema (2010: 172) argues that such unifying representations of rescue are precisely why the myth of trafficking is so powerful: "because it expresses the convictions of many different, and even opposed, social groups." Yet, as Nigerian novelist Chimamanda Adichie discusses, presenting complex narratives as single stories is especially dangerous because single stories "leave no possibility of feelings more complex than pity" (Adichie 2009). She goes on to say, "it is impossible to talk about the single story without talking about power ... How they are told, who tells them, when they're told, how many stories are told, are really dependent on power." By presenting people as "unable to speak for themselves and waiting to be saved"[9] anti-trafficking representations reproduce cycles of dehumanization and objectification. In turn, such dehumanization reinforces stigma and criminalization.

Thus, anti-trafficking discourses are used to justify and naturalize dominant approaches to national security and migrant rights, especially policy recommendations advocating for stricter border controls. They are similarly employed to formulate and advance anti–sex work laws that have little to do with human trafficking and that negatively affect individuals involved in sex industries. This book emphasizes that such bandwagon responses to violence reproduce the very structures and psyche that underpin the violence in the first place. After each emotional meeting, commitments to reinforce state powers are established and vows to abolish the sex trade – and, implicitly, sex trade workers – are affirmed. The identity of the rescue–saviour remains firmly intact and civility unscathed, while racist structures persist: women go missing, are murdered, and are disappeared through targeted violence, then criminalized, disciplined, and silenced by their self-purported saviours.

Yet, such decontextualized approaches to anti-trafficking have undeniably captured the social justice imagination, to such an extent that overt reproductions of sensationalized images advanced in anti-trafficking campaigns have become a spectacle in their ability to capture the settler colonial gaze. Spectacle, according to Toni Morrison (1997) "is the best means by which an official story is formed and is a superior mechanism for guaranteeing its longevity."[10] Despite bringing attention to "recurring humanitarian crises," anti-trafficking maintains a restrictive emphasis on "subjective violence – an outward violence that is symptomatic of an underlying structural violence, which the spectacle conveniently obscures" (Kapoor 2013: 115). Million (2013) further outlines that settler societies often position Indigenous suffering, in particular, as a *spectacle* based on the assumption that such suffering is inescapable and unending (i.e., natural).[11] At the same time, racialized migrants are constructed as potential threats to civilization and as projects of rescue, domestication, and assimilation.

In such a context, and as this book will trace, anti-trafficking has featured prominently in the nation-building project of Canada and the formulation of responses to trafficking has contributed to the production of settler identities.

Meanwhile, when faced with such ongoing forms of oppression, *willful subjects* continue to contest the imposition of rescue efforts that restrict their lives, security, safety, and land. Sara Ahmed (2014) illustrates her concept of willful subjects with the Grimm story of *The Willful Child* cited at the outset of this chapter:

> Once upon a time there was a child who was willful, and would not do as her mother wished. For this reason God had no pleasure in her, and let her become ill, and no doctor could do her any good, and in a short time she lay on her death-bed. When she had been lowered into her grave, and the earth was spread over her, all at once her arm came out again, and stretched upwards, and when they had put it in and spread fresh earth over it, it was all to no purpose, for the arm always came out again. Then the mother herself was obliged to go to the grave, and strike the arm with a rod, and when she had done that, it was drawn in, and then at last the child had rest beneath the ground. (Grimm and Grimm 1884: 125, as cited in Ahmed 2014: 1)

With particular significance to the Canadian context, this "story of the arm" was shared throughout the Truth and Reconciliation Commission of Canada (TRC) hearings as a narrative that was told to so-called willful Indigenous children by disciplinary Catholic nuns in Canada's residential schools. As Métis elder and writer Maria Campbell details, in the Canadian narrative, the role of the nun replaced that of the mother.[12] The message of the story is clear: those who resist dominant, colonial narratives are to be disciplined and silenced, even unto death. In Ahmed's words: "The punishment for willfulness is a passive willing of death, an allowing of death" (20114: 1). For our purposes, at this point in Ahmed's narration, it is worth turning our attention to the deaths of far too many sex workers, especially Indigenous sex workers, in Vancouver's Downtown Eastside, in Edmonton, in Calgary, in Saskatoon, in Winnipeg, and elsewhere: the passive *willing* of their deaths, enabled by material and structural violence and inequality, facilitated through an ongoing failure to recognize basic rights to security and safety of person – a failure to understand that individuals working in sex industries do not consent to violence or coercion.

However, as Ahmed goes on to say, "willfulness is also that which persists even after death: displaced onto an arm ... Willfullness involves persistence in the face of having been brought down, where simply to 'keep going' or to 'keep coming up' is to be stubborn and obstinate. Mere persistence can be an act of disobedience." (2014: 2) Here we can hear the songs of daughters, sisters, mothers, friends, community-members, and sex workers that have echoed every February 14 across Turtle Island during marches that began a quarter of a century ago in Vancouver's Downtown Eastside, led by Indigenous women, sex workers, migrant rights activists, and community members and allies who walk along in solidarity. Such solidarity is powerfully captured in the image of the 2013 Valentine's Day march taken by David P. Ball that is depicted on the cover of this book. Here, the willful arm raises beyond the grave: "Together, we form a network that is not in reference to a violent legal order ... We form a network of people walking in honour not only of the individual people we have lost to these interwoven violences, but also in honour of our ancestors who first fought against the onslaught of policies rooted in our dehumanization" (Hunt 2014: par. 11).

It is in this context of colonialism and dehumanization as well as resistance and organizing that I am critical of existing anti-trafficking responses and the use of anti-trafficking discourses to shape policies that are of little interest to trafficked persons and harmful to sex workers, migrants, and others. But I am by no means cynical. As Brown (2005: x) reminds us, "Critique is not equivalent to rejection or denunciation ... The call to rethink something is not inherently treasonous but can actually be a way of caring for and even renewing the object in question" (as cited in Dean 2015: 20). Rooted in this understanding of critique, I intend this book to be of use to academic theorizing, but I hope it might also prompt critical consideration among a broader audience, including – and perhaps at times especially – those with whom I disagree. The book does not provide a handbook or an overview of anti-trafficking initiatives, or an exploration of best practices; rather, it seeks to spur critical dialogue about anti-violence efforts by foregrounding the settler colonial context of ongoing structural and material dispossession in which violence and exploitation are negotiated. In doing so, the book troubles the ways anti-trafficking and other rights-based discourses reproduce settler colonial nation-building projects. In this, I hope it can incite critical dialogue among service providers, enforcement officials, journalists, policymakers, and human rights and migrant rights advocates, particularly since it is these perspectives that form the empirical basis of the work. I write from a place of deep gratitude and respect for all who took the time to meet and share their experiences with me and I sincerely hope this research will contribute to efforts to spark a more nuanced and constructive dialogue in the country about decolonizing rights-based claims and to stimulate further critical examination into the contested narratives of Canadian anti-trafficking discussions.

Empirical Basis of the Book

Although research on human trafficking traditionally adopts a truth-seeking methodology to uncover facts about who is being trafficked, how they are being trafficked, and what can be done about human trafficking, critical scholars have problematized the effects of erasing uneven social contexts from truth claims. As Suchland (2015: 5) argues, "the global apparatus to combat human trafficking has failed to address the problem as a symptom of complex economic and social dynamics *precisely because* the focus has been on defining and deciphering the proper individual victim" (emphasis added). Doezema (2010: 10) further outlines an approach that prioritizes "the effect of power on knowledge." Drawing on the work of Foucault (1975), Doezema (2010: 10) suggests an examination of "the way in which social power is exercised in knowledge creation, and the ways in which representations of people and problems are used to legitimate knowledge." This approach is particularly relevant in an area of inquiry dominated by misinformation and politicized discourses because it creates space to question how the truths or facts about human trafficking are interpreted and which interpretations are advanced to a legitimized form of knowledge – thereby influencing responses and policies – while considering the power relations at play in producing said knowledge about human trafficking and representations of trafficked persons. As Doezema (2010: 11) argues, what is missing from traditional accounts of human trafficking "is a critical examination of the power dynamics involved in producing knowledge about 'trafficking in women' and the ways in which dominant constructions of the issue emerge and are incorporated into policy."

Given the prominence of anti-trafficking discourses and sensationalized images currently underpinning representations of trafficked persons in Canada, an anticolonial understanding of power in knowledge construction is essential to an examination of representations of trafficked persons in the country. Various projects in Canada have executed fact-finding assessments of the nature and scope of human trafficking in the country,[13] with limited critical discussion of responses to trafficking[14]; such analyses remain detached from the broader structural inequalities in which they originate.[15]

To critically examine responses to human trafficking and the production of international and internal or domestic anti-trafficking discourses, the research informing this book prioritizes qualitative[16] one-on-one interviews. However, data were drawn from multiple sources, including focus groups, group interviews, and a document review of online news media[17] and websites of government and nongovernment agencies engaged in anti-trafficking efforts (see Appendix A for a list of organizations), as well as an examination of Canadian policy proposals, legislative debates, and adopted legislation. Using content and critical discourse analysis, the research explores how trafficked persons are represented in anti-trafficking initiatives and how anti-trafficking discourses reproduce power and inequalities (Peräkylä 2005).

The primary data were generated from fifty-six one-on-one interviews (sixteen in Calgary; twenty-one in Vancouver; and nineteen in Winnipeg) with representatives involved in various levels of anti-trafficking, including frontline workers,[18] representatives of nongovernment organizations, sex workers and sex worker–rights advocates, policymakers, politicians, immigration officials, judiciary, government officials, law enforcement, and some formerly trafficked persons (see Appendix A for a list of selected government and nongovernment agencies represented by participants in one-on-one interviews).[19] Interviews were conducted between October 2010 and February 2011 and took the form of face-to-face or over-the-phone conversations that involved open-ended discussions (see Appendix B for a list of questions used to guide the interviews).[20]

Frontline workers and others involved in anti-trafficking responses provided key insights about their perceptions of human trafficking. These participants were also provided with a description of the research to pass along to individuals who have been directly affected by human trafficking and/or anti-trafficking responses.[21] As there are few individuals who have experienced human trafficking represented in this study,[22] their experiences should not be taken as representative of trafficked persons as a whole. Nonetheless, the voiced experiences of individuals with lived knowledge of trafficking provide key insights into anti-trafficking initiatives and associated representations of human trafficking.

Other participants, such as representatives from nongovernment organizations, policymakers, politicians, immigration officials, judiciaries, city police, and Royal Canadian Mounted Police (RCMP) officers working in the area of anti-trafficking response, provided useful insight into how individuals directly involved in designing and/or implementing counter-trafficking strategies represent trafficked persons. A critical analysis of these representations further underscores the reproduction of power and inequality underlying the adoption of certain portrayals of trafficked persons that privileges crime control and criminal justice responses, on the one hand, and rights-based discourses, on the other. Both have proven not only incapable of transforming structural and material forms of violence and inequality, but also potentially serve to reinforce ongoing forms of oppression.

In addition to the one-on-one conversational interviews, two focus groups and three group interviews further examined key themes raised in the initial document review,[23] such as how anti-trafficking advocates understand human trafficking and their perception of the strengths and limitations of anti-trafficking responses (see Appendix B for a list of questions used to guide the focus groups).[24] Focus groups and group interviews enabled the conversational reflections of frontline workers and thereby provide key insights into the use of rights-based discourses and anti-trafficking representations.[25] To explore how the settler colonial state reproduces itself and the ongoing conditions of colonial gender violence that are naturalized in contexts of rights-based interventions, an examination of anti-trafficking discourses uncovers the way knowledge regimes "help make social realities" (Hua 2011: xviii). Focus group discussions also provided a rich foundation of data to inform the more in-depth questions that were posed in the one-on-one, conversational interview setting.

Although the selected Western Canadian cities cannot represent the country as a whole, they help inform how dominant national anti-trafficking discourses are negotiated within various localized contexts of settler colonialism. To this end, the analysis of each city's discourse is interpreted within the broader national discourse in Canada.[26] In addition to being underexamined, each of the three cities was selected because it has a high proportion of migrant and sex trade workers and is frequently referenced in anti-trafficking discussions. Both Vancouver and Winnipeg have been identified by RCMP intelligence reports "as 'hot spots' of trafficking in persons" (Oxman-Martinez, Lacroix, and Hanley 2005: 4). These reports also suggest that trafficked individuals

are rotated among Winnipeg, Vancouver, and Calgary "to avoid stay-
ing in one place for an extended period of time" (2005: 13). Moreover,
the RCMP further indicate that Vancouver and, in particular, Winnipeg were the Canadian cities with the highest levels of awareness of
domestic trafficking, including ongoing discussions about human trafficking in relation to Indigenous women and girls. The RCMP (2013: 30)
report *Domestic Human Trafficking for Sexual Exploitation in Canada*, for
instance, connects trafficking to "prostitution" of "primarily Aboriginal" individuals by suggesting "the money earned through prostitution
is used most predominantly as a means to fuel their [drug] addiction."
The report further indicates, "Manitoba is unique in that this province
is one of the few in Canada where street-level prostitution is prevalent." According to the 2006 census, Winnipeg also has the highest
urban Aboriginal population in the country, making up 10 per cent of
the city's total population. As accounts of internal trafficking centre on
representations of the "at risk" nature and vulnerability of Indigenous
women and girls located in communities affected by *legacies* of colonization and socioeconomic forms of inequality, this makes Winnipeg an
important city for understanding representations of trafficking in the
settler colonial context of Canada.

In order to critically examine anti-trafficking in the context of settler
colonialism, analysis of the interview and focus group data was two-
fold. First, thematic content analysis[27] explored the information from
the interviews and focus groups/group interviews for recurring and/
or significant themes and compared these themes with the findings of
the document review. By adopting a thematic approach, the research
remained sensitive to the ways in which participants represented and
identified with anti-trafficking approaches and experiences of human
trafficking. In other words, rather than presupposing specific concepts
or categories, the data were initially approached with an open, qualitative lens to uncover the thoughts, ideas, meanings, and constructions
of the research participants.[28] As this book is concerned with the depth
and nuances necessary to understand a diverse range of experiences,
such an approach uncovers how participants perceive and represent
human trafficking and anti-trafficking initiatives.

Second, from a postcolonial and anticolonial perspective, I drew on
ideas of critical discourse analysis to examine how the recurring and/
or significant themes demonstrate how power and inequality in anti-
trafficking discourses reinforce the power imbalance and inequalities
within which trafficking exists. Critical discourse analysis is concerned

with how texts produce and reproduce power and inequalities (Perä-kylä 2005). A core assumption of this approach is that the production and reproduction of power and authority occur through language use (i.e., through discourse) (Stenvoll 2002). In other words, interviews produce texts that uncover how participants negotiate the discursive landscapes in which they are situated. Rather than taking text at face value, critical discourse analysts recognize that discourses are a form of social practice produced through the dialectical interaction between language and social context (Fairclough and Wodak 1997). Merry (2003: 344–5), for example, outlines how the "battered women's movement has always relied on a criminal justice component to its activism, which encourages victims to see their violation as a crime and to turn to the legal system for help," yet individuals victimized by gender violence are often "slow to take on rights." Based on this, Merry then reveals that the desirability of adopting a formal rights-based approach and "rights-defined identity ... depends on the individual's experience with the law" (2003: 346). For racialized and criminalized individuals in settler colonial contexts, the state cannot be interpreted as a benign actor relied upon for help. Rather, resistance to colonial gender violence can look like a rejection of rights-based approaches while rights-based discourses can function to reproduce state-based priorities.

With this in mind, I built on the initial analysis of recurring and/or significant themes by adding the contextual elements essential to understanding the discourse.[29] Specifically, in the context of settler colonialism, I used a critical lens to examine the circumstances in which anti-trafficking discourses occurred as well as the potentially unequal effects of these discourses on the individuals involved. For example, an examination of the interaction between national security and the experiences of trafficked persons requires a contextualized understanding of what "national security" means as well as the potentially unequal racialized and gendered consequences of associating anti-trafficking with heightened border security. In this way, I explored how respondents represent trafficked persons within the context of such representations. Trafficking, from this perspective, forms an important site to examine the development of the Canadian settler colonial nation-building project, particularly in an age of securitization and ongoing dispossession.

Such an approach considers how anti-trafficking discourses reveal and negotiate a settler colonial landscape. This approach assumes that rights-based discourses emerge through an ongoing process of negotiation and interaction between representatives of formal policy and social and moral entrepreneurs, activists, and advocates. As Merry (2011: 125) highlights, "using human rights law as a social movement strategy domesticated human rights ideology." In other words, the rights-based ideology became legible only through "compromises and accommodations to the state" (Merry 2011: 25). With respect to discourses of human trafficking, national priorities become evident when examined through this negotiation between state actors, formal policies, nongovernment representatives, and others. Moreover, because critical discourse analysts are concerned with exposing and challenging the discursive reproduction of power and authority (Stenvoll 2002), this examination was aimed at uncovering how anti-trafficking policies and initiatives reproduce structures of inequality while remaining sensitive to practices that can transform systems and structures of injustice and actualize the sovereignty, rights, and self-determination of individuals negotiating the structural conditions of settler colonial domination.

Human Trafficking in Canada: Overview of the Book

This book examines the construction of human trafficking and anti-trafficking discourses by rooting these discourses in the context of settler colonialism and paying explicit attention to the "colonial continuities" underpinning anti-trafficking discourses. By exploring the boundaries delineated and naturalized by conceptions of trafficking as international or domestic, the book considers how anti-trafficking discourses produce and naturalize the national, racial, and sexual priorities of a settler colonial state – what Lee Maracle refers to as the "mountains" of oppression that form structural conditions in which trafficking and anti-trafficking is imagined.

Chapter 1 examines the construction of anti-trafficking representations and the separation of international versus internal or domestic trafficking representations as well as the colonial continuities embedded in these representations in the context of Canadian settler colonialism. Chapter 2 further situates Canadian anti-trafficking discourses within the "master narrative" of the nation and traces its construction in relation to the project of settler colonial nation-building. Chapter 3 analyses the delineation of "domestic" versus "international" in anti-trafficking representations by examining how anti-trafficking advocates in three Western Canadian cities negotiate these tensions. Discourses of labour trafficking, for instance, are discussed with the presumption of internationality yet sex trafficking is illustrated in both domestic and international terms. Such discourses function to naturalize conflations between trafficking and sex work while also producing subjects of "risk" and subjects of "intervention" within a settler colonial context. Chapter 4 extends this discussion by examining the reproduction of state violence against and discipline of sex workers along the lines of race, citizenship, and gender. This examination considers the differential negotiations of anti-trafficking in a context of silencing, restriction, and other ongoing forms of control. Chapter 5 considers discourses of internal and international trafficking by interrogating the role such discourses play in shaping restrictive immigration policies and border securitization. This chapter details how anti-trafficking initiatives use exclusion – such as the securitization of national boundaries – and inclusion – such as the incorporation of migrant labourers – to consolidate Canadian notions of nationhood through control mechanisms associated with precarious status and temporality. This chapter further details how such discourses elide the realities of setter colonialism and structural domination. The brief concluding chapter discusses the key findings and theoretical insights unpacked in the book along with the implications of the book for examining broader appropriations of social justice and the potentials and limitations of incorporating anti-trafficking into a transformative justice framework.

Chapter One

The Production of International and Domestic Anti-trafficking in Settler-Colonial Canada

[W]e started to shift our focus, certainly on international trafficking – the movies, the kidnappings, you know, that's certainly present, but to a bigger degree, and a more important extent, to get across to the public that trafficking is happening in our own backyards.

– Chair, faith-based anti–human trafficking network

Canada enacted laws to criminalize the trafficking of persons through the Immigration and Refugee Protection Act (IRPA) in 2002 and the Criminal Code in 2005. The initial focus of the counter-trafficking legislation and the corresponding anti-trafficking awareness campaigns emphasized migrant sex work as the primary site of trafficking in persons.[1] In particular, stereotypic images of international trafficking informed early frameworks that portrayed "young Eastern European women deceived into sexual slavery in the back rooms of strip clubs in Toronto, or young Asian women forced into prostitution in seedy massage parlours in Vancouver" (Sikka 2009: 1). Comparable to nineteenth-century accounts of white slavery, the signifiers "young," "foreign," and "deceived" provided the lens through which trafficked women became legible, that is, read only in relation to "sexual slavery" and "forced into prostitution" (Doezema 2010).[2] The use of "back rooms" and "seedy" spaces echoed early anti-prostitution campaigns and missions to civilize Canada, but emphasis was placed on international movement into Canada. By conflating human trafficking with sex work,[3] such discourses focus on the victimization of women coerced into various forms of sexual exploitation,[4] often through portrayals of a victimized Other.

In 2010, for example, the RCMP prepared a report for the Immigration and Passport Branch, *Project SECLUSION*, to serve as "a baseline of human trafficking activities affecting Canada" (2010: 1). The report emphasizes the trafficking of Eastern European, Asian, and African women and the "exploitation of foreign exotic dancers" (RCMP 2010: 8). Similarly, the National Action Plan to Combat Human Trafficking (NAPCHT) stressed the vulnerability of "socially and economically disadvantaged" migrants, new immigrants, women, and children as subjects *at risk* for trafficking based on assumptions regarding the victimization of national, racialized, and gendered identities (Public Safety Canada 2012a). Yet, far from focusing on structural or material violence faced by migrants and others deemed at risk, anti-trafficking discourses emphasize sex industries as the focal point in discussions of exploitation. Although the report acknowledges, "the extent of human trafficking in Canada is difficult to determine,"[5] (RCMP 2010: 8) the plan further states that "prostitution victimizes the vulnerable" and identifies demand for sexual services as a "contributing cause of human trafficking" (Public Safety Canada 2012a: 11). Despite the inclusion of broader conceptions of trafficking, such as various forms of forced labour and services, for many, "trafficking *meant* prostitution" (Doezema 2010: 163). Moreover, international human trafficking meant a "victim" crossed "an international border" (RCMP 2010: 8). Based on this reading, criminal justice interventions and police raids were deemed the appropriate mechanisms of response and migratory restrictions were interpreted as necessary strategies of prevention.[6]

The Canadian Department of Foreign Affairs and International Trade (DFAIT), in particular, was involved in shaping international conceptions of trafficking with an emphasis on restricting migration (Oxman-Martinez, Martinez, and Hanley 2001a). Although research on the relationship between migration and human trafficking has repeatedly suggested that anti-trafficking responses focus on migrant rights and enhanced migratory options,[7] anti-trafficking policies, such as those advanced in Canada, have a demonstrable tendency to create more insecurity by restricting migratory movement.[8] Nonetheless, from a foreign policy standpoint, the promotion of international anti-trafficking protocols and the adoption of anti-trafficking legislation are framed as both a matter of human rights and crime control.[9] As Jeffrey (2005: 33) highlights, anti-trafficking preserves and promotes Canada's self-proclaimed identity as "a good, helpful nation" while functioning as "an exercise in maintaining a particular gendered and raced neo-colonial identity."[10] In this way, identity policies that restrict migratory move-ment and impede the rights of sex trade workers are interpreted as part of the solution to human trafficking, and sex workers and migrants become the problem.[11] In turn, demands of sex workers for better working conditions[12] were effectively externalized into a foreign policy concern and imperialist norms of rescue and control were reasserted through the presumed victimhood of foreign bodies (Jeffrey 2005).

Critical responses to anti-trafficking emerged alongside the interna-tionalization of sexualized labour and the corresponding expansion of globalized labour markets.[13] Critical feminist scholars emphasized the agency of migrant women working in sex industries by examining the ways women negotiate the "restrictions imposed on their mobility by the social and legal position they occupied and by the relations of power through which these were sustained" (Andrijasevic 2010: 17).[14] When considering the structural and material conditions of individuals work-ing in sex industries, it becomes clear that sex work is often not identi-fied as a primary source of oppression and engagement in commercial sexual activity is not necessarily a source of further injury to individuals affected by structural violence. Rather, as Bernstein (2007: 3) points out, sex work can provide a source of escape from "more profoundly violat-ing social conditions." Therefore, "the accelerated entry of women, men, and transgendered individuals into the contemporary sexual economy" (Bernstein 2007: 3) must be interpreted in the broader context of struc-tural violence, including the conditions set by racism, poverty, gender inequalities, homophobia, and so on. These conditions include violation of colonial policies of assimilation enacted through moralized social interventions as well as formalized enforcement structures, what Bern-stein (2010) refers to as "militarized humanitarianism."

While many anti-trafficking advocates, especially individuals adopt-ing an "oppression" paradigm[15] (Weitzer 2012), argue for the criminal-ization of sex industries, particularly purchasers of sex – such as the Swedish approach – to protect women from violence, such arguments occur in the context of ongoing settler colonialism wherein heightened police intervention and criminalization further reinforce structural forms of inequality. In an effort to make violence against women visible, such approaches actually reproduce the subjects of colonial interven-tion as objects of colonial law, with limited substantive change to the conditions in which colonial gender violence occur (Million 2013; Deer 2011). When the settler colonial lens is removed, it becomes clear that criminalization and increased police visibility address neither societal vulnerabilities nor the reality that violence is rooted in multiple and overlapping systems of dominance that produce spaces of dehumanizing poverty, restricted choice, isolation, and commodification. Rather than reduce violence, criminalization produces another version of a long history of colonial state violence. This ongoing production of harm becomes especially apparent through sustained examination of anti-trafficking in the context of settler colonialism.

In response to anti-trafficking claims focused on the prohibition and suppression of prostitution, some sex worker–rights advocates argued for an "empowerment" framework, highlighting the benefits of sex work.[16] Although public discussions and policy debates remain highly polarized around ideas of victim/agent; coercion/consent; and oppression/empowerment, sociological literature on sex industries has established far more nuanced depictions that move beyond the "sex wars" to account for the heterogeneity of experiences represented by individuals involved in sex industries.[17] As Jeffrey and MacDonald (2006: 7) critique, both sides of the dichotomy "see agency in black and white terms: either one has it or one does not. One is either completely free or completely exploited. Both deny any resistance on the part of the sex worker to the powerful structures that shape all our lives."

Although scholars emphasize moving beyond restrictive categories of oppressed versus empowered, public discourses continue to be severely polarized along these lines.[18] Nonetheless, a frequent conversation that arises in feminist circles from women who offer a variety of perspectives is the idea that "there's just so much we agree on, why can't we move past this impasse?" Despite recognition of complexity and a desire to move passed divisive standpoints, the conversation continues to be severely polarized. Advocates frequently rely on war metaphors and images of violence in their descriptions of relations with "the other side." Both abolitionists and sex workers claim they are attacked by one another and the whole area is described as a "minefield" (provincial government representative, British Colombia). In such a context, it is simplistic to ignore the reasons why we can't just focus on what we agree on. Those working and living on the front lines of these conversations recognize that lives, freedom, safety, and security are at stake. Such concerns over security of person arise for both sex workers and former sex workers who reject anti-trafficking labels as well as individuals who identify as survivors of trafficking or forced prostitution.

From these perspectives, significant disagreements occur over the nature of legislative interventions – on the one hand, decriminalization, and on the other, arguments for the Nordic or Swedish model. Neither can address the inequalities constructed in a settler colonial context. However, dominant discourses of international and domestic trafficking generally contest the decriminalization of sex industries, maintaining that by criminalizing the purchasers of sexual services, societies can abolish sex industries. Although abolishment attempts are intended as an effort to address colonial legacies and the violence disproportionately experienced by Indigenous women working in sex industries (Native Women's Association of Canada [NWAC] 2014), such approaches naturalize and reinforce the ongoing power dynamics of settler colonial relations and the conditions underpinning such violence. In a context of spacialized justice that disproportionately oppresses Indigenous women, Razack (1998: 340), for example, asserts an argument about the "inherent violence of prostitution," not in terms of "prostitutes are victims and men are their victimizers,"[19] but in terms of a structural argument regarding the "the violence of prostitution and ... its sources in patriarchy, white supremacy, and capitalism." Yet, from this standpoint, sex workers are read as complicit in accommodating and reproducing structural inequalities: "to suggest as I have that the john is enacting a hegemonic masculinity does not preclude that a prostitute is exercising agency, but it does mean that how we read the collective impact of her action (as opposed to its individual dimension) changes from resistance to systems of domination to accommodation" (Razack 1998: 354). Such interventionist-based arguments are rooted in preconceived notions about how individuals and collectivities enact their resistance to structural oppressions and overlooks ongoing manifestations and resistances of gendered colonial violence, including resistances enacted by sex workers.

Furthermore, by placing the onus on sex workers for *accommodating* social domination and blaming sexualized labour for upholding and creating bourgeois conditions of hegemonic masculinities, such arguments fail to alter the structural conditions they aim to critique. Rather, by asserting the abolition of these spaces, such approaches simultaneously erase the racialized and sexualized individuals facing oppressive and spacialized injustice while upholding the colonial imperative that there is no space for such "repugnance" in "civilized" society (Razack 1998). Thus, in spite of Razack's significant contributions to understanding settler colonialism in Canada and the gendered and racialized nature of Canadian legal systems, the relevance of her own critique – and the importance of ongoing reflexivity as we consider decolonial approaches to anti-violence – becomes apparent here: "We cannot imagine that we are implicated in the crises we set out to solve." Erasing Indigenous, racialized, and sexualized bodies is precisely the colonial imperative, and strengthening formalized interventions onto such bodies perpetuates a prominent tool of enforcing this imperative.

By suggesting that targeting men (i.e., johns) through criminal mechanisms provides the solution to "prostitution as violence" in order to "disrupt the social relations," such arguments promote law enforcement as a means of protecting "victims" while failing to identify how such approaches further reproduce the lines between civility and incivility. Thus, the colonizer "has succeeded not merely in creating a place for himself but also in taking away that of the inhabitant, granting himself astounding privileges to the detriment of those rightfully entitled to them" (Memmi 1965: 8). Moreover, such reliance on legislative strategies to address colonial legacies negates the reality that "Canadian law is about the oppression of Aboriginal people" (Monture-Angus 1995: 59). At the same time, in both distinct and intersecting ways, the law also produces uneven rights and privileges for racialized migrants, and consolidates "racializing formations of the nation-state" (Dhamoon 2015: 24). The law, in this context, continues to be a productive tool of settler colonialism with which to reinforce national, racial, and sexual priorities.

Thus, arguments that blame sex workers for accommodating structural violence and emphasize the production of bourgeois identity through prostitution ignore how anti–sex work campaigns – and many anti-trafficking campaigns – establish bourgeois subjects. Also ignored is the role of such campaigning in the process of naturalizing state domination in a settler colonial context and the subsequent reproduction of structural inequalities and corresponding forms of social retrenchment in Canada through such domination. Limited efforts to recognize structural underpinnings of violence contribute to the creation of spaces of marginalization and stigma by downplaying the ongoing control of women's bodies by the state in their analysis of sex industries, the collusion of anti-sex work advocacy (frequently conflated with anti-trafficking) in producing subjective bodies, and the related imperative to intervene.

In the nation-building narrative of Canada, erasure of sex industries in particular is premised on the simultaneous erasure of sex workers. In the face of ongoing material and systemic violence, Indigenous women, migrant women, and non-heteropatriarchal actors involved in sex industries actively work to reduce the harms experienced, including issuing calls for self-determination, body sovereignty, and anti-violence approaches that address these material and systemic targeted forms of physical and sexual violence. Placing anti-trafficking discussions in the context of settler colonialism reveals the role of structural and material violence, the inequalities shaping the nature of dominant discourses, and the ability of such discourses to function in a hegemonic way to silence complex narratives.

In this context, many sex worker and migrant-rights advocates restated their position that structural inequalities necessitate the decriminalization of sex trade industries and migratory movements to establish safer working conditions and decrease instances of trafficking.[20] From this perspective, sex work should not be conflated with sex trafficking and other forms of coercion, exploitation, or abuse. Weitzer (2012: 16) summarizes this approach in his argument for a "polymorphous paradigm" that remains "sensitive to complexities and the structural conditions shaping sex work along a continuum of agency and subordination." The structural conditions of such a continuum include restrictions imposed by the boundary-maintenance practices of the state.[21] Of those who argue from this standpoint, some believe that trafficking must be interpreted "independent of the type of work" a person is engaged in (Parent and Bruckert 2013: 23) while others reject the use of trafficking terminology to emphasize "the extent of unfreedom"[22] experienced in migratory movements. Regardless, early anti-trafficking discourses in Canada emphasized international trafficking by conflating trafficking with migratory movements, particularly of individuals involved in sex industries.

Given the high standing human trafficking has received in being declared one of the world's most profitable global criminal enterprises,[23] alongside drug trafficking, arms dealing, and terrorism, anti-trafficking endeavours are highly politicized. Therefore, efforts to control the human trafficking narrative occur on a number of discursive fronts and anti-trafficking discourses are mobilized to shape a variety of policy areas, including border controls and national security, gender and sexuality, migration and labour, and human rights.

The role anti-trafficking discourses play in shaping contemporary boundaries of social organization raises a number of questions: How do anti-trafficking discourses portray what Yuval-Davis (1994: 628) refers to as the legitimate "boundaries of the collectivity" and the corresponding processes of inclusion and exclusion? How are anti-trafficking debates shaping the relationship between gender and state relations, such as the intersection between rights, sexuality, morality, and the law? How are anti-trafficking debates shaping existing boundaries of social organization, including discussions of human rights, citizenship, migration, and national security, especially the securitization of borders?

Considering how these discourses are produced and delineated in the settler colonial context of Canada adds to critical examinations of trafficking discourses by examining the role anti-trafficking discourses play in the reproduction of social boundaries: civility and incivility; citizen and subject; and victim and agent. Moreover, how do such discourses elide the negotiation and resistance enacted by gendered and racialized bodies? This requires an examination of how anti-trafficking discourses and responses participate in a "planetary consciousness" that naturalizes depictions of the Other and facilitates ongoing forms of colonial domination, what Heron (2007) refers to as "colonial continuities." By rooting the analysis in a development framework, we see the Canadian context as one that advances patterns of global economic and political "development," producing conditions vulnerable to trafficking while claiming to rescue trafficked women predominantly through criminal justice reform[24] as well as a growing and unreflexive body of rights-based claims. In other words, anti-trafficking discourses have provided a particular site for Canada to advance its global interests while naturalizing (i.e., rendering invisible) practices of imperialism, colonialism, paternalism, and racism: the mechanisms by which "the matrix of domination" constructs and upholds gendered, racialized, and state-based violence. In her seminal work on anti-racism, Patricia Hill Collins (2000: 228–9) refers to the "matrix of domination" as "the overall social organization within which intersecting oppressions originate, develop, and are contained." Drawing on anti-trafficking, Canadian systems of justice – embedded in settler colonialism – reinforce state control over migrating bodies and discipline gendered and racialized bodies for their *risky* migrations.[25]

These critiques are delineated through an examination of responses to human trafficking in Canada in relation to ongoing forms of restriction and control supported by a transnational crime framework in the context of settler colonialism, including an analysis of the treatment of migrant boats that arrived off the coast of British Colombia in 2009 and 2010 and the dismantling of the exotic dancer visa under the Temporary Foreign Worker Program (TFWP).

Exploring the Internal Shift: Discourses of Domestication

Despite revealing the imperialist imperative underlying efforts to define *victims* of trafficking as a form of racialized Other and rescue them through mechanisms of state control, discursive analyses of the appropriation of anti-trafficking are limited. In particular, casting human trafficking as one of many possible forms of appropriated humanitarian language ignores the specific importance of the discourse of trafficking, especially in a context of settler colonial domination. Beyond merely co-opting anti-trafficking language for alternate agendas, Canadian anti-trafficking efforts unite liberal and conservative rights discourses that portray trafficking policies and responses as a specific way to address colonial *legacies* while unreflexively reinforcing settler colonial domination and naturalized violence in colonial relations that were established through the very means articulated in anti-trafficking definitions. According to the United Nations Protocol to Prevent, Suppress and Punish Trafficking in Persons, Especially Women and Children (hereafter, UN Trafficking Protocol),[26] trafficking occurs "by means of the threat or use of force or other forms of coercion, of abduction, of fraud, of deception, of the abuse of power or of a position." These are precisely the means by which the settler colonial state was formed: forced dispossession from lands, abduction of children into residential schools, forced removal of children into state care, the violent abuse of power that aimed to dispossess Indigenous women from their lands and communities through the implementation of the Indian Act (Hunt 2008; Deer 2011). In this context, anti-trafficking aims to bring recognition to the legacies of colonization, but does so by emphasizing at-risk subjects as the object of concern while naturalizing and reinforcing the ongoing production of the settler colonial state,[27] the very space of dispossession where so-called "at risk" persons emerge.

Critical discursive analyses of trafficking also remain incomplete by restricting trafficking to a migration concern, while ignoring the shift towards the construction of domestic victims of trafficking. The Canadian anti-trafficking gaze, in particular, has expanded beyond immigration and foreign policy concerns. Alongside the adoption of the Criminal Code legislation in 2005, discussions materialized and have since proliferated to underscore domestic or internal forms of trafficking – trafficking within Canadian borders. These discussions have centred on the relationship between trafficking and the experiences of Indigenous women and girls.[28] In a study commissioned by the

Department of Justice, Oxman-Martinez, Lacroix, and Hanley (2005: iv) identify that marginalized socioeconomic circumstances underpin "the fact that a majority of people trafficked within Canada are Aboriginal women and children." The RCMP report *Project SECLUSION* further splits "international" human trafficking from "domestic" forms by conceptualizing "domestic" trafficking as "the phenomenon in which all stages of trafficking occur *within* Canada regardless of the victim's legal status" (2010: 8). The report emphasizes that "vulnerable, economically challenged and socially dislocated sectors of the Canadian population represent a potential pool of domestic trafficking victims." Despite this proposed framework, advocates and researchers argue that domestic trafficking has not received the same kind of attention as international trafficking. In particular, they bring attention to how mainstream understanding largely ignores the trafficking of Indigenous women and girls.[29] As Sikka (2009: 1) critiques, domestic trafficking has not received the same level of attention as international trafficking, "and the unique ways in which Aboriginal women and girls are being trafficked have not been put in the 'trafficking' picture." It is noteworthy that *Project SECLUSION* (RCMP 2010) does not specify the vulnerability of Indigenous women, given the RCMP's later emphasis on Indigenous women as "at risk" for trafficking.

Thus, as the quote at the outset of this chapter suggests, internal trafficking was framed in reaction to the stereotypic conceptions of international human trafficking in Canada: "we started to shift our focus, certainly on international trafficking – the movies, the kidnappings, you know, that's certainly present, but to a bigger degree, and a more important extent, to get across to the public that trafficking is happening in our own backyards." From this standpoint, the aim was to counteract the "apathy" of the criminal justice system towards Indigenous bodies (Sikka 2009). Although the criminal justice system has hardly been apathetic towards Indigenous women, as demonstrated by the stark overrepresentation of Indigenous women incarcerated in Canada,[30] the idea was that a trafficking lens could undermine colonial-derived images that portray Indigenous women and girls as perpetrators of crime rather than as victims.[31] By 2012, both an RCMP report and the NAPCHT specifically labelled Aboriginal women and girls as being at heightened risk for internal trafficking, highlighting that 90 per cent of cases in Canada are domestic. Further, in 2013, the RCMP report *Project SAFEKEEPING* specifically identified Aboriginal women as a "vulnerable population" to "domestic" trafficking.

This emergence of representations of Indigenous women as "domestically trafficked" begs the question of how Indigenous women's experiences are portrayed in Canadian anti-trafficking discourses. What frames are employed to interpret trafficking of Indigenous women? What mechanisms make Indigenous experiences with trafficking visible, and when are Indigenous experiences omitted? How has inclusion in dominant anti-trafficking narratives informed this visibility? And, in particular, what happens when Indigenous women are conceptualized as domestic or internal? The construction of an internal versus international trafficking dichotomy provides a generative site of analysis to explore how Canada negotiates boundaries and consolidates national entitlements.

Internally, the victim label associated with trafficking is bolstered as a mechanism to resolve racist and colonial constructions of Indigenous women. Yet such interpretations overlook how settler colonial forms of state control are particularly evident in Canada's role in, and response to, violence against Indigenous women. While anti-trafficking advocates assume themselves to be beyond the violence of colonization, often by the very virtue of addressing the legacies of colonization, they (we)[32] underestimate how anti-trafficking responses reproduce and reinforce colonial systems and structures of domination, criminalization, and marginalization.[33] Thus, anti-trafficking discourses assume Indigenous women and girls to be "domiciled" in Canada and propose as solutions the very processes that capitalize on the oppression of Indigenous people (Monture 1999: 17).[34] Framing Indigenous women as "internal" has a particular *domiciling* effect – both in language and in practice – and, as a result, implications for understanding Indigenous self-determination. In turn, the inclusion of Indigenous women in dominant understandings of domestic trafficking disproportionately serve to reproduce and naturalize the national, racial, and sexual priorities of the settler colonial state.

Anti-trafficking, in a context that naturalizes settler colonialism, underscores national entitlement by simultaneously situating migrants – and especially precarious-status migrant workers – as international, racialized Others to be excluded, while domesticating Indigenous communities and especially Indigenous women and Two-Spirit persons. Both exclusion and inclusion draw on forms of criminal justice intervention as well as right-based discourses of protection for at risk and/or risky subjects in naturalizing structural violence against gendered and racialized bodies.

Anti-trafficking and "Colonial Continuities"

Situating the trafficking industry and anti-trafficking responses within the context of settler colonialism, this book draws on critical feminist, anticolonial, Indigenous, and postcolonial development theories to understand the production and implications of internal and international anti-trafficking discourses and anti-trafficking responses in Canada. In response to Western-dominated development from colonialism through economic globalization, postcolonial and anticolonial theorists question representations of Otherness via the "Third World subject" and the failure of development to achieve its goals. Such studies are guided by the seminal work of Edward Said (1979), particularly his notion of Orientalism, that is, how representations of the "Orient" are produced and reproduced in relation to the "Occident," which includes an underlying assumption of Western superiority.

From this perspective, postcolonialism "does not refer to the 'end' of colonialism; rather, it speaks to the *continuations* and legacies of colonialism" (MacKenzie 2012: 9; emphasis added). This underscores Heron's (2007: 7) previously mentioned concept of "colonial continuities": the racialized and interlocking constructs of thought that "circulated from the era of empire, and today remain integral to the discursive production of bourgeois identity."[35] Contemporary forms of empire, as Razack (2004: 10) argues, "is a structure of a feeling, a deeply held belief in the need to and the right to dominate others *for their own good*, others who are expected to be grateful." By focusing on inclusion in anti-trafficking discourses and state systems of response as a means of addressing colonial legacies in Canada, the reproduction of colonial processes become visible. Thus, such inclusion becomes a site for the ongoing maintenance of colonial gendered and racialized identities while claiming to address the legacies of colonization: "calls to social justice ... that include indigenous peoples, if they are not attuned to the ongoing conditions of settler colonialism *of* indigenous peoples, risk deeming colonialism in North America resolved, if not redressed" (Byrd 2011: xxvi).

In the context of anti-trafficking, we see specific calls to action to address the trafficking of Indigenous women as a legacy of colonization that ignore the ongoing conditions of Indigenous women and communities in the midst of living and resisting settler colonial domination. Lee Maracle details a sociology of these conditions by centring her perspective as an Indigenous woman of Salish and

Cree ancestry and a member of the Stó:lō Nation. In *I am Woman*, she writes,

> I sometimes feel like a foolish young grandmother armed with a teaspoon, determined to remove three mountains from the path to liberation: the mountain of racism, the mountain of sexism and the mountain of nationalist oppression. I tire easily these days ... Sometimes I feel the tiredness is old, as old as the colonial process itself. On those days I am energized by the fact that it is not my fatigue but the fatigue of the oppressor's system which haunts me. On other days the tiredness is deeply personal. (Maracle 1996: x)

Situated within the "mountains" of oppression, and ignoring the conditions of such oppression, anti-trafficking calls to action exacerbate the exhaustion of those working towards resistance of colonial gender violence by arguing for increases in state powers and social interventions that reproduce and maintain colonial control and regulation of Indigenous and migrant bodies. For example, targeting individual traffickers (frequently construed as racialized men and youth) draws attention away from the role of the state in reproducing conditions in which Indigenous women and individuals who challenge gender binaries experience relentless and interconnected forms of violence. Thus, state efforts – produced and upheld by anti-trafficking advocacy – focus on criminalizing and increasing criminal sentences for traffickers, while avoiding transformations required to produce material changes to the levels of violence racialized and gendered bodies face on a day-to-day basis. In other words, anti-trafficking can be seen to reproduce unproblematic assumptions about the inherent *benevolence* of development and its associated priorities of rescue and aid, while naturalizing the structures and material conditions of privilege, domination, and inequality that compel the obligations of the helper.

Feminist postcolonial thinkers like Gayatri Spivak (1988) and Chandra Mohanty (1991), specifically underscore the problematic representations of women in development discourses. Spivak's (1988) discussion of the representation of the subaltern subject caused sustained reflection on how Western development discourses portray women of the Global South.[36] In this vein, Mohanty (1991: 56) criticizes representations of women from the Global South as "ignorant, poor, uneducated, tradition-bound, domestic, family-oriented, victimized, etc." As Heron (2007) argues, such representations and the associated obligations of rescue and aid occur alongside and are justified by a global awareness that assumes a comparative relationship, with the Other "somehow lacking." By defining the development agendas underlying colonization – and more recently globalization – as predominantly Western initiatives, postcolonial and anticolonial critiques allow for an examination of anti-trafficking initiatives in the context of the "economic, material, and cultural conditions" that shape the global system in which the postcolonial subject operates (Young 2001: 57). Despite a persistent focus on development as modernization or progress, very little has shifted in global hierarchical relations[37] since neoliberal economic practices furthered globalized capitalist social relations; instead, disparities have only increased both within and between nation-states.[38] In this way, the development project, from colonization to economic globalization,[39] has been rooted in Western forms of knowledge and power that, according to Kothari (2005), inevitably limit the adoption of alternate ways of organizing and achieving social change. Similarly, in the words of Escobar (1995: 39), development has "created a space in which only certain things could be said or imagined." Thus, numerous development and rights-based discourses, including anti-trafficking discourses, are dominated by singular, oftentimes hegemonic narratives derived from nationalist assumptions and perspectives. This comparison with non-national and racialized Others derives "a sense of entitlement and an obligation to intervene for the 'betterment' of the Other *wherever he or she resides*" (Heron 2007: 7; emphasis added). In anti-trafficking, such intervention reinforces state mechanisms of surveillance and control.

Although Heron's analysis focuses on the North–South divide of international development and the helping imperative of Canadian development workers in international contexts, "planetary consciousness" is not detached from internal expressions of settler domination. In a settler colonial context, racialized and gendered representations of Indigenous women and Two-Spirit persons provide the basis for colonial constructions depicted in Mohanty's "Third World" Other. As Acoose (1995: 55) argues, "stereotypic images of Indian princesses, squaw drudges, suffering helpless victims, tawny temptresses or loose squaws falsify our realities and suggest in a subliminal way that those stereotypic attitudes are us." She further argues that such representations promote cultural attitudes that underpin and naturalize

violence against Indigenous women. In addition to underlying violence, such cultural attitudes also shape preconceived ideas about
coercion and choice that inform responses to violence against racialized women, including anti-trafficking initiatives rooted in models
of rescue and control. In turn, such representations reinforce existing
structures, enabling "dominant cultures to continue their domination,
rather than shedding light on how social domination is reproduced"
(Elabor-Idemudia 2002: 231).

By questioning Western feminist attempts to "rescue non-European
and poorer women," postcolonial and anticolonial development and
Indigenous feminist thought allow researchers to not only consider
how uneven development feeds discourses of human trafficking, but
also to examine how structural forms of inequality underpin representations of trafficked persons and, in doing so, reproduce dominant discourses of Indigenous, migrant, and racialized Others. In a
settler colonial context, such representations produce and sustain
particular national, racial, and sexual notions of what it means to be
Canadian.

With respect to human trafficking, anticolonial examinations of
trafficking discourses move beyond mere description of how human
trafficking occurs in postcolonial and settler colonial contexts to examine how representations of trafficked persons are constructed and the
power dynamics underpinning dominant representations in anti-
trafficking discourses and policies.[40] With this in mind, researchers
need to remain attentive to the ways in which power and domination
are expressed in anti-trafficking discourses, which necessitates looking
beyond material forms of inequality without neglecting the everyday
material conditions that naturalize and reproduce violence.[41] Power,
from this perspective, refers to the unequal context in which the narrative of human trafficking is constructed by some and, by discursively
framing the issue, its ability to shape the response (i.e., anti-trafficking
and related policies). Moreover, in the context of settler colonialism,
notions of power point to the "matrix of domination" (Collins 2000) or
"cacophony" (Byrd 2011) whereby colonialism and imperialism "often
[coerce] struggles for social justice ... into complicity with settler colonialism" (Byrd 2011: xvii). Building on this analysis, Dhamoon (2015: 30)
recognizes that "there are multiple co-constituting horizontal struggles
of gendering, sexuality and desire, capitalism, and ableism that interact
with the cacophony of colonizer-colonized and other minority oppressions." In turn, discursive power has the ability to reproduce social and

political forms of domination between and among colonial and race–gender relations.[42] This matrix of domination is taken up to disrupt the ways in which dominant anti-trafficking constructions produce and define internal versus international discourses in a settler colonial context.

Settler Colonialism and Canadianness: Anti-trafficking on *"Our* Home and Native Land"

Anti-trafficking in Canada is constructed from and contributes to what Sunera Thobani (2012: 4) refers to as the "master narrative" of the nation. To be Canadian is to be an "enterprising" and "law-abiding" citizen. Canadians are "responsible citizens, compassionate, caring, and committed to the values of diversity and multiculturalism" (Thobani 2012: 4). Our national inheritance is perceived to have been won by those who overcame "great adversity in founding the nation" and multiple threats from "outsiders – Indians, immigrants, and refugees" (Thobani 2012: 4). To be Canadian is to elide foundational narratives of dispossession and violence.

In her lecture on the gender of the state and the ongoing gendered effects state violence, Kahnawà:ke Mohawk scholar Audra Simpson further unpacks this master narrative:

> In spite of the innocence of the story that Canada likes to tell about itself: that it is a place of immigrant and settler founding; that in this, it is a place that somehow escapes the ugliness of history. That it is a place that reconciles, that apologizes ... Canada is just quite simply a settler society. A settler society [whose] multicultural, liberal, and democratic structure and performance of governance seeks an ongoing settling of land. This settling is not, of course, innocent either. It is dispossession: the taking of our land from us. And, it is ongoing. It is killing our women in order to do so; and has historically done this to do so. (Simpson 2014b)

The discourse of being Canadian is a well-known and aptly parodied discourse of polite apology – apology that conceals the "ugliness" of history. From this place, Canadian national identity is characterized by democratic stability and enviable peace and prosperity. For example, discussing the financial crisis that began in 2008 at the G20 summit in fall 2009, the prime minister at the time, Stephen Harper, promoted the economic and political agenda of Canada, which he described as an "advanced, developed" nation to the benefit of "its citizens":

> Canada remains in a very special place in the world ... we are the one, major, developed country that no one thinks has any responsibility for this crisis. In fact, on the contrary, they look at our policies as a solution to the crisis. Everybody, we're the one country in the room, everybody would like to be. They would like to be an advanced, developed economy, with all the benefits that conveys to its citizens, and at the same time not have been the source or have any of the domestic problems that created this crisis in the first place.
>
> Secondly, Canada has broader assets. We should not, you know we're so, we're so, humble isn't the word, but we're so self-effacing as Canadians that we sometimes forget the assets we do have that other people see. We are a very large country, with a well-established, you know, we have one of the longest-standing democratic regimes, unbroken democratic regimes, in history. We are one of the most stabile regimes in history. There are very few countries that can say for nearly 150 years they've had the same political system without any social breakdown, political upheaval or invasion. We are unique in that regard. We also have no history of colonialism. So we have all of the things that many people admire about the great powers, but none of the things that threaten or bother them about the great powers. (as cited in Wherry 2009)

In promoting the Canadian narrative, the former prime minister expressed a complete disregard for the history of colonialism and the ugly foundation upon which current financial structures in Canada are built and continue to operate to the benefit of those with citizenship. Although his office responded to critiques of this statement with the suggestion that "the prime minister was giving some context and saying that unlike past global empires, Canada does not have a history of colonialism with respect to the financial market." With this response, the prime minister's office (PMO) further erased the "taking" of Indigenous lands as well as the "ongoing settling of land." In doing so, Indigenous bodies carrying the violence of dispossession and struggle for nationhood are simultaneously, discursively erased.

Situated in such notions of Canadianness, anti-trafficking purports to rescue vulnerable individuals from unscrupulous criminals who violate the law and human dignity. As Vic Toews, former public safety minister, declared, "[h]uman trafficking is one of the most heinous crimes imaginable, often described as modern day slavery. This crime robs its victims of their most basic human rights and is occurring in Canada and worldwide ... As part of our Government's *longstanding commitment* to protect the vulnerable, tackle crime and safeguard Canadians and their families in *their* homes and communities, we are taking action against these terrible crimes (as cited Public Safety Canada 2012b; emphasis added).

The idea of "longstanding commitment" harkens to another feature of Canadianness: to be Canadian is to disavow foundational narratives of racism, genocide, conquest, forced labour, and exploitation (Razack 2002; Thobani 2012; Simpson 2014a). Competing claims of sovereignty are undermined by docile narratives of inclusivity and safety for "families in *their* homes and communities."

In this context, the relationship between Indigenous sovereignties and migrant rights, particularly conceptions of what it means to be a settler and benefactor of Indigenous dispossession, remains contested. Sharma's (2006: 8) early exploration of "home" in relation to migrant workers in Canada, asserts that notions of "their" (i.e., Canadian) "home" establishes boundaries of national identity through a patriarchal "overlaying of the idea of *home* onto that of the *nation*." In a context of settler colonialism, "European colonization gave shape to notions of discrete, ethnically bounded *homelands*" that establish the boundaries between "members and non-members of the *national family*" (Sharma 2006: 9; emphasis added).[43] At the same time, such discourses naturalize settler colonialism established through the notion of terra nullius – the idea that "[I]ndigenous peoples were never *at home* on these lands" (Sharma 2006: 9; emphasis added). However, in an effort to distinguish differential forms of migration and to avoid the conflation of colonialism and unequal migrations that vary on a spectrum from voluntary to forced, Sharma and Wright's (2008) understanding of transnationalism places Indigenous sovereignty in opposition to migratory freedom. In doing so, such a binary approach extends critiques of nation-states to Indigenous forms of nationhood and thereby naturalizes the dispossession and erasure of Indigenous sovereignties (Lawrence and Dua 2005; Dhamoon 2015; Stark 2016). Rather, from a feminist, anticolonial perspective, Byrd (2011: 67) identifies the importance of tracing "how colonial discourses have functioned in geographies where there are multiple interactions among the different colonialisms, arrivals, and displacements at work." Colonial gendered violence, from this perspective, requires attentive consideration of a variety of areas of struggle, including, but not limited to, boundaries of gender, sexuality, labour, movement, land, and territory.

By definition, the political boundary of citizenship establishes membership in a polity and the relationship of the state to the Other (Brubaker 1992) through a "dialectical process between inclusion and exclusion" (Kivisto and Faist 2007: 1). Yet such boundaries are "imagined"[44] in a context of colonial and global economic relations that produce and reproduce structural forms of inequality[45] and differential freedom of movement.[46] Inscribed into laws and policies of Canadian justice, Canadianness naturalizes the national, racial, and sexual priorities of the state around the national subject and places this subject in hierarchical relation to Others: Indigenous, refugee, immigrant, migrant, and racialized women as well as LGBTTQQIA,[47] Two-Spirit, and gender nonconforming persons.[48] The gendered, raced, and national hierarchies that structure Canadian society become apparent when we unsettle Canadian anti-trafficking discourses by placing these discourses in the settler colonial context in which they are constructed.[49]

Postcolonial and anticolonial theorists argue that the idea of the nation and the incarnation of the nation-state is a relatively new construction that is reciprocally linked to imperialist development and the corresponding structural domination and inequalities associated with colonial expansion. In the words of Bhabha (1990: 59), "nationalism is an ideology that, even in its earliest forms in the nineteenth century, implied unequal development. Even though nationalism as an ideology came out of the imperialist countries, these countries were not able to formulate their own national aspirations until the age of exploration." Nations "discovered" through exploration provided the necessary boundaries of empire to produce nationalism in the "homelands," while postcolonial and settler colonial states reinforced and solidified notions of "nation-ness" in response to European ideas of nationalism. However, as Simpson (2014a: 177) underscores, "the story that settler colonial nation-states tend to tell about themselves is that they are new; they are beneficent; they have successfully 'settled'"; in doing so, such depictions conceal the coercive origins of ranking and dispossession underpinning missionizing as well as the sovereignty of Indigenous peoples that "interrupt" tidy narratives of inclusion and domestication.

The centrality of nation-building exercises led Anderson (2006: 3) to assert that such ideas of nationalism are "the most universally legitimate value in the political life of our time." For Anderson (2006), nations are "imagined communities" constructed through official and popular forms of nationalism. Officially, such communities and notions of belonging are consolidated through state institutions, such as the Indian Act, criminal codes, immigration policies, and formal social service. As Alfred and Corntassel (2005: 603) argue, "[c]ontemporary forms of postmodern imperialism attempt to confine the expression of Indigenous peoples' right of self-determination to a set of domestic authorities operating within the constitutional framework of the state (as opposed to the right of having an autonomous and global standing) and actively seek to sever Indigenous links to their ancestral homelands." In this context, rights-based claims, such as anti-trafficking, are sought through the addressing of colonial legacies and their associated vulnerabilities, yet, within the framework of legislative control and formal intervention, elide the role of ongoing forms of dispossession in producing and maintaining structures of inequality in which such vulnerabilities emerge. Moreover, such claims reproduce the notions of Canadianness wherein Canadians are responsible for intervening and addressing the perceived at-risk members (e.g. migrant and Indigenous women) of *our* society.

In addition to official policies of intervention, imagined communities of national belonging are also produced through popular forms of nationalism epitomized by the "nationalist": those who "belong" in and comprise the nation-state. Such belonging necessitates "white subjects, who actively enacted the dispossession of Native people on the ground, as they did the exclusion of 'non-preferred' races from equal access to land, mobility, and employment" (Thobani 2012: 84). White women, in particular, and the "mutually reproductive connection between bourgeois subjectivity and the subject position of development worker" occupy "the position of boundary markers of bourgeois 'civilization.'" (Heron 2007: 36–7). Although nation-states are in a privileged position to establish and enforce boundaries through rules and controls, Valverde's (2008) analysis of social purity campaigns reveals national subjects only "internalize" identities through active participation, often in the form of voluntary organizations that provide white, middle-class women an active role. As Valverde (2008: 25) notes, "many voluntary organizations were far more concerned about nation-building and even about strengthening the state than the state itself." Here, we see the role of national subjectivities as integral to the formation and continuance of nation-states and national identities.

According to Tilly (2003: 608), identities, and in this case national identities, comprise four component parts: "1) a boundary separating 'me' from 'you' or 'us' from 'them'; 2) a set of relations within the boundary; 3) a set of relations across the boundary; 4) a set of stories about the boundary and the relations." In Canada, the "story" of European immigration and settlement constructs notions of "Canadianness" and, in turn, demarcates citizenship boundaries whereby some individuals are warranted only conditional access to national space, such as migrant workers and refugee claimants, while others require assimilation or eradication in order to uphold national mythology, such as Two-Spirit, gender nonconforming, and Indigenous women (Razack 2002; Thobani 2012). As Audra Simpson (2010: 116) identifies, "this process of equality cum absorption required a vanquishing of an alternative or existing political order, an interesting problem in itself, which raises questions about how and why citizenship then might be a utilitarian good, when it requires or initiates a disappearance of prior governance." In this context, demarcation of boundaries through national subjectivities naturalizes dominance of national subjects (white, middle class, Canadian) in relation to "the Indian, the immigrant, and the refugee" (Thobani 2012: 5) and reinforces boundary maintenance through surveillance techniques, such as policing "at risk" communities, border securitization, and restrictive immigration policies that enhance state control over apprehension, detention, deportation, and refused entry for *protective* purposes. Anti-human trafficking discourses in Canada demonstrate limited ability for transformative engagement; rather, they predominately reinforce and naturalize mechanisms of control.[50]

Regularly framed through politics centred on criminal justice of protection, and supported by rights-based narratives of social intervention, anti-trafficking provides a focal point with which to examine how Canada demarcates the boundaries of the nation-state and the national identity of who is considered domestic or "at home" in ways that reproduce the national, racial, and sexual priorities of the settler colonial state. In this way, anti-trafficking in Canada is delineated within a context of resistance to identifying "benefactors and perpetrators of contemporary colonial relations of dominance, in '*our* home and native land'" (Gill 2002: 162). A decolonial approach necessitates a disruption of such systems of power whereby "marginalized peoples are systemically (even if unintentionally) operating within, across, and through a matrix of interrelated forms and degrees of penalty and privilege" (Dhamoon 2015: 30). Indigenous women, in particular, are framed as domestic – erasing claims to sovereignty and presuming assimilation into the Canadian home – while migrants are framed as international and thereby away from *their* homes and an imposition on, or a threat to, *our* (non-Indigenous) Canadian home, thereby naturalizing Canadian claims to sovereignty and ownership of the land.

Emphasizing safety from criminal activity, national anti-trafficking discourses further establish a boundary between *us* (law-abiding national citizens – "families in their homes and communities") and *them* (criminalized and generally racialized Others). As we will see, at this turn the "them" includes Indigenous families and communities – alongside migrants – who are blamed for perpetuating domestic forms of trafficking. Sharma's (2006) idea of nationhood as superimposing patriarchal structures of home onto the nation can be extended to justify this misplaced blame. By placing patriarchy at the starting point of the analysis of the nation, such claims assume homogeneity of nationalisms and nationhood as equally oppressive for all women while ignoring nationhood as a potential site of liberation. Conversely, insurgent and resurgent models of Indigenous governance decentre the settler colonial nation-state while advancing Indigenous sovereignty and nationhood "predicated on interrelatedness and responsibility" (Smith 2008: 311; Coulthard 2014). As Dhamoon (2015: 27) points out, an anticolonial feminist approach to nationhood "does not see Indigenous men as the root cause of problems facing Indigenous women; rather, the problem is the imposition of colonial heteropatriarchal structures in/as the nation-state." Such an approach disrupts the matrix of domination that reproduces uneven relational hierarchies. Nonetheless, in anti-trafficking, Indigenous persons are represented as both domestic and as "outside the boundaries" of Canadianness, both of which have implications for naturalizing settler colonial structures of the nation-state while mitigating struggles for Indigenous sovereignties. In all, the domestic (read as Indigenous)/international (read as migrant) anti-trafficking dichotomy conceals relations of domination that work together to reproduce national entitlement through modes of inclusion and exclusion.

Moreover, the nation-state continues to function as a mechanism of control to maintain the advancement of the global capitalist economic order in continuity with the civilizing mission associated with colonial expansion: regulating and restricting migration by, in part, disciplining "unruly" or "irregular" (i.e., illegalized and criminalized) migrants and asylum seekers. Hoogvelt (1997), for example, argues that the reproduction of the global economic order is "not an economic problem but a law and order problem." As this suggests, the state serves to legitimize and naturalize instruments of control and domination that demarcate and enforce national boundaries between *us* and *them*, such as policing, border securitization, and restrictive immigration policies that enhance state control over apprehension, detention, deportation, and refused entry for "protective" purposes. Anti-trafficking efforts highlight how nationhood in Canada is founded on and necessitates control over migration and Indigenous communities, both of which are tied to Canada's global political and economic position. In doing so, anti-trafficking advances the assumption that "trafficking is an aberration, rather than symptomatic of political economy" (Suchland 2015: 6). By constructing the Other in terms of potential risk, at risk, and a risky threat to the nation-state,[51] anti-trafficking discourses help facilitate the realization and racialization of exclusion and inclusion by naturalizing precarious labour in certain industries while restricting movement in others.

Chapter Two

Settler Colonialism and the Construction of Anti-trafficking

We cannot imagine that we are implicated in the crises we set out to solve.
— Sherene Razack, *Dark Threats and White Knights*

God in his providence has made you the guardians of the very fountain from which is to flow the latest and best streams of Christian Civilization ... the love of country and the hope of founding the noblest edition of national life to be an example to the world.
— Frederic Beal Du Val (1847–1928),
"The Problem of Social Vice in Winnipeg"

The concept of human trafficking entered international discourse in the early twentieth century alongside concerns over white slavery.[1] Initial discussions focused exclusively on the migratory movements (or "traffic") of women and girls and conflated trafficking with prostitution.[2] Dominant representations portrayed trafficked individuals as "innocent young girls being kidnapped, deceived, drugged or otherwise coercively obtained and forced to be prostitutes" (Doezema 2010: 15). *Innocence*, in the colonial imagination, was largely synonymous with whiteness and purity. In this context, the moral panic over white slavery enabled the consolidation of the purity movement precisely because prostitution was perceived as "*the* social evil" (Valverde 2008: 77) and was thereby able to mobilize advocates from a variety of interest groups, including doctors, lawyers, judges, journalists, suffragists, Christian social reformers, and others.

Given the centrality of political discussions about prostitution and white slavery from multiple perspectives, it is not surprising that prostitution and early conceptions of trafficking feature as recurrent themes of national identity formation. The narrative of white slavery and that of its descendant, human trafficking, provided a flexible discourse of varying local expressions as anti-trafficking advocates sought to construct and negotiate the realities of colonialism and settler colonialism in diverse regional contexts. Consistently, anti–white slavery campaigners and their corresponding vision of purity were juxtaposed against the "impure" – the prostitute, the Aboriginal woman, and the immigrant – in the burgeoning national narrative. At the same time, racialized constructions of impurity constituted spaces of intervention whereby campaigners assumed the responsibility for rescue and restoration. Moreover, this juxtaposition occurred in a context of ongoing colonial gender violence perpetrated against Indigenous women and naturalized through legal mechanisms of domination and the racialized separation of settlers from immigrants.

In 1904, the first international convention against white slavery was adopted. Emphasizing trafficking as prostitution – and, particularly, innocent young women and girls being deceived – the convention aimed to "suppress the 'criminal traffic' of women or girls compulsively procured for 'immoral purposes'" (Gallagher 2010: 13). Again, in 1912, the International Convention for the Suppression of the White Slave Traffic reiterated such representations by obliging states to punish "[w]hoever, in order to gratify the passions of another person, has, by fraud, or by means of violence, threats, abuse of authority, or any other method of compulsion, procured, enticed, or led away a woman or girl over age, for immoral purposes." Although historical studies concede there were actually few cases of white slavery,[3] moral reformers and feminists of the day condemned the abduction and relocation of white European and North American women for prostitution in South America, Africa, and Asia.[4]

Triggered by actual increases in women's migration (including the migration of sex workers)[5] and fuelled by misguided images of uncivilized – i.e., non-Western and Indigenous – Others, white slavery received significant media attention.[6] However, by 1927, references to white slavery were disregarded as "not reflecting the nature and scope of the problem" (Gallagher 2010: 14).[7] In this way, the earliest conceptions of human trafficking were shaped by discourses of moral panic and sensationalized representations of innocent victims, with the overarching aim of protecting the purity of (i.e., civilizing) young, white, immigrant, and working class women.[8] Meanwhile, the production of trafficked persons and broader experiences of the precariat naturalized by the settler colonial state remained intact. In Canada, social concerns accompanying colonial nation-building, rapid urbanization, and immigration from increasingly non-Protestant and non-British countries of origin (Valverde 2008) further integrated the white slavery narrative into the colonial project of civilizing the West.

Institutionalized racism was entrenched in federal policies that restricted Chinese and Japanese immigration. Moreover, in spite of claims to common legal memberships within the growing Empire, subjects of British India faced targeted restrictions to entering Canada (Macklin 2010). Such racialized exclusions served to naturalize the nation-building project of white, settler colonial domination and provided the foundation for implementing subjugation through civilizing missions. From 1885 until 1903, many Chinese immigrants were required to pay a head tax, ranging from 50 to 500 dollars (Marshall 2014). Measures of exclusion became further ingrained in 1923 when the Chinese Immigration Act explicitly denied entry to most people of Chinese descent and particularly to Chinese children and wives. Although few Chinese women arrived during this time, those who entered Canada were detained "for hours, days, or weeks in what family members described as the immigration 'prison'" (Marshall 2014: 111). Beyond such detention, Chinese women were presumed by white settlers to be "slaves or prostitutes" in need of rescue, moral regulation, and "proper domesticity" (Ikebuchi 2015: 35). As Ikebuchi (2015) documents, the Women's Missionary Society began the first Chinese Rescue Home in 1887 with the mandate of evangelizing and civilizing Chinese women within white constructions of respectability.

Japanese immigration appeared less restrictive through the adoption of the 1894 Anglo–Japanese Treaty of Commerce and Navigation, which Canada signed in 1905 (Macklin 2010). However, in a context of widespread anti-Asian sentiment, Macklin (2010) demonstrates that the Lemieux Agreement reduced immigration to 400 people annually. According to Macklin (2010: 9–10), "if the Chinese were treated as imported commodities subject to duty, then the Japanese were allowed to manage the emigration of their own population through voluntary export restraint." In both instances, racial dominance through mechanisms of immigration control reasserted settler claims to sovereignty over the land. In the words of Ikebuchi (2015: 31), settlement was "about creating and maintaining a hierarchy of race that solidified white settlers' rights to the land ... Thus, understanding settlement requires understanding the power relations and powerful relationships it fostered. If Aboriginal populations and non-white immigrants were seen as racial impediments to proper settlement, then white settlement depended on the taming of so-called 'savage' Aboriginal populations as well as the control, expulsion, and sometimes transformation of Chinese and Japanese 'sojourner' populations." In this way – by racializing and gendering conceptions of inclusion and exclusion that further reinforced white heteropatriarchy as normative of the state – settler colonialism naturalized interlayered forms of domination.

With high levels of anti-Asian racism and corresponding social anxieties about interracial marriages, procurers in the white slave trade, especially in the Canadian West, were conflated with "foreigners." As Hua (2011: 82) notes, anti-trafficking relies on the "racializing of patriarchies" as a means of constructing linkages of "Asianness to despotism and traditional practices of patriarchy in ways that gauge progress through the (cultural) exercise of liberal feminist principles. Such representational effects enable human rights to act as a site of (neo)colonial power." Thus, white slave traffickers were portrayed as a racialized threat to settler communities, offering promises of marriage to lure girls from their homes and families into prostitution (McMaster 2008). Forming a Committee on the Equal Moral Standard and Traffic in Women in 1912, the National Council of Women (NCW) decried that foreign influence was shaping urban immorality: "in the cities [of the West] most of the dens of vice are owned by Chinese and Japanese. No doubt many of the girl inmates are owned by them also." Whether citizens or not, the "foreign" character of white slave traders provided a racialized means of distancing them from authentic members of the Canadian national identity. Against this backdrop, the committee declared, "we rejoice in the fact that there is a general movement throughout Canada to suppress the business of social vice, including the white slave trafficking, for purity is the very foundation of national life" (as cited in Valverde 2008: 93). Purity, in this context, refers to freedom from social vice and from "foreign" contamination.

Such framing was a result of, and lent support to, racial hostilities and exclusionary immigration policies, including the Komagata Maru incident.[9] In 1908, the continuous-journey regulation, an amendment to the Immigration Act, restricted immigration from British India in spite of claims to legal membership within the transnational Empire (Macklin 2010). Such policies of exclusion were demonstratively performed against racialized bodies when, in 1914, the Komagata Maru arrived off the coast of British Colombia, but was denied entry by the Government of Canada. In the process of denying entry in order to preserve "cultural homogeneity" (Ward 2002: 91), the exclusion of the migrants provided a basis for European claims of being "at home" and "native" to the land. The arrival was perceived as a threat to the racial purity of the *new* nation in spite of the reality that the population of British Columbia was becoming proportionally more white during this time, while Indigenous populations and the population of Chinese arrivals remained numerically stable (Valverde 2008). Nonetheless, at a protest meeting calling for the deportation of the ship, Conservative Member of Parliament H.H. Stevens declared, "we cannot allow indiscriminate immigration from the Orient and hope to build up a Nation in Canada on the foundations upon which we have commenced our national life ... I hold that no immigration is or can be successful where it is impossible to assimilate and readily assimilate the immigrant" (as cited in Ward 2002: 91–92). In the context of settler colonialism, the "spectacle of sovereignty" characterized by such overt forms of exclusion functioned to naturalize settler colonial Canada as an independent sovereign state. The immigrant Other was thereby portrayed as a subject to be feared based on the perceived threat posed to the purity of "*our* national life" and national identity.

Thus, the focus on assimilating "the immigrant" and the exertion of state-based power to exclude entry into national territory provides a basis for determining sovereign Indigenous nations as "domestic dependent" nations (Byrd 2011). Macklin (2010: 2) points out the following:

> For the story of Canada as a nation of immigrants can only be recounted with pride (as it always is) if immigration is understood as a process of extending hospitality and membership by those entitled to do so, as opposed to governmentalizing ongoing invasion and occupation. The rendering of indigenous peoples as internal other – the alien within – must transpire in order that a settler society can usurp the epistemic privilege of identifying and excluding the external other. Without this move, the sovereign could not properly differentiate the flood of illegal aliens swamping the nation from the immigrants coming to build it.

Racialized discourses of exclusion and the potential for inclusion of the immigrant conceal settler colonial injury and efforts of domestication by painting Aboriginal Otherness as inferior, conquered, or already assimilated in the mind of the colonizer. The foundations of national life are thereby characterized by whiteness and assimilation to British conceptions of civilization. In turn, both Aboriginal and "foreigner" were deemed antithetical to whiteness, purity, and civility.

In the Canadian nation-building narrative, "the prostitute" and the related white slave in the early nineteenth century provided another counterpoint to the emerging national citizen. The prostitute was cast as "the antithesis of the pioneer woman – a moral icon that embodied the values of restraint, self-sacrifice, chastity, godliness, and civilization" (Erickson 2011: 79). As can be heard, the bodies of sex workers took on a similar antithetical position to the perceived impurity of the bodies of foreigners and Indigenous women in the colonial imagination. Missionaries "were horrified by Native attitudes towards sexuality" (Anderson 2000: 85). In many Indigenous cultures, women in particular were held in high regard and their bodies were generally seen as powerful, to be celebrated. Sex was seen as natural and women could initiate sexual encounters. In the words of Anderson (2000: 85), many Indigenous women "had a great deal of individual control over their own sexuality" (see also Green 2007). Moreover, Indigenous sexuality in many cases was premised on gender fluidity. As Cameron (2009: 201) highlights, "Gender orientation is not based on physical sex characteristics, but rather on the roles the person chooses to align with."

Nonetheless, the colonizers' racist and gendered perspectives of Indigenous women's autonomy over their bodies led to a view of "Native woman as prostitute" and "morally loose" in the colonial imagination. This conflation occurred within the context of ongoing physical and sexual violence towards Indigenous peoples. Further, it lent itself to the suppression of Indigenous cultural practices by associating them with the perceived immorality of "wayward" sexuality, such as the racialized notion (and subsequent ban) of the potlatch ceremony as "the ultimate sign of degradation" (Mawani 2002: 52)[10] and the aim of "total control" over Indigenous women's sexuality in the context of residential schooling (Barman 2004: 230). Given the colonizer's perspective of prostitution, i.e., through lenses of sexual morality and control, conflating Indigenous women with the stigmatized "prostitute" became a means to further separate both Indigenous women and sex workers from the bourgeois ideal of purity. Such conflation was demonstrated in sensational headlines of slavery and abduction, which "proved to be groundless" upon investigation.[11] Regardless of their validity, the claims motivated Indian agents, missionaries, and moral entrepreneurs to argue for more stringent laws, resulting in constructions of the emerging white national woman in relation to and against Indigenous women.

For the actors of the purity movement, the white slave could induce both pity and abhorrence, both of which necessitated the intervention of bourgeois philanthropy: "She is not wholly to blame for her fall and can therefore be pitied, rescued, and perhaps redeemed by compassionate philanthropists"; however "she can never be truly redeemed" (McMaster 2008: 90). True redemption required purity, which depended on virginity and whiteness. In turn, this enabled "reformers to seek harsh law-and-order measures while making a space for voluntary philanthropy" (Valverde 2008: 100). Bourgeois purity was thereby constituted both in opposition to and in management of the sex worker and the Indigenous woman, as Erickson (2011: 78–79) underscores, "Prostitutes' bodies, much like Aboriginal women's, became sites of inscription upon which competing interest groups – Christian social reformers, physicians, law officials, and feminists – wrote the deep-seated fears and ambitions for authority that accompanied their confrontations with modernity ... the prairie prostitute loomed large in the bourgeois imagination because she, alongside the dangerous and dissolute Aboriginal woman, was a female variant of the serpent of the wilderness." Colonial images of the sex worker as both "a source of danger and endangered" (Erickson 2011: 80) facilitated a dual process of dehumanizing and prohibiting that also underpinned colonial tactics of *civilizing* Indigenous women. Much like the colonial perception of Indigenous women, the sex worker was a figure to be simultaneously civilized and subjugated. The tools of subjugation overlapped in the Indian Act and in provisions made in the Criminal Code.

Canada passed the first statute that directly mentions "prostitutes" in 1839 in Lower Canada (Backhouse 1985). Although a diversity of responses shaped early efforts to regulate the "problem of prostitution" as a "necessary evil," a matter of moral order, or as a vector of contagious disease, early white slavery panics consolidated abolitionist readings around the need to eradicate prostitution.[12] In this context, "feminists, anti-feminists, socialists and conservatives, extreme racists and moderate assimilationists were all able to join the campaign by conveniently stressing one or another of the variegated analyses and images of white slavery" (Valverde 2008: 95; McMaster 2008). With social anxieties accompanying mass urbanization and entrenched fears about interracial miscegenation, toleration and regulation of sex industries was replaced with moral vigilance and efforts at prohibition. Frederic Beal

Du Val, cited at the outset of this chapter, for instance, perceived the pitfalls of urbanization as epitomized by the "fallen woman"; he goes even further to refer to sex workers as "noxious weeds" that will spread unless eradicated. Eradication of Otherness was necessary for the dominance of heteronomative patriarchy. Sex workers, alongside those cast as Other, were seen to contain the ability to undermine Canadianness and thereby threaten "the West's imperial destiny" (Erickson 2011: 90). Although early anti-prostitution laws in Canada were more punitive than their English models, missionaries, Indian agents, and first-wave feminists still argued for more stringent controls.[13]

Given the undoubtedly gendered and racialized nature of the Indian Act, it is not surprising that prostitution controls were included in the 1879 Act and later incorporated into the Criminal Code in 1892. The purpose of the Indian Act was to strip Indigenous persons from their lands and "was openly aimed at the elimination of Indigenous people as a legal and social fact" (Lawrence 2004: 33). Thobani (2007: 50), for instance, describes the intersecting processes of appropriating land and dehumanizing Indigenous people: "[A]s was the case with the deployment of the concept of terra nullius to claim European legal entitlement over territories emptied of Aboriginal presence, a corresponding humanitas nullius was deployed through the Act to empty Native peoples of their human status." In particular, the Act sought the erasure of Indigenous peoples through the dispossession of Indigenous women. The autonomy and sovereignty represented by Indigenous women posed a substantial threat to nation-building, which necessitated their subjugation to Victorian standards of "domesticity" through state policies (Eberts 2014). Under the Act, gender inequalities typical of settler patriarchal societies were formally institutionalized for Indigenous women who were legally denied Indian Status if they married a non-Status man.[14]

The legislation was thereby shaped by and contributed to the colonial project of naturalizing dominion through patriarchal gender violence that inscribed "hierarchy and domination on the bodies of the colonized" (Smith 2005: 23). As Boyer and Kampouris (2014: 6) detail,

Patriarchal laws, policies, legislation and regulations would be instituted that attacked Aboriginal women as their families' "anchors." The high social standing accorded by societies and cultures that held women in high regard was eroded. Eventually, women's effective participation in governing their societies and nurturing good social relations within their communities was substantially diminished, and, in some cases, eliminated with the imposition of the [Indian Act], residential schools, forced sterilization laws, mental health laws, forced removal of children and enfranchisement; all of these factors contributed to eroding the position of Aboriginal woman as caregivers, nurturers and equal members of the community. The perception that the original inhabitants of this land were "savages" fortified the notion that Aboriginal peoples were less than human and that women were free to be exploited.

Thus, the inclusion of prostitution in the Indian Act cannot be separated from the purpose of the Act. In a context that sought to dehumanize Indigenous women (humanitas nullius), appropriate Indigenous land (terra nullius), destroy Indigenous ceremony (cultural genocide), and discipline autonomous women in general through principles of civility founded in heteropatriarchy and hierarchical binary gender orders, anti-prostitution policies were conceived from a Victorian purity standard aimed at the domestication of women in general and the eradication of the status and power of Indigenous women in particular, especially those in matrilineal communities. Under this civilizing mandate, the Indian Act provisions targeted intraracial prostitution by criminalizing Indigenous women and men involved in sex industries, while ignoring non-Indigenous participation.

Thus, the conflation of Indigenous women as "promiscuous by nature" facilitated the colonial positioning of Indigenous women as farthest from white conceptions of civility and purity as a means to eradicate troubling bodies, either through criminalization, assimilation, or both. This occurred in a context of colonial sexualized violence against Indigenous women devalued of humanity (humanitas nullius), and was enacted through the introduction of punitive laws. As Stoler (2002: 47) argues, "regulation of sexual relations was central to the development of particular kinds of colonial settlements." Through such regulation, the Indian Act also produced and naturalized the making of different kinds of Indigenous subjects (Lawrence 2004). It is by controlling this "different kind of subject" that colonial Canada legally facilitated and continues to perpetuate a context of colonial gender violence. Although anti-trafficking advocates aim to resist and address such legacies of colonialism by denouncing the conflation of Indigenous women as "sexually available," this often occurs at the expense of addressing ongoing forms of domination and control, particularly at the expense of the agency, self-determination, and bodily sovereignty of Indigenous women and Two-Spirit, LGBTTQQIA, and gender non-conforming Indigenous persons.

Nonetheless, alongside specific representations of Indigenous women as *fallen* and in social positions of subjugation, such a stance further positioned the philanthropist and white social reformation woman as the standard of domestic purity and the regulator of sexual relations through notions of rescue: "stronger marriage laws and the abolition of [I]ndigenous marriage customs were necessary for the *protection* of Native women, the *prevention* of prostitution, and the *preservation* of white settlement" (Mawani 2002: 52; emphasis added). Such themes of protection, prevention, and preservation (particularly of moral purity) naturalized the settler as the saviour of Indigenous women, and remain dominant in anti-trafficking discourses as they intersect with anti-prostitution mechanisms of control. Given the centrality of criminalization in civilizing missions, "private philanthropic workers assumed quasi-police powers" and "the public police also came to see itself as exercising benevolent functions" (Valverde 2008: 100). The Salvation Army, in particular, argued that *forcing* individuals convicted of moral offences to submit to the "Army's care," would result in their rapid and voluntary conversion and reform (Valverde 2008).

In this context, vagrancy provisions in the Indian Act not only restricted Indigenous women from walking alone but also served the parallel civilizing function of producing "prostituted subjects" that required rescue, intervention, and control. As Lawrence (2004: 35) writes, "Indian agents were given the powers to enforce anti-vagrancy laws, the primary legislative provisions governing prostitution in Canada until the 1970s, which provided the Indian agents with the power to control Indian women through designating them as 'common prostitutes.'" In doing so, such intervention institutionalized violence perpetrated by the state and state-actors, including sexual violence, theft of land, removal of children, and cultural genocide in the context of colonial–gendered violence. Lawrence (2004: 49) further highlights:

> Clearly, if a white settler society modeled on British values was to be established, white women had to take the place of Native women, and Native women had to be driven out of the place they had occupied in fur trade society, a process that would continue through successive waves of white settlement, from the Great Lakes westward across the continent. The displacement of Native women from white society, and the replacement of the bicultural white society that their marriages to white men

created to an openly white supremacist society populated by all-white families, was accomplished through the introduction of punitive laws in the *Indian Act* concerning prostitution and intoxication off-reserve. These laws targeted Aboriginal women as responsible for the spread of venereal disease among the police and officials in western Canada and therefore increasingly classified urban Aboriginal women as prostitutes within the criminal code after 1892.

Building on provisions in the Indian Act, the Criminal Code further enacted laws that criminalized "prostitutes" for being found in a public area. As Backhouse (1985: 389) highlights, "she could be punished merely for *being* a prostitute. In large measure, it was the 'status' of being a prostitute that was unlawful." Thus, enforcement officials could detain any woman who "could not explain her presence in a public place to a police officer" (O'Connell 1988: 113). Guided by assimilationist policies, vagrancy was similarly applied to migrants, whose very existence was conflated with vagrancy: "the imposition of the idea that homelessness is akin to godlessness allowed vagrancy to be understood as a moral (and often a criminal) offence to the community of 'honest residents'" (Sharma 2006: 11). Migration, in this context, was a likewise criminalized "status" to that of "the streetwalker." Overall, the *status* of Otherness was institutionally criminalized in ways that, from the outset of nation-building in Canada, disproportionately affected individuals involved in sex industries, Indigenous women, and migrants from non-European countries. Anti-trafficking, through early discourses of white slavery, featured prominently in this nation-building project towards the production of Canadianness and the domestication of Indigeneity.

Thus, in the context of white slavery panics and colonial civilizing missions, early anti-trafficking discourses were characterized by settler colonial imperatives of rescuing "fallen women." Yet, there are noteworthy omissions in these foundational trafficking discourses. Abolishing white slavery was tied to anti-prostitution and moral reformation; however, more explicit forms of what we might understand as human trafficking were directly connected to the civilizing mission of creating "good" (domestic) women. The appropriation of Indigenous lands, in particular, required the subjugation of Indigenous women and part of this subjugation included abduction, enslavement, and coerced labour. As Smith (2005: 23) shows, "while enslaving women's bodies, colonizers argued that they were actually somehow freeing Native women from the 'oppression' they supposedly faced in Native nations." Although involvement in sex industries was interpreted through a trafficking framework, forced labour was largely disregarded as a necessary part of the civilizing process.

By way of example, in 1891 Qu'Appelle Industrial School "pressed more than twenty female students into service as maids, nannies, and household assistants" (Erickson 2011: 51). The school's principle, Father Joseph Hugonnard, "arranged the terms of service and payment" and "retained the majority of the students' wages, and provided their parents with only a small stipend" (Erickson 2011: 51). By isolating girls from their families and communities, the goal of the program was to prepare Indigenous girls for *Christian* marriages and to civilize them into the tasks of middle-class housewives. Although few were ever in a position to become housewives (Smith 2005), the training served the dual purpose of preparation for servitude in white middle-class homes. In the United States, children were similarly "involuntarily leased out to white homes as menial labour" where "they were taught domestic skills of washing, ironing, sewing, and preparing and serving at parties" (Smith 2005: 37). In short, "it was training in dispossession under the guise of domesticity, developing a habitus shaped by the messages of subservience and one's proper place" (Lomawaima 1994: 86, as cited in Smith 2005: 37). Despite the coercive and exploitative nature of such labour, this type of coercion was omitted from discourses of trafficking, which only became legible through its conflation of prostitution and white slavery.

Other forms of state practice also fall under the radar of trafficking advocacy, such as forced assimilation, abduction into residential schooling, forced relocation, and so on. In this way, early trafficking discourses provided a flexible rights-based narrative that mobilized moral, legal, and social reforms along the lines of national-identity formation through a civilizing process. In turn, such discourses helped establish and facilitate the reproduction of the legitimized boundaries of the nation-state. Therefore, we see trafficking discourses effectively reproducing the sexual, racial, and national priorities of the state, while offering very little in the way of transformative change to counter the structures of inequality that produce trafficking subjects in the first place.

The Construction and Deconstruction of Anti-trafficking Dichotomies in International Anti-trafficking Protocols

By 1927, references to white slavery were disregarded as "not reflecting the nature and scope of the problem" (Gallagher 2010: 14).[15] But in spite of waning interest in the white slave trade, concerns over prostitution continued. In this context, prohibitionist campaigns against white slavery joined forces with feminist campaigns seeking to abolish prostitution (Doezema 2010). As Bernstein (2010: 46) highlights, such "strange bedfellows" are united by "a shared commitment to carceral paradigms of social, and in particular gender, justice [carceral feminism] ... and to militarized humanitarianism as the preeminent mode of engagement by the state." Such coalitions were pivotal in the expansion of international conventions against trafficking.

Institutionalizing the conflation of human trafficking and sex work, Article 1 of the 1933 International Convention for the Suppression of the Traffic in Women states the following: "Whoever, in order to gratify the passions of another person, has procured, enticed or led away *even with her consent*, a woman or girl of full age for immoral purposes to be carried out in another country, shall be punished" (Organization of American States 2008; emphasis added). Based on abolitionist ideals, the convention built on previous agreements to portray trafficked women as innocent victims of the "passions" of others and expanded this perspective to deem the consent of women as irrelevant and fallible to the enticement of the luring practices of others, thereby denying agency. These sentiments were reiterated in the 1949 United Nations Convention for the Suppression of Traffic in Persons and the Exploitation of Prostitution of Others. Although few countries signed the 1949 convention, the abolitionist legislation informed domestic policy for most of the second half of the twentieth century and a number of countries continue to adopt abolition-oriented approaches to human trafficking that emphasize the abolishment of prostitution through criminal justice interventions as a means of protection and rescue for *victims* of human trafficking, particularly women and girls.[16] Meanwhile, contemporary campaigns against human trafficking parallel responses to the white slave-trade,[17] particularly by equating human trafficking with prostitution and relying on emotionally charged awareness materials to stir moral sentiments and potentially moral panic in the development of criminal intervention strategies to what advocates perceive as a new form of slavery.

Although interest in white slavery and trafficking declined after the Second World War, radical feminists concerned with sexual slavery[18] resurfaced abolitionist approaches and anti-trafficking discourses following the Vietnam War (Kempadoo 2005). In particular, due to the ongoing stationing of US military troops during the post-conflict reconstruction and post-war development period in Southeast Asia, feminists expressed concern over "sex tourism, mail-order bride arrangements, militarized prostitution, and coercions and violence in the movement and employment of women from poorer to more affluent areas at home and abroad for work in leisure, relaxation, and sex industries" (Kempadoo 2005: xi). Thus, at this time, trafficking debates focused on the transfer of people, particularly women, from contexts of poverty to affluence: from the Global South to the Global North and from rural areas to major urban centres.

In line with this shift, Sassen (2002) argues, for example, that contextualizing the experiences of migrant women under the broader restructuring policies of economic globalization reveals the disproportionate effect such policies have had on women (see also Chant 2006; Pearce 1978; Mies 1998; Oxman-Martinez, Martinez, and Hanley 2001b; Thorbek and Pattanaik 2002). Structural adjustment policies, in particular, led governments to scale back social programs, such as housing, health care, and education, and also led to increased migration of women searching for income-generating activities (Chuang 2006). This resulted in low-income women playing an essential role in the global economy; a dynamic Sassen (2002) coined the "feminization of survival," which refers to the increasing dependence of households, communities, and states on the migratory labour of women. Thus, resistance to models of development enacted on and against "third world" women, and rescue projects shaped by radical and carceral feminisms emerged.

In Canada, discourses emphasizing the criminalization and "moral culpability" of sex industry workers focused inward towards nuisance provisions of criminalization (Brock 1989; O'Connell 1988). Meanwhile, structural adjustment favoured discourses emphasizing global sex trade and risk, particularly risk "of violence, of entrapment, and seduction" (Hallgrimsdottir, Phillips, and Benoit 2006: 272; Sanghera 2000). Yet, as Aradau (2004: 253) details, notions of *at risk* and *risky* become intertwined in anti-trafficking: "As illegal migrants, prostitutes and (potential) criminals, trafficked women are a cause of insecurity; as victims, they are also simultaneously vulnerable and made insecure themselves." Such discourses facilitated the advancement of Canadian foreign policy concerns through the adoption of the "victimist view of migrant sex-work as trafficking" and the corresponding securitization of borders alongside the adoption of anti-trafficking protocols and legislations (Jeffrey 2005: 37).[19] In this way, feminist humanitarian efforts to rescue and develop the Other simultaneously reinforced the boundaries separating *us* from *them* and the ongoing criminalization of migrants to Canada.

Meanwhile, a new form of feminism spread from the Global South to critique the "gynocentric" philosophies of Western feminists and the positioning of "poor bodies" as objects of intervention and subjects of risk (Saunders 2002: 11).[20] Such approaches asserted the agency of women in a "highly gendered and racialized world order" (Kempadoo 2005: xi). From this perspective, women can be victimized by global sex industries in the same way victimization occurs in unskilled or semi-skilled professions increasingly filled by a feminized workforce. As a result, certain trafficking discourses were polarized: victim versus agent and coercion versus consent. As O'Connell Davidson (2013: 177) argues, the "forced/voluntary dyad has much wider currency (it is used in relation to [for example] labour, prostitution, and marriage), and has its origins in a liberal tradition of Western post-Enlightenment thought that tends to conceive of reality in terms of binaries or dualisms." Although such polarization continues to be problematized in the critical anti-trafficking literature, the conflicting claims shaped the adoption of current international protocols and continue to shape their implementation and ongoing public discourses in national contexts.

Plagued by moralizing ideologies and dichotomous discourses, politicized coalitions of nongovernment organizations became especially influential in framing international definitions of human trafficking. Claiming to draw on the experiences of trafficked women, polarized coalitions – such as the Human Rights Caucus (HRC) and the Coalition Against Trafficking in Women (CATW)[21] – argue their research and ideology protects the rights of women in the sex trade. Yet, their polarized positions limited the advancement of anti-trafficking measures that protect the rights and security of trafficked persons or consideration of proactive measures to prevent trafficking in the first place.

Formed by the International Human Rights Law Group, the HRC established a global network of nongovernmental organizations (NGOs) that distinguish between trafficking and sex work, arguing that sex work (as work) is a form of labour. Trafficking, on the other hand, requires some form of coercion or deception. By acknowledging the right to voluntarily engage in sex work, the HRC sought to develop a framework to protect the labour rights of women working in sex industries in the negotiations leading to the UN Trafficking Protocol.[22] At the same time, the HRC argued for an understanding of trafficking that acknowledges men, women, and children are trafficked into a number of positions, including forced prostitution, marriages, domestic services, agricultural labour, and/or factory work (Jordan 2002). From this perspective, anti-trafficking initiatives must target all forms of trafficking by focusing on the abuse, coercion, and human rights violations that affect trafficked persons, rather than seeking to eradicate the particular areas of labour (Sanghera 2005). Weitzer (2012: 7) refers to the ideas underlying the HRC perspective on trafficking as the "empowerment paradigm." However, the language of "agency" is more reflective of this approach, considering – as Weitzer (2012: 10) himself notes – few scholars and advocates would "define sex work solely in terms of empowerment." Nonetheless, at its extreme, empowerment approaches are as "one-dimensional and essentialist" – particularly in their erasure of intersectional forms of violence – as their counterpart, the "victim" or "oppression" paradigm adopted by the CATW.

The CATW argues that trafficking and prostitution are synonymous.[23] From this "oppression paradigm" (Weitzer 2012: 10), prostitution is symptomatic of patriarchy and male domination[24] and women are portrayed as incapable of offering consent because they are perceived as inherently exploited and thereby victimized through the very act of engaging in prostitution. To ensure this point is dominant, accounts of human trafficking circulated by feminist and abolitionist groups draw on "melodramatic narratives" in their graphic depictions of violence, their warnings about the prevalence and growth of trafficking industries, and their calls to action (Doezema 2010). In doing so, an "ideal victim" of trafficking emerges: a young, naive, female victim – often from a "Third World" or racialized context – who was innocent, economically desperate, and ignorant of what awaited her before being deceived by her trafficker. Such depictions underscore discourses that separate "domestic" trafficking from "international" trafficking through varying interpretations of "innocence."

Further, they contribute to the objectification of trafficked individuals as passive victims, as exemplified by Bales's (1999) depiction of "disposable tools." Similarly, Janice Raymond (2004: 1183, as cited in Weitzer 2012), co-executive director of the CATW, suggests that "prostitution is something done to women." In this way, advocates of a "victim" or "oppression" paradigm claim to protect the rights of women by protecting "prostitutes" from the "inherent violence of 'prostitution.'" Simultaneously, an image of anti-trafficking advocates emerges: compassionate individuals with a call to rescue the most vulnerable and restore the innocence of "victims" of trafficking.[25] I doing so, however, such interventions often ignore or discredit the voices of individuals involved in sex industries.

These unresolved debates persisted during the signing of the 2000 United Nations trafficking protocol supplementing the UN Convention

Against Transnational Organized Crime (i.e., UN Trafficking Protocol). In this context, Canada signed the Protocol in December 2000 and ratified it in May 2002. According to the UN Trafficking Protocol, trafficking in persons refers to the following:

> [T]he recruitment, transportation, transfer, harbouring or receipt of persons, by means of the threat or use of force or other forms of coercion, of abduction, of fraud, of deception, of the abuse of power or of a position of vulnerability or of the giving or receiving of payments or benefits to achieve the consent of a person having control over another person, for the purposes of exploitation. Exploitation shall include, at a minimum, the exploitation of the prostitution of others or other forms of sexual exploitation, forced labour or services, slavery or practices similar to slavery, servitude or the removal of organs. (United Nations Office on Drug and Crime [UNODC] 2000)

For clarity, the definition of trafficking is frequently broken down into three separate parts: an activity, a means, and a goal.[26] Activities include recruitment, transportation, transfer, harbouring, or receipt of persons.[27] While recruiting or harbouring trafficked persons is included in the definition, some anti-trafficking advocates have argued that movement was, in fact, intended to be a core element of the definition (Jordan and Burke 2011). These advocates emphasize the abuse and possible risk, even death, which can occur through the process of transportation. By emphasizing the importance of movement, advocates also aim to distinguish human trafficking from other forms of sexual labour (Jordan and Burke 2011). Others have argued that movement is not – and should not be – an essential element of the trafficking definition, emphasizing that the focus should be on the exploitation of the "victim of crime," rather than whether or not the "victim" was moved (Perrin 2010b). Omitting movement, from this perspective, facilitates the characterization of sex work as trafficking.

Significantly, under the Criminal Code of Canada, movement is not a necessary provision in human trafficking cases. However, mirroring confusion at the international level, criminal justice authorities and frontline workers in Canada debate whether movement of some kind is a required element of the offence, with some interpreting movement as a mandatory element. As one legal representative commented, "I think if you read within the context of the definition there, the person who's charged doesn't have to be solely responsible for the movement; they can facilitate, they can counsel, they can assist, but ultimately there has to be a movement of a person and then the servitude of the exploitation." Said another way, "[I]n my opinion, that there has been a movement of a person and the conduct has assisted in that movement for the purpose of exploiting the victim, and I've come from that opinion because there's not a lot of case law on that."

Similarly, in applying the legislation, some law enforcement officials rely on the element of movement as the defining factor for determining whether to lay human trafficking charges.[28] As one law enforcement representative indicates,

> I had a file where someone thought she was just going be working as like a stripper, or a dancer at bachelor parties and she got mentally forced into doing prostitution as well, which wasn't her main goal but then she just kept getting hounded and hounded and hounded so much that she definitely did stay in it because she felt forced to. However, that doesn't fall under human trafficking because *she wasn't taken anywhere* but she was forced to work in the sex trade, which is stuff we do prosecute and we see that more often. (emphasis added)

As this excerpt suggests, movement is sometimes perceived in the field as the primary distinguishing factor used to determine whether a case falls under the *trafficking in persons* legislation versus pursuing charges under a related section of the Criminal Code. In the quote, this dominance of movement is evident even when perceived forced labour occurs. Although beyond the scope of this book, an exploration of whether movement is similarly constructed in conceptions of nonsexual labour trafficking would prove insightful. Despite such applications of the Criminal Code definition, at the time of writing, eleven of the twelve cases that have obtained convictions involved domestic sex trafficking – i.e., cases in which the trafficked persons were not moved across international borders. Although some cases involved transport between cities, others appear to involve no movement.[29] Thus, the necessity of movement continues to pose interpretive challenges.

The second element of the international definition of human trafficking, the "means," refer to the method(s) used to facilitate human trafficking. These can include threat, force, coercion, abduction, fraud, deception, abuse of power, or bribes (UNODC 2000). Finally, the "goal" of human trafficking is the overarching purpose of exploitation, which, according to the UN Trafficking Protocol, can include the exploitation of the prostitution of others, sexual exploitation, forced labour, involuntary servitude, slavery or practices similar to slavery, or the removal of organs.

While debate over the definition continues, common interpretations of the UNODC definition assert that at least one of the elements from each of the three criteria – activity, means, and goal – has to be met for a case to be considered human trafficking (Smith and Kangaspunta 2012).[30] However, in the case of children and youth, the means of trafficking are deemed irrelevant; under the Criminal Code of Canada definition of human trafficking specifically, the means are not a required consideration at all in cases involving children or adults in Canada.[31] However, as Kaye and Hastie (2015: 94) point out, the Criminal Code conception "imports an implicit *means* element in understanding what is meant by 'fear of safety,' and the fact that this is not explicit and in line with the [UN Trafficking Protocol] has only added to confusion at the interpretive and implementation levels." In particular, the "fear of safety" clause potentially restricts perceived application to non-physical forms of coercion, which functions to restrict "non-sexual forms of labour" as potential sites of human trafficking.

Conversely, in cases involving sex industries, Roots (2013) reveals how the vague nature of the Criminal Code's trafficking legislation creates challenges in distinguishing trafficking from other offences, such as procurement. As the fear of safety standard is well established in procurement cases, the distinction between human trafficking and procurement is blurred. This blurring results in placing the "discretionary power of interpretation in the hands of individual law enforcement officials to evaluate the situation based on their own moral compass" (Roots 2013: 23). This leads to violations of the rights of sex workers and creates greater insecurity for individuals involved, willingly or not, in sex industries (Roots 2013). For example, Clancey, Khushrushahi, and Ham (2014: 7) highlight how conflating trafficking with sex work or sexual exploitation "ignores significant structural factors and root causes of human trafficking such as gender inequality, poverty, increasingly stringent immigration policies and, in Canada among Indigenous girls and women, colonialism." As Benoit et al.'s (2014: 19) detailed examination of sex industries in Canada further reveals, "much of the vulnerability experienced by some sex workers has little or nothing to do with sex work." In spite of this, examinations of trafficking in sex industries frequently omit both the recognition of the heterogeneous nature of experiences of individuals working in sex industries and its necessary grounding in structural forms of inequality, and therefore fail to consider how a variety of factors intersect and constrain opportunities available to women in general and women in sex industries in particular.

In theory, rights-based approaches to anti-trafficking efforts necessitate collaborations with organizations that are focused on self-determination in sex work and migrant sex work because such partnerships allow for a more clear representation of sex workers who are best positioned to identify human trafficking in sex industries. Along these lines, Roots (2013) argues that conflating trafficking and procurement offences in Canada results in cases of human trafficking going undetected by law enforcement and reinforces a climate of distrust between individuals in sex industries and law enforcement. This is understood as restrictive when considering the compounding structural and social factors – trafficked persons risk stigmatization, deportation, loss of financial livelihood, and other forms of insecurity when reporting experiences of exploitation. However, as Timoshkina and McDonald (2011) highlight, coordination on trafficking responses requires navigating potentially irreconcilable differences in interests, ideological perspectives, and attitudes between and among migrant women, immigration systems, law enforcement, service providers, varying feminist factions, ethnic communities, and the general public. Such differences become particularly apparent when situated within the realities of the settler colonial nation-building project.

In the end, despite inherent differences, both victim and agency advocates claim to have "won" the lobbying debate to shape the UN Trafficking Protocol towards their respective standpoints.[32] This reflects the compromises established in the UN Trafficking Protocol as well as the ambiguous nature of the document and ongoing struggles to shape trafficking discourses and anti-trafficking agendas (Lepp 2002). From an agency perspective, the UN Trafficking Protocol successfully diverges from the abolitionist roots of the 1949 convention by connecting trafficking to multiple labour sites and the use of threat, force, or coercion (Doezema 2002). At the same time, the UN Trafficking Protocol includes stipulations about the abuse of "a position of vulnerability," which refers to "any situation in which the person involved has no real and acceptable alternative but to submit to the abuse involved" (UN Interpretive Footnote in Jordan 2002: 4). This stipulation is seen to draw on victim discourses that suggest trafficking can occur in the absence of coercion to include persons who have "no culturally acceptable or legal means to refuse and so they 'submit' to the situation" (Jordan 2002: 8). Women's agency advocates argue that such a stipulation can be used to silence the voices of women from economically marginalized situations by declaring them passive victims of their circumstances, while victim advocates insist it considers the hidden forms of manipulation that traffickers use to lure women into trafficking for sexual exploitation.[33]

By criminalizing the "exploitation of the prostitution of others," rather than all forms of prostitution, the UN Trafficking Protocol maintains national government autonomy over the question of whether all forms of prostitution constitute trafficking or, as the majority of governments agreed, if only "involuntary, forced participation in prostitution would constitute trafficking" (Lepp 2002: 92).[34] In turn, the ambiguous relationship between prostitution and human trafficking provides a basis for ongoing lobby efforts of both victim and agent perspectives. As O'Connell Davidson, and Anderson (2006: 14) argue, the vague nature of the definition of sex trafficking means "diametrically opposing proposals for the reform of prostitution laws can each be presented as contributing to the struggle against 'trafficking.'" This debate continues to drive public discussions of human trafficking. For instance, a background paper discussing the international obligations of Canada, specifically conjoins the trafficking protocol and prostitution legislations, arguing, "signatories must criminalize anyone who brings another person into prostitution, even if this is done with that person's consent" and "all parties must agree to take measures for the prevention of prostitution, as well as for the rehabilitation and social adjustment of victims of prostitution" (Barnett 2008: 2). In the end, the criminalizing and prohibitionist tendencies of abolitionist perspectives continue to dominate Canadian anti-trafficking discourses,[35] often to the detriment of trafficked persons and others affected by anti-trafficking responses.[36]

Overall, the UN Trafficking Protocol has been criticized for taking a weak stance on matters of human rights.[37] Although the law enforcement elements of the UN Trafficking Protocol are mandatory for signatories, the provisions to protect and assist individuals victimized by human trafficking are discretionary.[38] As a result, issues of national security and border controls have taken precedence, raising important questions about the appropriation of rights-based discourses and the potential for rights of migrants in general (O'Connell Davidson 2006) and trafficked persons in particular (Gallagher 2001; Jordan 2002) under anti-trafficking paradigms. Further, rights-based discourses that emphasize polarized distinctions – such as forced/voluntary, trafficking/smuggling, sexual exploitation/sex work – have been employed to obscure the complex processes of migratory movements and the politicized nature of anti-trafficking discourses.[39] According to Kempadoo (2005), human rights violations continue to escalate despite the anti-trafficking policies derived from the UN Trafficking Protocol. In a report prepared for the Global Alliance Against Traffic in Women (GAATW), Dottridge (2007: 2) indicates that existing anti-trafficking measures are "counter-productive" in their attempt to help trafficked persons and some "victims" have refused to participate in such programs or felt revictimized by their participation. Stagnated by ongoing cycles of definitional casuistry and ideologically driven discourses of the victim or agent status of trafficked persons, the trafficking protocol failed to offer appropriate measures for addressing the structural violence underpinning trafficking experiences or improving the conditions in which human trafficking occurs. Such critiques find their basis in broader discussions of human rights under the confines of existing boundaries of the nation-state that exclude non-citizens, such as refugees, non-status migrants, and, at times, trafficked persons, and fail to address Indigenous claims of nationhood and self-determination.

Constructing Anti-trafficking in Canada

Canada was one of the first countries to sign and ratify the UN Trafficking Protocol. Representatives from the Department of Foreign Affairs and International Trade (DFAIT), Status of Women Canada (SWC), and Justice Canada were key advocates in the negotiations leading to its adoption (Oxman-Martinez, Hanley, and Gomez 2005). Given Canada's global–economic position as a settler colonial country, it is clear from the departments represented in the negotiations that trafficking was perceived as a matter of interest to foreign policy and trade, a matter of criminal justice, and a women's issue. Consistent with the three-pronged approach outlined in the UN Trafficking Protocol (i.e., "the three Ps"), the federal government suggests it "works with partners to *prevent* human trafficking, *protect* victims, and *prosecute* offenders" (Department of Justice 2016; emphasis added). The following provides an overview of existing anti-trafficking responses in the areas of prevention, protection, and victim assistance in order to contextualize the negotiation of anti-trafficking discourses in localized contexts.

Canada's prevention efforts have centred on education and awareness raising activities. In 2004, the federal government established the Interdepartmental Working Group on Trafficking in Persons (IWGTIP) to coordinate their anti-trafficking efforts and develop a national strategy to address human trafficking. The IWGTIP sought to raise awareness through the dissemination of pamphlets and posters as well as through conferences on human trafficking. Although the group aimed to formulate a national strategy to combat trafficking in persons in Canada,[40] the national action plan did not come into fruition until Public Safety Canada assumed primary responsibility for anti-trafficking policy and initiatives. Advocating for the advancement of a national action plan, a government representative summarized the perceived limited progress of the IWGTIP in coordinating the Canadian anti-trafficking response, and also provided insight into the nature of anti-trafficking discourses in Canadian policy formation:

> [T]here were some aspects of the working group that have been very good, but you know you work with all departments, you work with the decision makers, and *you try to speed it up* ... because it's bureaucracy, it's a very large room, it's a very big challenge ... Departments need to work to make sure there are policies and they don't always do that because they themselves – the different departments – have different political views and they might not like the minister or maybe they *don't believe in the cause*, so the challenge is working together. In every department you have good and bad and indifferent. (emphasis added)

The excerpt points to the limited contribution of the IWGTIP as well as definitional discrepancies informing the varying interpretations of the nature and extent of human trafficking that affect anti-trafficking policy formation. Although the statement "they don't believe in the cause" likely refers to limited awareness and/or apathy about human trafficking, the statement also points to the perceived urgency and singularity of the cause. This underscores the central framework adopted by anti-trafficking advocates, who emphasize the pervasive nature of what they refer to as "modern forms of slavery"[41] by reiterating frequently cited statistics and the pressing need to develop counter-trafficking strategies based on the assumption that instances of human trafficking are widespread and rapidly expanding.[42]

Although the global scope and national conceptions of human trafficking remain vague at best, and existing figures are highly contested,[43] advocates rely on notions of urgency in order to rouse moral sentiment akin to those of the abolitionist movement that dismantled the transatlantic slave trade. In doing so, contemporary abolitionists cast themselves alongside now-heroic figures, such as William Wilberforce: "a passionate proponent of abolishing slavery – *an abolitionist*" (Perrin 2010a: 6; emphasis added). Such casting erases the racialized nature of anti-slavery politics wherein "some of the white figures that are today held up as icons of that movement did not regard the black brethren they sought to release from the bonds of slavery as fit for inclusion as equals in white political society" (O'Connell Davidson 2013: 93). Wilberforce, in particular, viewed former black slaves as "so 'uninformed' and 'debased' as to be 'almost incapacitated for the reception of civil rights' (Festa 2010: 14, as cited in O'Connell Davidson 2015: 83). Thus, regulatory interventions aimed to stop the "influx of uninstructed savages" (Jordan 2005: 180, as cited in O'Connell Davidson 2015: 93) were conjoined with anti-slavery, while simultaneously reproducing racialized exclusions from the growing national citizenry represented by the white settler colonial figure. In working against the aims of antiracism, such framing also elides the institutional nature of racism evident in transatlantic slavery and the continuities of ongoing human trafficking discourses that situate racism and other forms of colonial violence in the past while perpetuating ongoing forms of systemic inequality in a settler colonial context. As Hua (2011: 101) highlights in the context of the United States, "[l]inking human trafficking to transatlantic slavery makes possible the rewriting of a US history of racial discord and exploitation into a national mythology of progress towards pluralism, equality, and liberty – American principles and ideals – that help legitimate the U.S. role as leader in the global effort to combat trafficking and other women's human rights abuses." Hua (2011) goes on to state that such an approach erases ongoing racial and gender violence, while ignoring the fundamental role of such violence in the nation-building project. In a similar way, Canadian anti-trafficking discourses relying on the trope of modern-day slavery evoke national images of Canadians as inclusive, humanitarian benefactors at the expense of examining the ongoing violence of settler colonial domination.

Further, by sensationalizing human trafficking narratives, the modern-day slavery narrative serves to exclude broader experiences of institutionalized precarity and exploitation as well as the experiences of individuals affected by anti-trafficking legislation and responses. According to O'Connell Davidson (2010: 245), such approaches "enable

the moral condemnation of slavery to coexist with the continued imposition of extensive, forcible restrictions on individuals deemed to be
'free.'" By marginalizing "that which might challenge the status quo
or is messy or unmanageable," such campaigns effectively sanitize the
messy realities of human trafficking in relation to sex industries and
the politicized nature of anti-trafficking discourses into singular, one-
dimensional narratives. In turn, alternate narratives "register as deviance" (Kothari 2001: 148) and are silenced, disciplined, or expelled as
being "the bad and indifferent."

Although the IWGTIP had limited effect, the primary site of response
to human trafficking in Canada was situated within the offices of Public Safety Canada. Therefore, from a criminal justice basis, the Government of Canada released a National Action Plan to Combat Human
Trafficking (NAPCHT) in Canada (Public Safety Canada 2012b).The
plan promised to further Canada's commitment to combatting human
trafficking; however, the plan presented a unified conception of trafficking – "one of the most heinous crimes imaginable, often described
as modern-day slavery" – that necessitated enforcement-based crime-
control response models, while also mobilizing human rights arguments towards the reproduction of the settler colonial state. As Hua
(2011: ix) reveals, such responses "[allow] for the appropriation of
feminist and antiracist language for ends that neither support feminist
or antiracist goals."

Despite the NAPCHT's claim of presenting a unified approach to
human trafficking, a number of participants in the research informing
this book indicate that limited consultation informed its development.
Interestingly, this exclusion includes state-based actors. For example, in
the words of one national law enforcement representative working on
anti-trafficking responses, "I did read through the plan, but unfortunately we weren't consulted on it so there are some things that … could
have been different." Another provincial government representative
leading a province-wide anti-trafficking response said, "we asked to
be a part of it and [they] shut us right down … and that means it's just
[their] document, it's nobody else's so it's not even relevant to the rest
of the country if they haven't done consultation about it." Others indicated they were consulted, but were given a very restricted opportunity
to provide input. In the words of one frontline worker, "there was a
draft of a national plan of action or national strategy, and it kind of came
across our desks, and it was the middle of summer and the deadline for
us to get it back was like the week after." Thus, while the drafters of the

plan claim extensive consultation, it appears the consultation drew on an already established network. One federal government representative involved in the drafting stated that "consultations were very extensive"; however, the representative went on to say, "well, being in it for ten years, I know where to go to, what questions to ask I think that gave me an advantage, it gave me a huge advantage ... I didn't have to find [anyone]. I knew where they were ... I did the specific interviews with people that I took out of my bank of people and that included victims, NGOs, and police officers."

In alignment with much research on human trafficking, the representative claimed "extensive" consultation, while limiting such consultation to individuals already included in their "bank of people." Of note, this was said to include individuals who self-identify as "victims," as well as NGOs and law enforcement. Yet, many NGOs and law enforcement organizations, as well as migrant and sex worker rights groups, suggest they were not consulted in the formulation of the national action plan. As such, the plan provides key documentation about political conceptions of human trafficking and related statistics regarding charges, convictions, and the issuing of temporary resident permits (TRPs) in the country; however, the strategies outlined in the national action plan should be interpreted as part of a broader political discourse about human trafficking in Canada. Nonetheless, the plan has significantly shaped law enforcement and informed the uptake and funding mandates of anti-trafficking initiatives, while further alienating sex worker and migrant rights organizers.[44]

The plan included sizable resources for anti-trafficking work related to criminal justice initiatives, including more than $5 million towards criminal justice–based responses.[45] In turn, Canada's purported prevention efforts are rooted in enforcement-based measures that strengthen state-based interests while reproducing the overarching socioeconomic factors that underlie human trafficking practices and anti-trafficking responses. Significant awareness campaigns have been launched throughout the country to warn potential migrants of the "risks" and "indicators" of trafficking, while simultaneously restricting access to migratory routes. At the same time, two of the primary funders of anti-trafficking initiatives in Canada, the Canadian Women's Foundation (CWF) and the SWC, frequently conflate anti-trafficking with anti-prostitution. As Clancey, Khushrushahi, and Ham (2014) document, "the majority of funding calls we encounter in Canada reflect an anti-prostitution analysis of trafficking, in which sex work is either confused with trafficking or considered one of the main drivers of trafficking." Such approaches effectively rely on rights-based discourses in the reproduction of the national, racial, and gendered priorities of the settler colonial state.

In the areas of protection and prosecution, three key instruments guide anti-trafficking from a criminal justice basis in Canada. First, in November 2002, the Immigration and Refugee Protection Act (IRPA) criminalized trafficking in persons under Section 118, which "prohibits deliberately organizing the entry into Canada of one or more persons through the use of force, threats, fraud, deception or any other form of coercion." Portrayed as important for identifying and prosecuting human traffickers, the IRPA offers no provision for individuals victimized by human trafficking. Moreover, rooted in immigration control, the legislation reproduces colonial-derived notions of protection in targeting trafficking from international contexts while rendering migrating persons vulnerable to criminalization (Oxman-Martinez, Hanley, and Gomez 2005).

Second, in 2005, Bill C-49 added human trafficking–related offences to the Criminal Code. Specifically, Section 297.01 "prohibits the recruitment, transportation, harbouring or transfer of a person for the purpose of exploitation or to facilitate their exploitation," whereas Section 297.02 "prohibits persons from knowingly benefitting from trafficking in persons" (Standing Committee on the Status of Women Canada 2007: 8).[46] Further, sections 279.02 and 279.03 criminalize the material benefit gained from trafficking in persons and withholding or destroying documents for the purpose of human trafficking. Finally, Section 279.04 defines the concept of exploitation in human trafficking cases.[47] However, the definition of exploitation has proved particularly problematic in human trafficking cases. Specifically, the onus has been placed on the individual victimized by trafficking to demonstrate that they believed "their safety or the safety of a person known to them would be threatened if they failed to provide, or offer to provide, the labour or service" (Criminal Code, R.S.C. 1985, c. C-49, s. 279.04). On the one hand, individuals fitting the narrowly defined conceptions of a "trafficked persons" do not always wish, or are not always able, to cooperate with enforcement agencies given the potential consequences (e.g., possible job loss, deportation, threats against family members, and so on).[48] In these instances, respect for autonomy can be violated by responses that link "victim" cooperation to service provision or prioritize the prosecution of perpetrators above the rights of trafficked persons. Nonetheless, the restricted ability to gain the "trust" of trafficked persons is often employed as an argument for increasing enforcement resources and coordination with and between NGOs, despite the problematic implications of intervention and enforcement within the context of ongoing settler colonialism. Such conceptions of exploitation assume trafficking is an aberration – rather than symptomatic – of the ongoing functioning of settler colonial relations. As Suchland (2015: 7) indicates, anti-trafficking has exposed some forms of exploitation *"and has simultaneously* obscured the greater sea of exploitation."

In addition to placing the onus on trafficked individuals in a context of structural and material inequalities, the definition of exploitation also narrows the scope of emphasized experiences by focusing on physical forms of threat or harms, rather than the financial threats and precarity before the law commonly used in other definitions of labour exploitation.[49] In June 2012, Bill C-310 added more factors for the courts to consider when determining whether exploitation had occurred in cases of human trafficking.[50] However, the revised Section 279.04 failed to modify the problematic "threat to safety" provision. Again, on November 26, 2013, Bill C- 452 passed the House of Commons and received Royal Assent on June 18, 2015. The bill further amends the Criminal Code offence to provide consecutive sentences for convictions related to trafficking, such as living off the avails of prostitution. However, both the Supreme Court of Canada and sex workers rights groups have raised significant concern that anti-prostitution legislations reproduce and furthers harm by violating sex workers' rights to safety and security in Canada. Alongside this, Bill C-452 also adds a presumption that, in the absence of opposing evidence, living with or being "habitually in the company of a person who is exploited" constitutes proof of an exercise of control, direction, or influence. Lastly, Bill C-452 adds human trafficking to Canadian offences that warrant the forfeiture of criminal proceeds. Again, the problematic "threat to safety" provision of the trafficking legislation remains intact.

The conflation of trafficking and sexual labour in Canada was particularly apparent in efforts to harmonize the trafficking in person legislation with the prostitution provisions in the Criminal Code. In September 2010, in Canada v. Bedford, the Ontario Superior Court of Justice ruled that three provisions of the Criminal Code legislation related to prostitution were unconstitutional: prohibiting brothels, living off the avails of prostitution, and communicating for the purpose of engaging in prostitution (Bedford v. Canada 2010, ONSC 4264). The conservative government then in power appealed the decision and, in March 2012, the Court of Appeal for Ontario overturned portions of the decision.[51] While denouncing some of the country's prostitution laws by indicating they violate the constitutional right of sex workers to protect themselves from harm (Court of Appeal for Ontario 2012).[52] The federal government appealed the decision to the Supreme Court of Canada.[53]

On December 20, 2013, the Supreme Court of Canada issued a unanimous ruling in favour of all three constitutional challenges. The Supreme Court suspended the effects of the decision for a one-year period to allow the government to consider the implementation of new legislation, indicating that "concluding that each of the challenged provisions violates the *Charter* does not mean that Parliament is precluded from imposing limits on where and how prostitution may be conducted, as long as it does so in a way that does not infringe the constitutional rights of prostitutes" (Canada v. Bedford, 2013 SCC 72). By drawing on discourses of human trafficking, particularly among abolitionist advocates and advocates adopting an oppression paradigm, these legislative battles provided a national context for ongoing and highly politicized anti-trafficking lobby efforts to shape Canadian prostitution policy.

Following this decision and parliamentary discussions, Bill C-36, the Protection of Communities and Exploited Persons Act (PCEPA), passed into law. Replacing legislation that criminalized acts associated with selling sexual services, Bill C-36 instead criminalized the purchase of sexual services and partially decriminalized sex workers. Advertisement of sexual services and communication in public for the purpose of prostitution remained constrained under the law. Relying on discourses advancing the Swedish model, the stated goal of the PCEPA was to decrease demand, which would result in decreased supply and eventual elimination of prostitution. While ignoring reports from Sweden of increased harassment of sex workers by police and a decrease in their experience of health and safety, and by criminalizing sex industries de facto, the Canadian legislation continued a repressive approach to prostitution while drawing on claims of "progressive" anti-trafficking narratives. Further, in an effort to harmonize the Criminal Code's trafficking in persons legislation and prostitution legislation, the PCEPA framed sex work as morally *exploitative* by relying on overlapping conceptions of exploitation. In turn, the government ignored scholarly and experiential evidence to the contrary, especially evidence presented by migrant and Indigenous sex workers, during Parliamentary hearings (Lawrence 2015: 5). Thus, the changes made under Bill C-36 perpetuate a repressive approach that is "achieved in large measure at the expense of the health and human rights of sex workers" (Corriveau 2013: 35).

The centrality of the concept of exploitation in criminal definitions of trafficking in Canada has also created controversial discussions regarding the relationship between trafficking and the sexual exploitation of children. Although the trafficking of children and youth are beyond the scope of this manuscript, anti-trafficking discourses frequently draw on discussions of sexual exploitation of youth under the age of 18 years.[54] In particular, the RCMP (2012) suggests "teenage runaways, as well as those who may be lured to urban centres or who migrate there voluntarily" as particularly "at risk" for trafficking, which is read as youth sexual exploitation. In most Canadian provinces and territories, the sexual exploitation of children and youth has been included among "the criteria for classifying a child as in need of protection," which enables child protection to remove children "at risk of prostitution and to place them in the child welfare system" (Barnett 2011: 13). Both British Columbia and Alberta refer explicitly to prostitution in the context of child protection. However, in Alberta, the Protection of Communities and Exploited Persons Act (PCEPA) further permits police and child welfare to involuntarily detain children engaged in prostitution. Manitoba, as we will see, extends the child protection approach "to deal with adults exploited through trafficking in persons as well" (Barnett 2011: 13). Under this legislation, both adults and children can be placed "in protection" in instances of sexual exploitation or trafficking in spite of the documented rights abuses perpetrated through "forced rehabilitation."[55]

While advocacy groups and some provincial mandates tend to emphasize trafficking for the purpose of sexual exploitation, national anti-trafficking legislation, law enforcement, government bodies, and international discussions often focus on human trafficking as a form of organized criminal activity, frequently conflated with or placed in opposition to migrant smuggling. In doing so, these discourses emphasize simplistic representations of human trafficking and migrant smuggling by polarizing heterogeneous experiences into dichotomous categories of "deserving victim" and "complicit criminal."[56]

From this basis, another federal anti-trafficking policy was adopted in May 2006 by the Department of Citizenship and Immigration Canada (CIC) to provide TRPs to trafficked persons. Initially for 120 days, TRPs now offer a potential means for trafficked individuals' to attain legal immigration status in Canada for up to 180 days (CIC 2009). Potential trafficked persons are interviewed by immigration officials to assess their eligibility for a TRP. Based on the interview, immigration officials may also permit access to health care and other services, such as trauma counselling and work permits, with the stated aim of assisting individuals victimized by human trafficking. The program claims to shift the treatment of trafficked persons as "illegalized migrants" to "victims" and thereby "deserving" of temporary access to legal status and basic support services.

However, service providers perceive the TRP to be particularly challenging for trafficked persons to access (Kaye, Winterdyk, and Quarterman 2014). Given the varying definitions of trafficking employed by government and nongovernment agencies and limited understanding of how to interpret and apply the legal definition of trafficking in Canada's Criminal Code or the IRPA, there is little clarity about whether specific cases will meet the undefined threshold of CIC, who issues TRPs. Moreover, the TRP is further employed as a key reason for coordinated responses and partnership between government and NGOs. Kaye, Winterdyk, and Quarterman (2014:19) argue that "although social serving agencies may be best situated to identify the broad ranging experiences of human trafficking, it is law enforcement and government agencies that have been mandated with key aspects of victim assistance and support." Regardless of the role of service providers, because the nature of the interview for accessing a TRP includes both CIC and law enforcement officials, potentially trafficked persons are, in essence (albeit not in policy),[57] required to report their experiences to law enforcement. This implicit reporting requirement is especially problematic for individuals who are criminalized within the restricted bounds of the nation-state. In this context, the TRP remains an ineffective mechanism to support trafficked persons or precarious status migrants and will go underused so long as it is perceived to create, rather than reduce, insecurity imposed by the state, especially in a context that reproduces inequalities through legislated temporality and precarity.

As one frontline worker indicated, there are considerable "gaps between the legislation and the realities." In this context, the framing of trafficking as a foreign policy and criminal justice matter by Canadian authorities as well as the mobilizing of right-based discourses result in multiple and intersecting challenges for migrant workers, including migrant sex workers, alongside gendered and racialized bodies reproduced as subjects of settler colonialism in Canada.

Chapter Three

Anti-trafficking in Canada: Negotiating "Domestic" versus "International"

The politicized nature of anti-trafficking continues to intensify in Canada and public discussions about victim/agent; coercion/consent; sex/labour; domestic/international remain prominent frameworks employed by anti-trafficking advocates; however, local narratives complicate the construction of such polarized representations. Although definitional debates over the nature of human trafficking persist in each city and dominant anti-trafficking tropes inform the uptake and implementation of anti-trafficking responses, key local narratives shape the discursive treatment of trafficking in each city. Provincial variations are particularly evident in definitions of trafficking and in how anti-trafficking advocates negotiate conceptions of domestic and international trafficking. This chapter examines prominent anti-trafficking responses in each city under investigation – Vancouver, Calgary, and Winnipeg – and analyses how anti-trafficking advocates negotiate conceptions of trafficking and the production of anti-trafficking responses. The chapter considers how representations of international and internal trafficking are constructed in each city and the corresponding resistance or reification of dominant representations in different regional contexts.

Anti-trafficking in Vancouver, British Colombia

Vancouver is situated on unceded Indigenous territory belonging to the Coast Salish peoples. This includes the territories of the xʷməθkwəy̓əm (Musqueam), Skwxwú7mesh (Squamish), Stó:lō and Səl̓ílwətaʔ/Selilwitulh (Tsleil-Waututh) Nations. In Canada, Vancouver represents the city with the third-largest population of Indigenous persons. A port city along the coast of British Columbia, Vancouver is a rapidly growing metropolis and is proclaimed as a key destination for newcomers to Canada. Between 2006 and 2011, Vancouver grew at a rate of 9.3 per cent, compared with the 7.4 per cent national average of metropolitan growth (Statistics Canada 2011). The city also boasts a multicultural makeup, highlighting that in 2011 40.3 per cent of census respondents in Vancouver indicated their mother tongue falls into the category of "nonofficial language" (City of Vancouver 2015). The perception of Vancouver as a global city alongside ongoing settler colonial relations with a significant population of Indigenous persons and continued racialized exclusion provides the context whereby anti-trafficking advocates differentially negotiate conceptions of domestic versus international trafficking.

The Ministry of Public Safety and Solicitor General established the formalized anti-trafficking response in British Columbia with the creation of the Office to Combat Trafficking in Persons (BCOCTIP) in Victoria, British Columbia in July 2007. The office was developed as part of the Community Safety and Crime Prevention Branch of the provincial government. Initially, the office received funding from the Victims of Crime Fund, Deputy Solicitor General, and the Ministry of Children and Family Development. The BCOCTIP was mandated to coordinate the response to human trafficking in the province and aimed to do so by partnering with key provincial ministries (such as the Migrant Services Program in the Ministry of Children and Family Development), federal departments (such as the Interdepartmental Working Group on Trafficking in Persons [IWGTIP] and Citizenship and Immigration Canada [CIC]), municipal governments, nongovernment and community-based organizations, including First Nations' organizations, as well as law enforcement agencies (such as the RCMP "E" Division Border Integrity Program) and academics to develop an integrated response to human trafficking in the province.

This response initially focused on international forms of human trafficking, which restricted anti-trafficking attention to cross-border movement. As a government representative from Vancouver indicated, "[W]e were looking at how do we deal with trafficked persons, primarily across the border, we weren't talking about domestic trafficking at that point, just international."

As the first provincial response model in the country to receive full government funding, the office was perceived to be "leading the way nationally in responding to human trafficking" (Province of British Columbia 2013). However, four years after its inception, the position

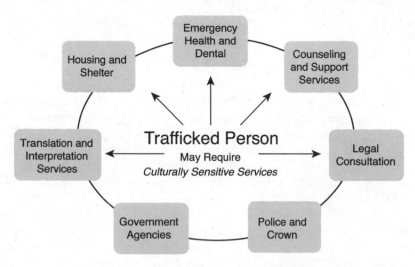

Figure 3.1 British Columbia Office to Combat Trafficking in Persons (BCOCTIP)
Service Model. Source: Province of British Columbia (2010: 10).

of Executive Director was cut from the office and the funding provided
by the BC Victims of Crime Fund was eliminated. Despite remaining
consistent during the early days of the office's operation, the annual
budget was also subsequently reduced.[1]

In a highly polarized and politicized environment, BCOCTIP was
constrained in its ability to fulfil its primary aim of offering effective
collaboration. The problematic construction of international versus
domestic trafficking in particular prevented the office from effectively
engaging with efforts of transformative change. Rather, attempts at service provision and service coordination produced unnecessary harms,
rendering the BCOCTIP a predominately awareness-raising entity with
limited capacity to address systemic barriers experienced by trafficked
persons and individuals affected by anti-trafficking initiatives.[2] In turn,
the redirection towards awareness appears to have shifted the focus of
the BCOCTIP away from certain forms of trafficking, especially international sex trafficking, towards reproducing and naturalizing conceptions of "at risk" bodies within Canada: youth, vulnerable workers, and
Aboriginal women. In 2013, for instance, the BC Action Plan to Combat
Human Trafficking (British Columbia Ministry of Justice 2013) detailed
a three-year plan prioritizing 1) the sexual exploitation of youth;

2) labour trafficking of vulnerable workers; and 3) domestic trafficking of Aboriginal youth and women. It is noteworthy that "labour trafficking" of "vulnerable workers" appeared to exclude individuals involved in sex industries and focused rather explicitly on international cases of live-in caregiver workers. Of further note, only live-in caregivers (predominantly women) are represented among vulnerable workers, even though other temporary migrant worker programs in British Columbia are identified as a potential site of trafficking (Public Safety Canada 2012a) and a significant number of men and boys are represented among these temporary workers. Moreover, of the anti-trafficking interventions framed as domestic (but largely conflated with prostitution), only Aboriginal women appear represented among victimized adults. Far from empowering individuals involved in sex industries or enhancing self-determination, anti-trafficking in this context serves to reinforce colonial constructions of Indigenous women as "impure," "at risk," and in need of rescue and domestication.

Negotiating Domestic and International: Migration, Sex Work, Disappeared Women, and Olympic Fever

Anti-trafficking discourses in Vancouver initially centred on experiences of coercion faced by migrant women. In this context, and against the backdrop of highly publicized arrivals of migrant ships off the coast of British Columbia, trafficking was largely conflated with migrant smuggling and immigration controls. However, alongside international discussions about the relationship between human trafficking and prostitution, some advocates working in the area of migrant rights and others working in exit-based responses to prostitution renegotiated their work in relation to resurgent anti-trafficking discourses. The following account from a representative of a women's rights organization details this type of shift in discussing entry into anti-trafficking advocacy:

> Well, it happened to us, as much as anything. I mean, we've always dealt with prostitution, but when the Fujian boat people were delivered off the shores of Vancouver and dumped into the waters, we began participating in a coalition in order to try and intervene on their behalf ... And that was a quick humanitarian response to a new consciousness of how desperate people were to migrate. We had to figure out what we actually thought about international trafficking and why all of a sudden this phenomenon was now being described as trafficking ... Since then, we've had to

articulate for ourselves who are we in this and what are we doing in this ... So we've kinda been in it up to our necks ever since.

We were just trying to apply what we understood about violence against women and what we understood about prostitution domestically and trying to apply it to the plight of women who were in a situation of such desperation that they would migrate across the border. And it didn't take us very much to realize there's not much difference migrating from Fujian Province than migrating from Prince George ... so, you know, we've had to learn quickly as we went: What's it [trafficking] got to do with immigration policy? What's it got to do with laws against prostitution? What is our understanding of the rhetoric? ... It was already clear that they [Fujian migrants] were in the hands of gangs and profiteers in a way that our police forces didn't interfere with, didn't touch; and if you deal with violence against women, you know that all the same issues exist for a white [woman] calling police as for a trafficked woman calling police, so we just kinda stumbled through each issue as we went.

As the advocate details, from a "violence against women" framework, their work in the area of prostitution was renegotiated in light of international trafficking discourses and the arrival of migrant ships off the coast of British Colombia (disparagingly referred to as "boat people" in Canadian discussions). This process highlights the internationalizing of anti-prostitution advocacy by using "what we understood about prostitution domestically" to understand trafficking as an "intensified" form of international violence against women (i.e., the "plight" of migrant women). While ignoring the foundational treatment and institutionalized racism directed at a variety of precarious migrants in Canada, migrant women were emphasized as being in particular need of rescue through mechanisms of regulation and control. The reading of international trafficking alongside violence against women, in turn, led to a reinterpretation of "domestic prostitution" as trafficking. In this context, the organization "rearticulated" itself in relation to trafficking through the conflation of trafficking as prostitution. As the representative goes on to state, "we don't see much of a distinction other than somebody else's arbitrarily defined border between trafficking and prostitution."

Significantly, it is through this framework that the unintentional erasure of intersecting forms of oppression occurs. The advocate highlighted that her organization became involved in "international" trafficking because of the arrival of the boats and the lack of police intervention. Such police inaction was interpreted as "all the same issues" experienced by white women (who are distinguished from "trafficked women)." In doing so, the advocate elides the experiences of racialized women facing overpolicing and underprotection. By forefronting a generalized stance about violence against women, the interlocking oppressions experienced by migrant and racialized women are erased and the roles law enforcement, white women, and anti-prostitution play in producing and reinforcing such oppressions are overlooked. Moreover, the advocate perceives that migrant women are interpreted through "a new consciousness"; however, the advocate's representation of migrant women echoes the stereotypically common depiction of Otherness as "poor" and "tradition-bound" through discourses of desperation. Such advocacy and the representation of "desperate" and "at-risk" bodies reinforce state control over migrating women, control that is advanced through anti-trafficking discourses, especially when conflated with anti-prostitution.

In addition to the erasure of interlocking oppressions experienced by migrants, reconstituting anti-prostitution advocacy in international terms further facilitated the reconstruction of "national" depictions of Canadianness and the domestication of Indigeneity. The representative continued,

> We've added globalization and the international context, which for me, changes everything and reconfirms and reintensifies everything. When I think back [to] the girl who was Aboriginal, I just didn't see the significance of her being Aboriginal at the time in the same way that I do now. It's clear to me that prostitution – national and international – preys mostly on the dispossessed and preys mostly on whole nations of women at a time, Orientalizing them, exoticizing them; or, diminishing them, as they do with Indigenous women ... It's in many ways a class fight as well as a race and gender fight, and I know which side I'm on.

The representative critiques the "Orientalizing" of women in "national and international" contexts. However, Aboriginality here only emerges – and is only understood in relation to – the internationalization of stigmatized notions of anti-trafficking as prostitution. In doing so, the migrant-rights advocate domesticates anti-trafficking discussions by viewing migrant and Indigenous bodies through the same lens as "dispossessed" and "diminished" women. In turn, advocates working in areas of migrant rights are portrayed as haphazardly entering the trafficking discussion through globalized conceptions of poor, racialized, and gendered bodies requiring intervention. In turn, this elides the construction of such oppression through material and structural inequalities naturalized in the context of settler colonialism.

Similarly, individuals working in the area of service-based responses to prostitution in Canada discuss a shift towards international advocacy in relation to anti-trafficking frameworks. According to a representative of a faith-based service provider,

> I saw the connection between human trafficking, prostitution, and domestic abuse ... We have not yet had an international trafficked person, but you know, as I say, I can see the connections, it's the same principles ... domestic abuse, child abuse, incest, pornography, you name it, all of those [are linked] and it's the same dynamic of power and control, which is unfortunately male over female.
>
> I was invited to numerous conferences on human trafficking and started to realize that we needed to educate the public, so I did a lot of public [speaking] ... You see that's what I think a lot of people don't understand: they don't equate prostitution with human trafficking, and they think of human trafficking as an international issue. They're not seeing, and that's why I try to make those connections for people.

By foregrounding "male over female" power dynamics associated with patriarchy, this representative equates trafficking with a variety of complex areas of violence and contested areas of feminist organizing. Yet it is through the discourse of international trafficking that the representative perceives the conflation of trafficking and prostitution in Canada. Prostitution, in this context, is differentiated from the international (i.e., the migrant), but "the prostitute" and the migrant are legible together through their shared relationship to trafficking. In other words, international trafficking discourses permitted the representative to understand prostitution and multiple forms of violence through a trafficking framework that provided a platform of "numerous conferences" and "a lot of public speaking" to advance this position.

Other anti-trafficking advocates in Vancouver produce and negotiate a split between international versus domestic trafficking by emphasizing the sensationalized awareness attained by international trafficking and the perceived responsiveness of the state to this form of trafficking, while highlighting the lack of attention and "political will" directed towards recognition of trafficking of Indigenous women. In particular, while ignoring the critiques of state-based criminalization of migrants through anti-trafficking, state-based "apathy" is discursively employed to draw attention to differential power dynamics between government-funded and nongovernment-funded organizations. Nongovernment, in this way, is framed as the keeper of legitimized understandings of trafficking and, in its critique of the state, perceives itself to be address-ing the racist and colonial *legacies* of law enforcement and government agencies. However, in doing so, the discursive practice renders invis-ible the broader structural constraints faced by the women on behalf of whom it seeks to intervene and the ongoing role its own interven-tions play in the reproduction of systemic forms of violence. In turn, such discourses reinforce narratives of Otherness while simultaneously replicating settler colonial depictions of Indigenous women as domes-tic. The following exchange, which took place in the context of a focus group with self-proclaimed abolitionist anti-trafficking advocates, demonstrates this process:

> SOPHIE: I have found, for me I have found I'm not a fan of VPD [Vancouver Police Department] {NADIA: No, I'm not either}. I have found that they have beyond dropped the ball on women's issues in this city ... But the RCMP that we have dealt with in the trafficking division and the border, this is what they do and they, allegedly, do investigations and these sorts of things so they're pretty fairly trained and we consulted with them on a training video ... It was interesting when I read the script of how they're portraying it cause it was such a weird, clean kind of case. I mean, the woman is Asian and this man is grabbing her and the whole deal, right? So you have kind of clean, innocent "Victim A," right, whereas this Aboriginal girl that wouldn't be clean enough for them right? Surely she did something or whatever, it's like blaming the victim. And in this video they use for training all across the country the cop is the one who saves the woman and is the "knight in shining armor" which is hilarious because as if she would immediately trust him, right? But at least they have some idea of it definitionally ...
> NADIA: And I think the VPD's got other things to protect itself from, right?
> SOPHIE: That's right.
> NADIA: The point is they have been, like, absolutely, uninvolved in protecting women of that community.
> AMELIA: Particularly First Nations women.
> NADIA: Particularly First Nations women I mean.

As the interaction reveals, sensational representations of international trafficking –"Asian" and "clean, innocent victim" – are considered against colonial portrayals of Indigenous women as "uncivilized": "she wouldn't be clean enough for them." Despite providing an important critique of law enforcement representations, including historical and ongoing forms of racism associated with their lack of responsiveness to violence against Indigenous women,[3] the critique ignores the intersecting forms of institutionalized racism and the criminalization of Asian bodies in the nation-building project. Rather, the critique is employed in this context to suggest that increased enforcement-based responses are needed to address trafficking as it affects Indigenous women. In this context, the critique of "the cops [as] the one who saves the woman" is mediated through a lens of the women not "immediately" trusting the enforcement officials, which suggests this trust is merely something to be built, rather than symptomatic of structural violence and inequalities. Here, the nongovernment advocates go on to discursively place themselves as the interloper to negotiate the constrained relationship between victims and law enforcement.

As was seen later in the discussion, the anti-trafficking advocates shared an exchange about the challenges they face in responding to human trafficking. In addition to "sexism," issues of social class were also raised. However, although class was initially noted in reference to the experiences of individuals affected by domestic trafficking, the central focus of the statement emphasize class in terms of power imbalances and associated lack of coordination in government versus nongovernment interactions.[4] In turn, the discourse elided the privileges of individuals working in the nongovernment anti-trafficking sector. When asked about the central challenges of their work, the following exchange took place:

SOPHIE: Sexism.
AMELIA: Sexism exactly plays a huge part. I think a victim-blaming
    mentality that's still very alive and well in people who have positions of
    authority, this is a significant problem. I think a lack of education, you
    know, about what human trafficking is and isn't … I think it's also a
    challenge for Canadians as a whole, right? To embrace the fact that this
    really does happen in our own country. I think it's really easy to have
    a feeling about some of the international situations that we hear about,
    but I think there's a real resistance to recognize when it's happening in
    your own country and in your own city … I think to come to terms with
    that as a nation also forces you to look at how you've been complacent
    yourself, how you've been participating in … [You] know you look at the

people who come down, the johns who come to the Downtown Eastside, they're not residents of the area, you know, so that's a whole other issue that as a country, as a city, you know Vancouver would really have to start to take a look at it and I think there's resistance to do that –

SOPHIE: – Uh, I would add to [sexism] that classism is a big piece especially with domestic trafficking [AMELIA: Absolutely] … it is difficult, the lack of cooperation between I'd say various sectors. The NGO community has a pretty, at least there's a pretty good group of us who have a decent connection and, you know, are able to source each other on various things, but where it breaks down? I really think it breaks down at CBSA. Big time. CBSA and RCMP, at first I came in really naively thinking oh they're both government, they're both law enforcement, surely they work well together and VPD has their own thing.

NADIA: Yeah, I think that's a huge problem.

SOPHIE: It is a huge problem and, I mean we've heard from various different avenues and various routes over, say, the last 10 years that women get picked up when they arrive, they're held in detention, and then they're deported. So we know that. Well, the one time that we got contacted is when this one woman saw this case that was fishy – it wasn't just fishy it was like the most blatantly clear case [AMELIA: Hmm!] of human trafficking I've ever heard of, I mean it was so blatant, and this woman had been held in detention for seven days, which means she's criminalized, right, and they had her out in pre-trial [NADIA: Oh God] which is a pretty rough place and I know, so um, and so someone from there must've just talked to OCTIP and they called me and said, "hey are you free to go down tomorrow to go to this hearing?" And it was just this very casual, I'm thinking are you kidding me? You know? … We don't have any kind of funding for that and it's a difficult thing to have funding for something that just comes up on the go and we're always on the go. We're always able to cobble it together, but the burden always falls to the NGO community and the government takes no responsibility whatsoever – at all!

NADIA: Other than giving her a "nice place" to stay for a week before they deport her.

As is seen in this conversation, the advocate is positioned as the responsible, yet disenfranchised (often oppressed) partner in collaborative interventions. Class distinctions are thereby employed to draw attention to power imbalances between government and nongovernment organizations, and the aim becomes bridging this divide in order to establish coordinated intervention in cases of trafficking. Meanwhile, the role of such interventions in reproducing a victimized Other, erasing structures of domination between victim and intervener, and criminalizing gendered and racialized bodies remains concealed. From this perspective, the experience of the individual "held in detention for seven days" and likely "deported" is seen as a result of an imbalanced coordinated response and limited funding for nongovernment sectors, rather than the natural functioning of a settler colonial state that is premised on the policing of gendered and racialized bodies and facilitating such policing through anti-trafficking discourses.

As well as mediating the relationship between victim and law enforcement, nongovernment advocates are also portrayed as holding the responsibility of challenging Canadian notions of national identity that suggest Canada is not a country where "that kind of thing happens." Of note, in line with abolitionist advocacy for the criminalization of purchasers of sexual services, the idea of having to look at "how you've been participating in [prostitution read as trafficking]" is understood in relation to public awareness and the role of "johns" (i.e., clients). As discussed in Razack (2000: 107), anti-trafficking advocates root the problem in spacialized injustice in which men "come down" to the street, or, as Razack states, men's ability to conquer "impure" spaces and emerge "unscathed." The argument suggests that legal protections should extend to racialized "spaces of immorality" by no longer participating in the complicity of protecting white "respectable" bodies from moving in and out of these spaces. In this context, raising awareness highlights ongoing stigmatized notions of individuals involved in sex industries as "uncivilized victims." Moreover, such analyses omit the roles of bourgeois advocacy in the construction of law and state intervention in the creation of gendered and racialized notions of "impure" and "uncivilized." The burden of trafficking, therefore, falls to nongovernment advocates, placing pressure on governments to formulate and enforce rights-based responses adjacent to criminal justice interventions and responses. In turn, the violence experienced by residents of the Downtown Eastside is naturalized and the voices of residents and acts of resistance are omitted.

This production and reproduction of boundaries between "liberated," bourgeois women and Others (read as "still oppressed" in relation to men) becomes evident in the process of negotiating conceptions of international and domestic trafficking. The excerpt from the following faith-based anti-trafficking advocate further exemplifies the discursive practice of delineating such boundaries:

> Like, internationally, the state wants control of the border and it wants to only let in the workers it wants to let in when it wants to let them in, legally and illegally, so there's plenty of room for women to come in and do domestic labour. Clearly taking care, and illegally taking care of the sick, the young, the old, and men's sexual needs. I mean, it's like they're importing the wives that we don't want to be anymore ... North American men still demand what they always demanded, but we've had enough progress as a liberation movement that many women are no longer willing to feed their egos and supply them with what they're demanding and they can get it from women with less opportunity. I think locally, in Vancouver, Vancouver's just a crucible of the whole thing. It's amazing. We know that in the illegal brothels, which the state is absolutely tolerating, it's disproportionately Asian women and, you know, poor women migrating from around the Pacific Rim. It's perfectly clear to us. And on the other hand, in the street, it's Indigenous women who are migrating from the interior. We have a situation in which our local authorities, pressed with the problem of the disappearing women and the violence in the streets and the secondary problems of prostitution, decided well the thing to do is not charge women with prostitution, not criminalize the women quite so much, not so directly any way. They still do it indirectly, but the price was they don't charge the men.

The construction of "poor women" as the means of importing Victorian conceptions of domesticity that "liberated" women are no longer willing to fulfil conceals the imposition of patriarchy on migrant and Indigenous women through the civilizing practices of disciplining autonomous and sovereign women in the process of nation-building as well as the role bourgeois women played in advocating for legal structures that served to subjugate and dispossess racialized women. In the context of settler colonialism, the "liberation" of white women occurred through processes of subjugation and domestication of a racialized Other. Yet, in turn, "liberated" women in anti-trafficking are constructed as the benefactors of women who are falling behind in social progress and thereby still filling roles "many [liberated] women no longer wish to fill." In this progress-oriented narrative, the ongoing settler colonial rendition of Indigenous women and racialized bodies as "backward" and "needing to catch up" with the help of colonial interventions remains apparent.

As Alfred (2005: 135) details, "Settlers can remain who and what they are, and injustice can be reconciled by the mere allowance of the Other to become one of Us." Bourgeois subjects are framed as the "liberators" of poor, racialized bodies. Meanwhile, there remains no perceived need for accountability of practices of cultural genocide and ongoing policies of intervention that benefit bourgeois subjectivities while undermining the autonomy, power, and self-determination of Indigenous and racialized subjects.

The analysis of discursive practices of negotiating domestic and international trafficking underscores how arguments that aim to situate sex work in relation to patriarchy and colonial legacies serve to hide ongoing settler colonial relations that shape all aspects of gendered and racialized lives. What remain unchallenged are stigmatized notions of individuals negotiating gendered, colonial forms of violence and the embodiment of resistance that has emerged in response to such violence, particularly through the organizing of sex workers in Vancouver's Downtown Eastside. The case of serial killer Robert Pickton and the experience of watching many friends, sisters, and colleagues go missing, especially from the Downtown Eastside significantly shaped the role of anti-trafficking advocates and the mobilization of sex workers' rights advocates in the "battle" to control the language of human trafficking. As Ferris (2015: 1) identifies, "from 1975 until 2001, at least 65 women – more than half of whom were Aboriginal, and many of whom were street-involved – disappeared from Vancouver, British Colombia." Although women had been going missing for decades from Vancouver's Downtown Eastside, government and police authorities paid little attention to friends, families, and advocates, including sex workers, seeking justice in their disappearances (De Vries 2003; Ferris 2015). After sustained pressure, a Vancouver Police Department and RCMP task force was formed in 1999 that led to charges against Robert Pickton in 2002. Pickton was convicted of murdering six women that were disappeared from Vancouver (Dean 2015); however, in a controversial decision, the crown prosecutors opted not to try him for an additional twenty murder charges that were pending against him because he would already serve the maximum penalty. In the end, many disappeared women remain unaccounted for and disappearances continue at alarming rates (Ferris 2015).

A later exchange among the abolitionist anti-trafficking advocates highlights the role of the Pickton trial, which they suggest is responsible

for the lack of coordination in anti-trafficking responses in Vancouver
and the related contested nature of anti-trafficking discourses:

> SOPHIE: Vancouver is such a liberal city and people are very well educated …
> I'm amazed by the amount of people here who are involved in NGO work
> who also have really solid analysis of gender, class, and race. So people are
> just very, very aware … I don't know if it's passion around Pickton –
> NADIA: Yeah, that's what I was just going to say.
> SOPHIE: I think Pickton's been a big piece. {NADIA: Yeah} And experience
> that women's organizations have had with the cops, you know?
> NADIA: And, you think about the enormous amount of anger that there is
> around that one specific thing {SOPHIE: Yeah} like I'm afraid of some of
> those ladies, like they freak me out and there's an enormous amount of
> anger that doesn't allow for anything else to be spoken of …
> AMELIA: And holy cow like some women are saying that [disappearances
> and killings were] going on in the late '70s so that's a, that's a huge
> root, right {NADIA: Mm hmm, yeah} in the community. And I think
> the Downtown Eastside is a very unique {SOPHIE: It is very unique}
> community in the country –
> SOPHIE: – but I would answer a differently, I would probably answer a little
> differently around international trafficking. The problem, I mean the
> thing is, when you're talking about domestic trafficking you're talking
> pretty directly about prostitution – you are in both, but the groups that
> work here more directly with domestic [cases]would be [working with]
> prostitution and that's where that stuff is so SO electric.

Again, we see nongovernment advocates emerge as "very aware,"
which enables the reading of "passion" and "anger" surrounding the
Pickton trial and critiques of uneven responses to violence facing Indigenous women and women working in sex industries as a constraint
to anti-trafficking coordination rather than a resistance to the way
such discourses are enacted on the bodies and lives of sex workers.
Thus, the incorporation of "prostitution as trafficking" and the associated imperative of intervention from spaces of privilege was perceived
as "so SO electric" in a context where sex workers have resisted the
imposition of advocates speaking over their lived experiences. In this,
centring the experiences of "women's organizations" "with the cops"
erases the experiences of criminalized women in their interactions with
police by foregrounding the relationship between "organizations" and
"cops." Interpreted through Foucault's (1975) premise that the ability

to control language and discourse serves as the most powerful means of discipline and regulation, the negotiation of an "international" and "domestic" split in anti-trafficking discourses is seen to remove conceptual space for the very existence of women who claim a place of agency in sex work or racialized women who claim autonomy over their movements. This supports Doezema's (2010: 168) observation that the constructed definition of trafficking "leaves 'room' for sex workers to exist only outside the protected space carved out for trafficking victims. However, within the trafficking discourse itself, there is no 'room' for the sex worker." Such discursive silencing and disciplining through anti-trafficking advocacy will be discussed further in the next chapter. For now, it is important to note that the negotiation of domestic and international discourses provides the location where hegemonic anti-trafficking constructions consolidate at the expense of erasing problematic narratives, whether through *passive permission* of ongoing violence and restricted access to safety or through *direct silencing* of alternate voices and experiences.

Another prominent area where the negotiation of domestic and international discourses becomes evident was in the context of the "global stage" when Vancouver hosted the Olympics. Media accounts and anti-trafficking advocates, especially faith-based advocacy, predicted an "explosion" of trafficking and sex tourism in the lead up to the Olympics (Lepp 2013). The discrepancy between claims of increased trafficking in relation to major sporting events and actual increases in human trafficking has been well documented (Global Alliance Against Trafficking in Women [GAATW] 2011)[5] As one frontline worker indicated, "there was a huge brouhaha about the thousands of women who were going to be trafficked." However, no charges of human trafficking were laid during the Olympics.[6] Nonetheless, since 2004, such events have been criticized as "fertile grounds for human trafficking" based on the assumption that international events will increase demand for commercial sexual service (Lepp 2013: 252). For example, faith-based organizations adopting an abolitionist stance, such as Resist Exploitation, Embrace Dignity (REED) in Vancouver, suggest, "any time that you have a mega event … trafficking goes up because the demand goes up. Any time you have men traveling away from their social networks [to a place] where they enjoy a degree of safety and anonymity, they're more likely to pay for sex." (as cited in GAATW 2011:14). Linking "demand" for purchasing sexual services to a significant growth in trafficking discursively conflates trafficking and sex work. However, as GAATW (2013) highlights, "there was no strong evidence of a significant spike in male demand for paid sexual services during the Olympic Games." Despite the unsubstantiated nature of such claims of increase, REED launched a "Buying Sex Is Not a Sport" campaign in the lead up to the Olympic games. This anti-trafficking message, connecting the purchase of sex services to sporting events and trafficking, was in line with government- and law enforcement–based depictions of trafficking.

Although some organizations identified trafficking cases among migrants working on the development of infrastructure in preparation for the Olympics (GAATW 2013), the migrant labourers (predominantly men) were deported instead of being treated as "victims" of trafficking. Regardless of whether trafficking occurred in these instances, it is significant that these cases did not fit the picture of trafficking painted by mainstream media, law enforcement, government, and nongovernment, which focused almost exclusively on human trafficking for the purpose of sexual exploitation in relation to women. The following excerpt from a law enforcement representative in British Colombia demonstrates this omission:

> We haven't here done any big [labour trafficking] investigations. I've got to be quite frank with you, I put a much greater value on the female victims of human trafficking in the sex trade. Twenty men from Mexico or Africa who are forced against their will to work under horrible conditions is very, very bad, but you know their lives probably aren't in danger, they're not going to get raped, they're not going to get beaten. So I don't want to minimize that because those are very valuable investigations, but we do focus more on female victims and there's some female victims in forced labour as well, and we do look at those, but it's not as high priority as female victims in the sex trade.

The implementation of the law, from this standpoint, reflects a bias towards women as vulnerable, fragile, and helpless victims needing rescue, while also, problematically, interpreting sexual assault as nothing more than male violence against women at the expense of intersectional forms of oppressions. Sex industries are prioritized for investigative purposes and the abuses suffered by individuals victimized by violence within sex industries are distinguished from the violences experienced in other industries, such as those framed as forced labour. Even more interesting is the context in which these statements occur, considering sex workers fought to have the violences they faced acknowledged by police for a number of years and were consistently ignored (Oppal 2012). The next chapter will discuss how such an interventionist standpoint has been mobilized by law enforcement in British Columbia to publicly criminalize and deport migrant women working in sex industries. By foregrounding "female victims," trafficking is interpreted as naturalized within sex industries, while its precarious relationship to the law, vis-à-vis anti-prostitution and immigration programs, is reinforced.

In the period leading up to the 2010 Olympics, the well-known faith-based organization, the Salvation Army, further mobilized the world stage to develop awareness campaigns about sex trafficking. A representative discussed how the Salvation Army negotiated decisions about where to focus their attention:

> So in 2004, the Salvation Army internationally made it a global priority to fight human trafficking. Because we were seeing people from one part of the world showing up in other parts of the world enslaved, and not just sexual trafficking but labour trafficking, and although there is some of that in BC – with the buildup to the Olympics and the historical influx of trafficked victims into a community when the world stage is set, we decided to focus on human sexual trafficking of females in the buildup to the Olympics and in our response to the Olympics. And we very strategically created a three-pronged approach: build awareness, to educate the public, and to have a response of somewhere for the victims to find freedom. We met lots of challenges, people who thought we were going after the sex trade and trying to exploit that that wasn't our goal.

As this comment highlights, such campaigning was met by resistance from sex worker rights' advocates who argued that organizations such as REED and the Salvation Army were using the international stage of the Olympics to advance their campaigns against prostitution (Lepp 2013). In turn, they felt such campaigns ignored calls for increased safety measures for individuals in sex industries and undermined sex worker concerns about displacement and criminalization, especially for street workers, in efforts to *sanitize* the stage for the Olympics (Bowen and Shannon Frontline Consulting 2009). In the context of settler colonialism, such sanitization is reminiscent of national identity–building work that relied on civilizing missions and racialized constructions of purity in order to isolate and criminalize deviations from the sovereign, white, settler colonial citizen-subject.

Nonetheless, the anti-trafficking advocacy leading up to the Olympics further provided a platform to shift discourses towards domestic trafficking. Responding to the critiques of sex worker rights organizations, the Salvation Army relied on a design company to prepare a sensational and highly contested anti-trafficking campaign. As the faith-based representative went on to describe,

> We engaged a company who worked for free for us, a creative company … they created a campaign for us under our banner "The Truth Isn't Sexy." The whole objective of that was to raise awareness, and so we had it in transit shelters, TV ads, radio ads, all making people aware that this was not only a global problem, that is, it was a global problem, but it was also a local problem – it's not just international people being victimized in Canada or Canadian girls being victimized. We went very public and met some criticism and we managed all that criticism, had all of the social partners involved – so the police, the judiciary, the government all have an office to combat trafficking in persons. We were all working together towards the same objective and that was to make sure there wasn't a peak during the Olympics, but also recognizing that sexual trafficking is happening in Vancouver now or in the province now, and this would continue during the Olympics and would be here afterwards.

As the representative discusses, the aim of the campaign was to convey the message that trafficking, interpreted solely through the lens of sex trafficking, is a "local problem" in addition to being an international or global problem. The aim of communicating the enduring nature of trafficking – a problem that "would continue during the Olympics" and "be here afterwards" – fits with the longstanding involvement of the Salvation Army in anti-trafficking advocacy. Of note, the role of the Salvation Army in colonial and militarized forms of humanitarianism and in ongoing efforts to naturalize experiences of violence within sex industries is concealed as "managed criticism" through partnerships resembling early social intervention campaigns, particularly among law enforcement, government, and judiciary.

In this context, the Truth Isn't Sexy campaign (The Salvation Army 2008) included lurid images of women and slogans: "Imagine being stolen. Raped repeatedly. Beaten repeatedly. Sold. Trafficked. Forced into sex work." The images were displayed on transit shelters, in men's washrooms, and posters depicting "women being beaten, kicked, choked, and brutalized" (Lepp 2013: 262). Other materials developed as part of this campaign depicted "the bruised faces of women from various racial backgrounds with the statement 'I am the face of sex trafficking'" (Lepp 2013: 262). In these images, the emphasized shift in focus on "Canadian girls being victimized" intentionally portrayed the depictions of "innocent" victims as "the girl next door." As Major Venerables of the Salvation Army describes, "The photographs are non-sexual and depict *the innocence* of each woman or girl. The overall effect is haunting ... The girls depicted could be your next door neighbour, your daughter or niece – and this truly is the reality, the face of human trafficking" (as cited in Lepp 2013: 263). The discursive link between "innocence" and "non-sexual" (i.e., passive, pure, and domesticated) echoes purity campaigners' previous claims about white slavery that underpinned early policies of targeted criminalization against migrant women, Indigenous women, and sex workers.

The faith-based representative went on to describe the campaign as "creative stuff" and "very bold": "It put the Salvation Army and sex in the same sentence. It wasn't branding for our sake, it was – we come across as the rescuer of many, the church of many – we are just whoever comes to us, we help, right? So we weren't going for any credit, we were just trying to make a difference because we realized if we didn't, who else was going to step up because the legislation wasn't there." Similar to other advocates, the shift into anti-trafficking was perceived as accidental – the natural result of "just trying to make a difference." However, such depictions unreflexively elide the specific role of the Salvation Army in reinforcing foundational conceptions of rescue, colonial discipline, and control through carceral forms of anti-trafficking intervention. Moreover, reproducing efforts to construct legal controls and maintain order (civility) in the deficiency of laws, the advocate highlights that action was necessary in the absence of legislation to intervene. In keeping with advocacy for legislative controls that reproduce civilizing missions, the Salvation Army also works alongside formal law enforcement in their operation of safe houses for trafficked persons.

Describing the safe house, the representative indicates, "it's a place where the police can deliver, or the referrer can deliver, someone in an underground parking garage to an elevator exclusive to this space within this facility. All the meals are provided, they never have to leave their area." Operated alongside a secure transition house for women in detention, the safe house has come under scrutiny for its detention-like practices in the face of critiques advanced by sex workers. As Goodyear and Auger (2013: 221) highlight, "[s]ex workers identified forced reha-bilitation as just another form of victimization, suggesting that being provided with tools for self-help was more empowering and that alter-natives to sex work such as dependency on the welfare state or mini-mum wage were not very attractive and certainly not liberating."

Although women are technically free to leave the Salvation Army shelter, the policy detailing the criteria for admission indicates that while "it is their right to choose to leave ... police and/or immigration will be notified of a pending release if the client is in danger and plans to return to the 'pimp,' or is potentially in the country illegally." Regard-less of perceived freedom to leave, in each of these instances the poten-tial for coerced restraint and/or revictimization and criminalization are possible, given the serious constraints precarious immigration status places on migrants as well as the limits on agency imported through the highly subjective nature of how "danger" is defined – particularly from the standpoint of an external observer who perceives all sexualized labour as trafficking and any form of relationship with a sex worker, aside from the well-intentioned intervener, as potentially exploitative.

Similarly, the perceived absence of legislation appears to provide the basis for faith-based organizations to "rescue as many as we could" (in the context of the Olympics) and to encourage and support state-based intervention strategies (in general). When discussing the criticisms the campaign received and how the Salvation Army managed such criti-cism, the representative argued that "all of the social partners" shared a similar objective; however, only the "the police, the judiciary, the government" are identified as partners. By restricting involvement, the campaign erases sex worker concerns and ignores the role and voice of sex workers in formulating anti-trafficking responses, while reinforcing criminalization and displacement. However, it should be noted that not all law enforcement shared the Salvation Army's objective. In response to the campaign, Vancouver Police Inspector John de Haas "argued that information campaigns should be grounded in facts and 'not cause hys-teria'" (GAATW 2011: 18). Nonetheless, in the absence of consultation, and especially consent, and in light of the stigmatizing nature of the campaign, sex worker rights advocates responded in an open letter to the Salvation Army:

> Vancouver's sex workers are distressed and angry over your "The Truth Isn't Sexy" anti-trafficking campaign. Sex workers are appalled that you

never consulted the sex work community before launching this highly offensive campaign. Research has repeatedly found that involvement of sex workers is critical to the success of anti-trafficking campaigns … Sex work is the exchange of money for sex, while trafficking is the coerced migration of someone through the use of force, threat of violence, physical or psychological abuse, abuse of authority, fraud, debt bondage, or deception. Conflating sex work and trafficking leads to policies and enforcement strategies that endanger workers and violate their rights. (FIRST 2009: 1)

Of note, rather than reject anti-trafficking discourses, the representative requested inclusion in anti-trafficking discussions in a way that mitigates the effects of conflating trafficking and sex work. Significantly, the sex worker rights advocates prioritize movement, particularly "coerced migration," as the distinguishing feature of human trafficking.

In spite of its negative effect for the rights and safety of sex workers, the sensational human trafficking discourses leading up to the Olympic games captured the public imagination, helping transform human trafficking into a matter of substantial public concern: said a provincial government representative, "we hadn't been expecting the media hype and it just ramped up and ramped up … it just blindsided." Although the extensive public attention was short-lived, it had a lasting effect on the public politicization of discourses, the establishment of domestic trafficking in relation to prostitution in the public imagination, and the corresponding production of the imperative to intervene to "rescue" the "innocent." Leading to the Olympics, Vancouver became a "battle zone" between sex workers' rights organizations and abolitionist groups focused on curbing male sexual demand (GAATW 2011: 18). As agencies working outside the realm of sex workers rights, such as the Salvation Army, took up the anti-trafficking cause in order "to make a difference," safety, resources, and a platform to raise awareness were detracted from sex workers. In this context, the role of advocacy in reproducing racial, national, and sexual priorities of the state remain hidden and ongoing discursive "battles" persist.

Winnipeg, Manitoba: Domesticated Trafficking as Sexual Exploitation

The City of Winnipeg is situated on the land of the Anishinaabeg, Cree, Oji-Cree, Dakota, and Dene peoples, and on the homeland of the Métis Nation. The city expanded rapidly after establishing itself on the

Hudson Bay Company's anchor hold at Upper Fort Garry. Located at the crucial junction of the Assiniboine and Red rivers, the growing city served the settler colonial society's mercantile interests. By 1881, the Canadian Pacific Railway extended its service westward from Ontario to the newly formed municipality (Monks 1992). After roughly ten years, the newly confederated Canadian state was well into expanding west to the prairies of the recently ceded Northwest Territories. As the city grew into the twentieth century it became the major Canadian urban gateway to western interests; a "white, middle to upper-class suburban enclave" expanded outward while an impoverished, racialized inner-city became the epicentre of gendered and racialized violence (Seshia 2010). According to single-origin ancestry data gathered throughout the last quarter of the twentieth century, besides Edmonton, Alberta, Winnipeg, Manitoba had the highest Aboriginal urban population in Canada (Peters and Starchenko 2005). In particular, the Aboriginal population in the inner city of Winnipeg during this time was 3.6 per cent of the total population. As Peters and Starchenko (2005) indicate, dispossession and displacement resulted in lower housing costs, access to services, and the presence of other Indigenous families pulling rural or reserve-based Indigenous people into the inner city of Winnipeg. Whether living on reserve or in the city, the rise of settler Canadian prairie society dislocated Indigenous communities and the role and status of Indigenous persons, particularly of Indigenous women. In this context, the survival sex industry became a restricted means of enduring colonial imposition for some community members (Monture 2007) and a primary site at which the domesticating effects of anti-trafficking coalesce.

In a context of targeted dispossession, anti-trafficking discourses in Manitoba focus on the sexual exploitation of children and youth, especially Indigenous children and youth. Although the Manitoba strategy attributes the vulnerability of children and youth to a number of factors, *legacies* of colonialism and the associated dispossession of Indigenous communities were seen as dominant indicators. Specifically, vulnerability factors include "poverty; racism; colonization; the legacy of residential school experiences; social and cultural isolation; marginalization; peer pressure; past abuse or trauma; sex-based discrimination; medical problems such as mental health, neurological or developmental disorders; system gaps or inaccessible services; and other social and financial inequalities" (Manitoba Family Services and Housing 2008: 3). In the context of colonial legacies and racism, it was perceived that placing the emphasis on children would invoke responses and interventions that are not afforded to Indigenous women.

For example, discussing the provincial emphasis on children, one anti-trafficking advocate suggests, "the general public is a lot more sensitive to children, more sympathetic to children. So I think that was strategically, by the community organizations done. The community organizations working with children were still working with adults." In light of the vulnerability factors identified by the province of Manitoba, the strategy further specifies that Aboriginal children are disproportionately represented among sexually exploited youth, especially if they have been involved in the child welfare system, and have disproportionately "experienced childhood abuse such as sexual abuse and physical abuse (Manitoba Family Services and Housing 2008: 3). Connecting childhood victimization to experiences of Aboriginal women, research conducted by the Native Women's Association of Canada (NWAC) (2010: 3) further indicates the effects of colonization are "most evident in the rates of violence against Aboriginal women" whereby Aboriginal women are the group most *at risk* for issues related to violence in Canada.

The effect of colonization and the systemic gendered racism Indigenous women experience as a result of colonial processes feature most prominently in discussions of anti-trafficking responses in Manitoba. In the words of one frontline worker from an Indigenous-led organization, "[W]hen you have very vulnerable populations that have been so profoundly impacted by the intersections of class, race, gender and sometimes other forms of sexuality, you create conditions for the commodification of humans ... it's an old story, not a new one. Like I think Indigenous women have been trafficked right from the beginning of colonization. I think we have been used as sex objects." As the representative details, colonial sexual violence forms a long history in Canada whereby the dispossession of Indigenous lands and laws occurred alongside ongoing physical and sexual violence as well as legal impositions that naturalized violence against Indigenous women. As Sweet (2014: 2) indicates, "for indigenous people, human trafficking is just the new name of a historical problem. They have experienced exploitation by outsiders in many different areas of the world for generations."

Nonetheless, in the context of settler colonialism, an emphasis on domestic trafficking was seen to provide a framework that could invoke a response to such violence and promote inclusion of Indigenous women in justice-based strategies. Similar to the emphasis on children, the language of trafficking was interpreted by some as capable of eliciting a response: "If [the public] hear human trafficking, particularly if they hear human sex trafficking, they're like "oh, you know, I want to fight against this," but if they hear sexual exploitation or even child sexual exploitation, child abuse, they are more apathetic towards it … around that time we started making that connection that human sex trafficking and particularly commercial sexual exploitation, aka prostitution, were very much interlinked."

The first phase of Manitoba's strategy for responding to sexual exploitation focused exclusively on children while phase two of the strategy, Tracia's Trust, launched in 2008, comprised the coordination of services for all ages (i.e., children, youth, and adults) and emphasized human trafficking for the purpose of sexual exploitation and, especially, domestic trafficking of Indigenous women and girls (Government of Manitoba 2012). Supported in part by Tracia's Trust, the Salvation Army and the RCMP lead the Human Trafficking Response Team in Winnipeg, which included coordinating partnerships with law enforcement agencies, government departments, and nongovernment organizations. Depending on the type of human trafficking and service-provision needs of the victimized individual, the goal of the team was to activate appropriate members once notified of a case through a dedicated phone number.[7] In addition to these provincial strategies, in 2009, SWC provided funding to the Assembly of Manitoba Chiefs to develop education and awareness programs aimed at preventing human trafficking, particularly trafficking for the purpose of the sexual exploitation of Indigenous women and girls.

Domesticating Indigenous Women

Tracia's Trust is dedicated to Tracia Owen, a young girl who spent her life in and out of the care of Child and Family Services, a time during which she became addicted to drugs and a sexually exploited youth. In 2005, Tracia took her life at the age of 14 while under provincial care, resulting in an inquiry that concluded as follows: "Although Tracia Owen died in August 2005, a review of the testimony suggests the foundation for her tragic death was laid many years before" (Provincial Court of Manitoba 2008: 51). Disregarding the role of "provincial care" and forced removal and relocation, the Manitoba strategy for responding to child sexual exploitation built on this inquiry to extenuate intervention to "adult sex trafficking" based on the following claim: "Most adults involved in the sex trade report that their victimization began at a young age, some as young as nine years old. The average age that adults involved in the sex trade were sexually exploited for the first time is 13 to 14 years"[8] (Manitoba Family Services and Housing 2008: 3). Relying on contested claims about the early age of entry, the strategy suggests children's experiences of sexual exploitation and of trafficking are indistinguishable from adult experiences, arguing that exploitation in adulthood is an extension of childhood sexual exploitation. In the words of a Manitoba provincial government representative,

> Exploitation and trafficking are the same to me; certainly in my experience, sex trafficking is the same thing just a different word for it. People are being moved, forced, having their [identification] held. So the definition in the Criminal Code has been happening for a long time for women and children who are being sexually exploited. And back then [sexual exploitation] was kind of the catch phrase … human trafficking has just widened that scope, so it's given law enforcement definitely more ability to look at that issue. But to me personally, it's the same thing.

As this representative reveals, the dominant anti-trafficking discourse in Manitoba equates all forms of prostitution and child sexual exploitation with human trafficking. Of note, the representative highlights the additional tool that anti-trafficking legislation provides to law enforcement officials and their ability to investigate sexual exploitation. Strategies of criminal intervention combined with those of child welfare intervention were a particularly dominant theme in Winnipeg, raising important critical questions about the connection between anti-trafficking discourses and the ongoing forced removal of Indigenous children and criminalization of Indigenous families.

Although the initial Manitoba strategy focused on "children exploited through prostitution," Tracia's Trust considers all forms of sexual exploitation, including prostitution, pornography, sex trafficking, sex tourism and internet luring" (Government of Manitoba 2012). As one frontline worker identifies, the strategy emphasizes "trafficking" as an umbrella term for multiple forms of sexual exploitation:

> It originally started off with just children and youth who have been exploited to the sex trade, then trying to open the doors for adults; our strategy now is expanding to Internet luring, child pornography, even though there's been very specific initiatives on that. We're just trying to

pull it all together under one umbrella. And, you know, we use the word "trafficking" in our strategy like along with "exploitation" – trafficking: it's sexual exploitation, right. So it's all the same thing.

In this context, a number of respondents from government and non-government agencies interpret human trafficking as "new words" to discuss the "longstanding" problem of sexual exploitation, which is seen as indistinguishable from sex work. In the words of one frontline worker, "domestic sex trafficking *is* the sex trade that we've had here, it's not a new thing."

Funding mandates, in particular, significantly influenced the adoption of anti-trafficking discourses. For instance, as one provincial government representative argues, not applying the terms "human trafficking" and "sexual exploitation" to women's experiences could result in a lack of funding for women and the stigmatization of women in sex industries based on the assumption that any abuse that is experienced as a sex worker was a result of participating in the industry by choice. Thus, the representative suggests the need to extend the label of "sexual exploitation" to include "human trafficking," for women especially, to subvert the stigmatization and apathy directed towards sex workers: "I really think people are just more okay with funding services for kids rather than adults. Once people turn 18 there is really that opinion that 'well, it's their choice' … If they are in a massage parlour or trafficked into strip clubs … it's their choice. They can leave,' people always say." While such arguments aim to ensure services are available for women and to discredit a false public perception of "deserved" abuse, in practice the blanket adoption of anti-trafficking discourse has led to the silencing of some women's experiences and restricted access to appropriate support. In the words of one frontline worker,

> [Human trafficking] reminds me of sexual exploitation … how that terminology was used and abused by people in power and different agencies in order to attract and keep funding. To portray a certain light or shine a light on everybody in one way. To use the same brushstroke to label everybody, which wasn't true. A red flag should go up when one term is used to describe everybody. And that's the problem with sexual exploitation: some are exploited and some aren't. And so it's wrong to use that term for everybody. It causes a lot of damage. So another term comes up: trafficking, used much in the same way … and so that way people can get funding for their program.

As this excerpt suggests, anti-trafficking discourses have facilitated access to funding, but in the process have also withdrawn funding of other supports, especially in the areas of harm reduction and those principled on self-determination.

This interpretation of trafficking as sexual exploitation emerges through a negotiation of the "new language" of trafficking in the context of domestic versus international conceptions of trafficking. A frontline worker, for instance, shared the following response to concerns raised by Manitoba's justice minister about formulating an anti-trafficking strategy for the province:

> I had to sit down with [the Minister of Justice] and tell him what traffick-ing was all about. Because he was concerned that he didn't have a strategy on trafficking. Like, "you've had one for a long time now, we just called it something different." It's international trafficking you didn't have a strat-egy on, but we don't have a huge problem with that and then, it's certainly the labour stuff … To check out whether you're on the right track, it's just new words. But we already have a strategy on trafficking, basically, on the domestic sex trafficking you know, so we already have done work on domestic sex trafficking for years in Manitoba. So it's no different.

As this representative suggests, "international trafficking," which is interpreted as "sex trafficking" and as "labour stuff," is not perceived as a significant problem in the context of a prairie city, which further lends itself towards understandings of trafficking as a "domestic" mat-ter within a "trafficking as sexual exploitation" framework. Similarly, a former immigration and security official indicated, "I think partially because of the inland nature of the region … we weren't seeing those [international] cases." However, in spite of low incidence, the repre-sentative perceives international trafficking as a more heinous crime in comparison to experiences of "residents" working in sex industries. From this perspective, "being deceived" forms the primary basis of cases involving migrants:

> In the large scheme, I think the numbers are relatively low … But the real-ity is that it's so heinous. I mean it's one thing as a resident of Canada and you decide I want to work in this business, it's a way, "I'm going to pay my way through university" or "I've got a drug habit and I've got to sup-port it because otherwise my kid's gonna starve." That's one thing, but actually deceiving a person to believe that they're coming into to Canada

to do something quite benign and then forcing them into prostitution is abhorrent and you know even if there were one case a year we should have provisions to stop that, now we do.

In this context, international trafficking was interpreted as a matter of enforcement-based protection of women that emphasized restrictive immigration. As the representative further discussed, "I think the young women are almost invariably the victims."

Of note, the possibility of interpreting the *victims* as passively deceived is applied only to international conceptions of trafficking; domestic subjects are read through stigma-informed notions of responsibilitizing blame. This type of framing underpins arguments for the inclusion of domestic subjects in trafficking discourses. By downplaying constraints faced within Canada – including the example of someone who is "drug addicted" and working to feed "starving children" – erases the role of Canadians in the production and continuation of widespread inequalities. Thus, only in the context of international movement are persons involved in sex industries considered to be "deceived" and thereby "real victims." While such discourses are premised on assumptions regarding the naivety of migrating women and especially women migrating in sex industries,[9] they also conceal structural and material forms of inequality by pitting (and stigmatizing) the decision to "work in this business" against the "heinous" crime of being deceived. In turn, it is precisely this form of "apathy" towards the material conditions of Indigenous women that Sikka (2009) and others argue underpins the unresponsiveness of law enforcement in incidences of violence facing Indigenous women in sex industries. However, rather than centre the self-determination of women in sex industries negotiating complex inequalities and structural forms of violence, reactionary responses aiming to address colonial legacies draw on anti-trafficking discourses to forefront victim-centred narratives and corresponding mandates of formalized intervention. In doing so, domestic trafficking in Manitoba is discursively linked to the sexual exploitation of Indigenous women and girls, foregrounding efforts to rescue, intervene, and protect, while simultaneously reproducing the mechanism of intervention that led to the dispossession of Indigenous people from their lands and that perpetuate ongoing physical and sexual violence against Indigenous women.

Childhood sexual abuse, connection to gang activity, and intergenerational sexual exploitation were cited as key explanations for emphasizing "domestic trafficking" in relation to sexually exploited Indigenous children and youth in Winnipeg. As one frontline worker highlighted, "It's intergenerational abuse stemming back to residential schools ... we often see intergenerational sex trade happening. Mothers putting their daughters out, or daughters going out because they're scared their baby sisters are going to have to go out. Protecting her for a little while, but then her joining in as well. It's very sad to see it happen, but it's not uncommon."

By emphasizing the intergenerational experiences of sexual exploitation, the province further argues that no distinction is necessary between the experiences of women and children in sex industries; rather, all are seen as victims of the exploitative practices of sex trade industries. Emphasizing intergenerational experiences of exploitation and the "victim" status of sexually exploited children and youth represents an important evolution from discourses of deviance and corresponding perceptions of "children as prostitutes." In the words of one frontline worker, "We have been so focused on sexually exploited youth and how that language has evolved and become so used. And that's good. We don't want "teenage hooker" to be used. So that's good, but on the other side are almost the people that are harder to reach because they are hiding themselves ... Probably, it's a lot like being in the closet."

However, as the passage above suggests, by drawing on intergenerational experiences of sexual exploitation to argue for the conflation of sexual exploitation, prostitution, and human trafficking, the province negates important contextualization: "stemming back to residential schools" and other state-based interventions of colonial dispossession. In turn, the province participates in silencing the complex experiences of individuals in sex industries and, at times, creates more insecurity for individuals who cannot or refuse to self-identify as a victim of human trafficking.

Nonetheless, anti-trafficking discourses emphasizing the experiences of sexually exploited Aboriginal youth and children in Manitoba have led to the adoption of some effective, traditional healing programs in the province, especially for Aboriginal women, youth, and children. For example, the experience of one trafficked individual represents the profile of sexual exploitation and trafficking the province prioritizes and aims to address by emphasizing traditional healing mechanisms that target sexually exploited, Aboriginal youth: "I'm a transgendered Two-Spirit individual ... I moved to Winnipeg at a young age and started sex trade work ... 12 years old and that's when I pulled my first trick and since then I was in the trade where I would exploit myself and people would exploit me. I was also pimped. I was also trafficked across Canada west."

The participant goes on to discuss the role traditional forms of healing played in facilitating a recovery experience from addiction:

> My Aboriginal background was what really helped me stay sane. Learning about the medicines, the drum, playing the drum, being involved in community and community organizations was also a big part of my sobriety. I've tried the [Alcoholics Anonymous/Narcotics Anonymous/ Cocaine Anonymous] thing, it just didn't work for me because the Bible was being thrown at me and I didn't accept that and I couldn't accept it because in the Bible, the statements on sexuality in the Bible, I wasn't too fond of that so I turned to my ways of being Aboriginal to really work on myself to pursue my sobriety.

In this instance, anti-trafficking discourses emphasized by the province subverted other interventionist strategies to provide an effective framework for healing and recovery that foregrounds self-determination of youth recovering from substance abuse, human trafficking, and sexual exploitation.

At the same time, narratives of intergenerational abuse are referred to in order to justify formal detainment, intervention strategies, and ongoing efforts of rescue, conversion, and civilization that echo early white slavery campaigns in the country. The follow excerpt from a faith-based representative clearly depicts this process:

> [O]ur solution is always change their heart, bring them to Jesus Christ and then they will make the changes in their lives and if they're enslaved in certain situations God will deliver them from that, you know, but a lot of times they don't even know any other way. If your mother has used you to earn an income for her, for her crack habit since you were, you know, an age of interest to men, which could be, sad to say, you know, very young … what does that girl think of life, she's gonna think it's what it is and she's gonna go and do the same thing with her own children.

In the context of settler colonialism, such ongoing efforts to Christianize resemble early intervention strategies aimed at assimilation. The representative elides the role of missionaries and Christian churches in the dispossession of Indigenous women, while reinforcing notions that intergenerational forms of exploitation are the result of "bad mothers"[10] failing to "change their heart." Colonial processes frequently construct Indigenous women as "bad mothers," particularly in a context where children were abducted into residential schools because Indigenous families were deemed unfit to parent, educate, and civilize (i.e., nurture citizens). The representative goes on to discuss the failure of state-based interventions and apprehensions:

> Even in the foster home they come back. We have so many resources here, I don't see any change at all or anything, the money just keeps pouring in, the resources keep pouring in and nothing changes … so when we come along and try and tell them that Jesus can change their life, they have no clue what that means and then if we start talking about turning from your sins, repenting of your sin and you know, turning your life to Christ and following him with all your heart, mind, soul, and strength and carrying your cross, they have no idea what any of those things mean anymore, to them it's the gulf – I think they think is so wide between themselves and suburbia that they would be like "why try to attain it?"

Of note, the representative critiques the amount of resources "pouring in" to state-based interventions that fail to create change; however, rather than reviewing these failings in a context of longstanding colonial interventions aimed at the destruction of Indigeneity – including mass removal of children into foster care systems – the respondent further emphasizes the importance of Christianizing. The individual indicates, "they have no idea what those things mean *anymore*" (emphasis added), which discursively erases the violent conditions in which "those things" were imposed on Indigenous communities and the intergenerational violences and ongoing familial disruption imposed by the abuses suffered in residential schools. Interpreted in the context of ongoing civilizing missions, the ultimate goal is constructed as "suburbia" and is seen as an unattainable space. This further elides the way inner city communities negotiate the ongoing gentrification and dispossession affecting many urban Indigenous persons and responsibilizes Indigenous people for their inability to access "suburbia."

In the context of settler colonialism, the role of movement also provides an important discursive device to negotiate distinctions between "domestic" and "international," with particular implications for the reproduction of national, racial, and sexual priorities. As a faith-based anti-trafficking advocate discusses, the linking of sexual exploitation and trafficking became possible through the framework of domestic trafficking wherein "there is no necessary movement of people at all." As the representative further discusses, "[I]t's been happening for centuries unfortunately, and what it would look like in Winnipeg would be basically people from the North End, you know mainly Aboriginal people, being exploited and girls unfortunately, too, whether they're coming in from reserves to the city or whether they're already in the city." Thus, anti-trafficking is perceived as a mechanism with which to respond to legacies of colonial gender violence through the inclusion of Indigenous women in state-based forms of "protection" that reinforce the state as saviour.

Further underscoring the distinction between movement in international trafficking and the importance of a domestic framework whereby "domestic sex trafficking is the sex trade," a frontline worker indicates,

[W]e don't have lots of people who take young Aboriginal or even non-Aboriginal kids. Actually we probably have more non-Aboriginal kids who get moved. Yeah, because there's a certain pimp culture that will move people, some just stay within Western Canada, some move out East, you know, you've probably heard this, you know there's different circuits right. … And then we do have the gangs here in Manitoba that are now more into the on-reserve and rural communities that, you know, might bring some girls down here to the city. But there's not lots of that going on and there's not lots of any of our girls going to Japan or you know … there use to be more where there was lots of movement with women and young girls being moved across Canada, but the culture has really changed, certainly here in Manitoba where we don't have that part, like, we have more gangs who are running the sex trade versus single, independent pimps.

The disclaimer "we don't have lots of people *who take* young Aboriginal" (emphasis added) children aims to distinguish domestic forms of trafficking from stereotypical representations of international trafficking (i.e., "girls going to Japan") through means of abduction (i.e., being taken). Once again the racializing work of anti-trafficking discourses is evident in naturalizing constructions of sex trafficking as the cultural conditions of an Orientalized Other. As Hua (2011: 73) reveals, anti-trafficking campaigns "affirm and recirculate the racialization of Asian difference as perpetually foreign." The Asian body, in anti-trafficking, is thereby constructed over "bodies identifiable as white, black, or indigenous," denoting differential claims to national belonging (Hua 2011: 75).

Meanwhile, the discussion also conceals the role of government and law enforcement agencies in the vast forced movement of Indigenous children in Canada, including movement into residential schools, but also substantial, ongoing, and disproportionate movement in child welfare and criminal justice systems, the latter of which is directly fueled by ongoing removal and forced apprehension in response to sexual exploitation. The representative further highlights attention to organized criminal activity, which is specifically noted as "on reserve" gang activity underpinning the sex trade in the province. When asked why the representative thinks movement has changed in the province, the response further drew on racialized characterizations of "individual pimps" as opposed to "on-reserve" gangs, noting the latter remain in Manitoba in spite of changing economic conditions:

> Reserve folks, especially if you look at – sorry, I'm going to be stereotypical here – but certainly among the individual pimps, when you're looking at, the black community, right, whether they're Caribbean or, lots of those guys, we use to have lots of those guys in Manitoba, but they don't tend to stay [*Laughing*]. It's too cold! Or, sometimes you know, for awhile there Winnipeg wasn't a big money-making place. So it's the *local people* who stay here, right? And we do have tons of issues for our Aboriginal people here in Manitoba, right. Like there's tons of struggles. For on-reserves who have no frickin' water you know. To just the lack of opportunity and all the historical stuff that have just really impacted our First Nations people, it's just destroyed a whole culture and it's going to take years for folks to get back to their roots, and back to stability, and back to having decent land, you know, just that whole impact. And because we do have one of the highest urban Aboriginal populations in Canada we are going to see more issues of gangs and people in the justice system, and in child welfare, and around like 70 percent in those different systems are from our First Nations communities. So that's probably more of Manitoba's flavour; however, same shit, different pot, right?

The representative's reference to "our Aboriginal people" signifies the perceived domestication of Indigenous persons within the context of settler colonial relations in the province. In this context, the struggles of Indigenous persons and the perceived destruction of Indigenous culture are seen through the lens of a "lack of opportunity and all that historical stuff," while the agents of colonization remain uncontested despite recognition of a stark overrepresentation of Indigenous children in "child welfare" and "those different systems." In other words, from the standpoint of colonial *legacies*, such overrepresentation appears as a result of a long process of Indigenous people trying to get back to "their roots," rather than an ongoing working out of a settler colonial state system intent on the destruction of Indigenous culture and communities.

Significantly, the language of "Manitoba's flavour" points to gendered, racialized, and sexualized violence against Indigenous children, yet the discussion of "sexual exploitation" was also seen to erase the relevance of structural inequalities in a settler colonial context. This can be seen in the same representative's mention of sexual exploitation training the represented agency provided in Eastern Canada:

> We did training [in Newfoundland and Labrador] ... a lot of young, white, Irish kids in Saint John's [are] being exploited. Because that's predominantly what's there. Certainly some smaller First Nations communities, but not like here. It was mainly all these little white girls. But same shit, different pile, it's still just somebody who's being exploited. I don't care what colour you are, somebody is being exploited and there's somebody doing that. ... If you have missing kids in your small community, then you're going to have kids who are being exploited. Because they're vulnerable.

Here, the overrepresentation of Indigenous children and youth as "victims of trafficking" in Manitoba is interpreted as a result of "predominately what's there." In this, the exploitation of "white girls" is interpreted as the "same shit, different pile," which obscures the role of ongoing colonial violence facing Indigenous communities. The focus becomes the "missing kids" (i.e., those vulnerable and at risk) and "somebody doing that" (i.e., criminals or perpetrators). In turn, ongoing interventions to protect vulnerable children and enforcement of tough-on-crime policies continue to be justified as central anti-trafficking responses, while colonial, racialized, and gendered violence is largely disregarded. Thus, without rooting understanding of violence in the context of ongoing colonial oppression, responses in Manitoba reproduce the very structures underpinning overrepresentation and criminalization in "those different systems." In doing so, the political economy conducive to the trafficking of persons is also reproduced.

Anti-trafficking in Calgary, Alberta:
Cross-Sector Coordination

Calgary is located on lands of the Blackfoot and is in Treaty seven ter-ritory of the Siksika, the Piikuni, the Kainai, the Tsuu T'ina, and the Stoney Nakoda First Nation as well as the current home of Region III of the Métis Nation of Alberta. The city appeared as the twentieth-century corporate centre of prairie enterprise against a background of dispos-sessing pre-existing Indigenous networks under colonial dominion. In 1850, the Blackfoot Confederacy of T'suu T'ina/Sarcee, Stoney, Siksika/Blackfoot, Kainah/Blood, and Piikani/Peigan First Nations ranged along the eastern steppe of the Rocky Mountains from Edmonton to Great Falls, Montana.[11] While the Numbered Treaties gave the Domin-ion of Canada legal rights to prairie Indigenous lands between 1871 and 1921, the introduction of disease and increasing starvation also reduced the Confederacy to restricted Native Reserves in southern and northern Alberta.[12] Building upon a strategy of *conquest by treaty* based on a terra nullius and humanitas nullius view of the continent, European settlers collectively established businesses and livelihoods and extended capi-talist market pursuits in line with the state-building goals of the 1867 Canadian Confederation.[13] Following the resource boom in Alberta in the early twentieth century, the corporate centre of Canada reached westward from Toronto–Montreal to Calgary–Vancouver. In line with efforts to control the land and the extraction of resources through poli-cies of assimilation, Alberta had the most residential schools out of any of the Canadian provinces.

Calgary maintains its position of prominence in a resource-based economy, and is commonly referred to as the "head office capital" of Western Canada. Specifically, the city hosts the largest concentration of head offices in Canada, particularly in the energy and financial ser-vices sectors, as well as manufacturing, transportation, logistics, and retail sectors (Calgary Economic Development 2011). Priding itself on low corporate and personal taxes alongside a high quality of life and leisure, Alberta's GDP was almost double the national GDP before the recession in 2008.[14] Given the resource-driven economy, the prosperity of the province is directly linked to global geopolitical relationships and the expansion of resource-extraction industries made possible through assimilationist and land-theft policies of settler colonial regimes.

In Alberta, the Action Coalition on Human Trafficking (ACT) Alberta is the provincial response to human trafficking in Alberta. It was established in 2010 following the adoption of the Criminal Code's Trafficking in Persons legislation and an environmental scan of Calgary, Edmonton, and Winnipeg conducted by the Centre for Immigrant Women in Edmonton, Alberta. Based on these origins, initial concerns in Alberta emphasized the relationship between the experiences of migrant women and human trafficking. The environmental scan, "Trafficking of Women and Girls to Canada," targeted social services, law enforcement, health care, faith-based, and immigration and settlement agencies. In this way, the emergence of anti-trafficking in Alberta was founded on the perceptions of the social services sector and directed specifically towards migrant women and girls arriving in Canada. The scan identified that 45.5 per cent of respondents perceived they were coming into contact with cases of human trafficking in their city (Trompetter 2007), and recommended specific education and training for service providers who may come into contact with trafficked persons.

As a result, ACT Alberta was formed to "increase knowledge and awareness on human trafficking, advocate for effective rights-based responses; build capacity of all involved stakeholders and lead and foster collaboration for joint action against human trafficking" (ACT Alberta 2012). ACT Alberta is a nonprofit organization mandated with establishing a coordinated response network to encourage collaboration and partnerships among stakeholders – nongovernment organizations, social serving agencies, health care providers, law enforcement, and government agencies.

The often-repeated notion of "stakeholders" is an important signifier of who has a *stake* in anti-trafficking responses. Similar to other anti-trafficking responses in the country, in Alberta, individuals who are most directly affected by human trafficking and anti-trafficking responses remain disassociated from the human trafficking terminology and from those deemed to have a stake in the response. As an intersectional examination of trafficking in Alberta highlights, individuals accessing services designed in response to trafficking rarely identify themselves as trafficked and at times are alienated by the language of trafficking (Kaye 2015). For example, a research and evaluation manager from southern Alberta highlights, "I feel that most victims do not use the language of human trafficking" (as cited in Kaye 2015: 31). Thus, while ACT Alberta does engage people who have been directly affected by human trafficking in forming the response, the engagement of stakeholders predominantly refers to mechanisms of social service, intervention, and enforcement.

As Quarterman, Kaye, and Winterdyk (2012: 9) show, ACT Alberta "mobilizes stakeholders to identify and respond to human trafficking through prevention efforts, ensuring adequate protection and support for trafficking persons, supporting the prosecution of the criminals involved, and encouraging effective collaborative partnerships." Further, "ACT broadly defines a response to human trafficking to include any activities aimed at preventing human trafficking from occurring, raising awareness within communities on the issue, building the capacity of service providers to assist trafficked persons, supporting the use of existing laws to prosecute traffickers, and advocating for a victim-centred and rights-based approach" (Quarterman, Kaye, and Winterdyk 2012: 10). Although there are many interpretations of the coalition signifier in the ACT Alberta organizational title, the organization has predominantly settled into a coordinating body that emphasizes the identification of human trafficking and the coordination of responses in instances of trafficking and other abuses.

Presently, ACT Alberta receives funding from the Government of Alberta: Justice and Solicitor General, Victims of Crime Fund,[15] Human Services, and the Community Initiatives Program. The Government of Canada has supported ACT Alberta via project-based and time-limited funding through the Department of Justice Victims Fund and SWC. Previous projects have received support from the Civil Forfeiture Office and the Human Rights and Multiculturalism Fund at the Government of Alberta. Since its inception, the number of chapters has varied. In 2012, ACT Alberta comprised five chapters, including Calgary, Edmonton, Grande Prairie, Fort McMurray, and Red Deer.[16] At the time of writing, there are two remaining chapters in each of the largest urban centres in Alberta: Calgary and Edmonton. The Calgary-based chapter of ACT began in 2008 with the establishment of an information-sharing network that facilitated collaboration when cases of trafficking were identified or referred to the network. In this way, the ACT Alberta chapter coordinators have acted as ad hoc case managers, coordinating service provision, such as immigration support, health care, legal guidance, and basic needs, and worked with government and law enforcement agencies (Quarterman, Kaye, and Winterdyk 2012). The service provision paradigm informing the Alberta protocol aims to offer a coordinated response model that places the trafficked individual at the centre of a network of services and interventions (ACT Alberta 2012).

In a case study of service provision agencies and frontline workers providing services to trafficked persons or populations considered vulnerable to human trafficking in Calgary, this kind of coordinating body was identified as particularly beneficial for bringing diverse perspectives and resources to the table without duplicating services or funnelling resources away from existing supports and into trafficking mandates (Quarterman, Kaye, and Winterdyk 2012). While beneficial from the perspective of identifying victims as they are legislatively defined and offering streamlined services in response, the reproduction of inequalities experienced by individuals centred in this model are negotiated within broader social, structural, and material contexts created through the dynamic interactions that occur between advocates and government actors (Merry 2003). As this book examines, it remains important to consider such benefits in the broader social context in which they emerge, which includes an exploration of how rights-based discourses and interventions function towards the reproduction of settler colonialism in Canada and why resistance to colonial gender violence can, at times, appear as a rejection of right-based interventions.

ACT Alberta collects data when they provide support for individuals victimized by trafficking and other abuses. The most recent statistics represent individuals with "confirmed or significant" elements of human trafficking that have had some form of contact with ACT from 2010 until just before March 2015.[17] The following percentages are based on 91 cases in which significant elements of trafficking were identified. However, it should be noted that these cases do not represent the total number of cases referred to ACT Alberta or where services were provided by ACT. From 2010 to 2015, ACT Alberta received a total of 208 referrals. Of these referrals, ninety-one were instances that ACT or partnering organizations either defined as trafficking or had significant elements of trafficking based on the UN Trafficking Protocol definition. According to ACT figures, 77 per cent of individuals assisted by ACT whose cases comprised significant elements of trafficking were female and the average age was 26 years (slightly higher among males, at 28 years).[18]

Of the cases identified, the types of trafficking represented include sex trafficking (57 per cent), labour trafficking (34 per cent), labour/sex trafficking (8 per cent), and organ trafficking (1 per cent). In addition, 56 per cent of cases were identified as internal trafficking and 44 per cent international. The place of origin (by continent) for victimized individuals included Canada (47 per cent); Asia, including the Middle East (38 per cent); Africa (7 per cent); North America (4 per cent); and other

(3 per cent). Of the individuals whose country of origin was Canada, 21 per cent were reported as Aboriginal.

ACT Alberta also documented the immigration status of cases whose origin was not Canada: 57 per cent, temporary foreign workers; 14 per cent, visitor visas; 14 per cent, no status; 5 per cent, student visas; 5 per cent, permanent residents; 2 per cent Canadian citizen; 2 per cent, refugee claimant; and 2 per cent, work permit. In addition, ACT Alberta identified the locations from which individuals were referred to ACT Alberta: 40 per cent from Edmonton, 20 per cent from Calgary, 13 per cent from British Columbia, 9 per cent from Red Deer, 9 per cent from Alberta (other), 7 per cent from Canada (other), and 2 per cent from other countries. Last, ACT Alberta reported substantial increases in the number of cases referred to them. These increases have been ongoing for the past few years and are attributed to heightened levels of education in the province. In light of this, such increases are anticipated to continue for the coming years.

While such data provide a picture of the perceptions and the corresponding identification of trafficking in the province, there remains a "general confusion surrounding the relationship between legal definitions of human trafficking and other forms of exploitation and abuse" (Kaye, Winterdyk, and Quarterman 2014: 10). In general, awareness efforts and other representations in the province include an overreliance of images of victimized women in the sex trade and emphasize criminal definitions. In this context, ACT provides education about the barriers created by human trafficking myths. For instance, in an infographic depicting the "Myths vs. Realities" of human trafficking in Alberta, ACT Alberta situates labour trafficking, trafficking of men, and trafficking of Canadian Citizens as important underrepresented areas of human trafficking and further states that trafficked individuals typically know their abusers and that trafficking occurs in legal businesses, not just in "unregulated industries like prostitution and gangs" (ACT Alberta 2015). In a context of significant definitional ambiguity and politicized representations (Kaye and Winterdyk 2011), ACT Alberta collects and disseminates "facts" about victims of human trafficking in Alberta and, in doing so, becomes an interloper of interpreting "real victims" under anti-trafficking legislations and protocols vis a vis other forms of exploitation. From the conception adopted by ACT Alberta, trafficking occurs by location (i.e., international and domestic) and by type (i.e., sex and labour).

In negotiating highly polarized discussions regarding the relationship between sex trafficking and sex work, ACT Alberta's interpretation of a "victim-centred" standpoint is to maintain a position of "neutral-ity." In particular, with the aim of maintaining an inclusive response that incorporates a broader range of services, ACT Alberta does not take a stance on the relationship between trafficking and sex work (although this approach has taken different iterations based on the context of the coordinating chapters). In Edmonton, for instance, where ACT Alberta headquarters are situated, ACT negotiates within a context of domi-nant abolition perspectives. This is apparent in the sensationalized public campaigns in Edmonton, which sought to represent sex work as human trafficking, such as the Chrysalis Anti-Human Trafficking Net-work that launched a website depicting a young girl next to the state-ment, "Now Recruiting: Child Sex Workers ... Start a Rewarding Career Today" (Chrysalis Anti-Human Trafficking Network 2013). The fake advertisement provided a link to the website "sexwork4U.com" that automatically redirected users to the campaign website "stoptraffic.ca." In this context, efforts to maintain an apolitical or neutral standpoint are interpreted as the most inclusive approach to uphold an emphasis on the broad spectrum of human trafficking experiences. In turn, such an approach is perceived as having the potential to include as well as alienate abolition and sex worker rights advocates. However, in light of the dominant national harmonizing of anti-trafficking and anti-prostitution legislations, there remains little space to interpret neutrality as an apolitical stance in spite of – and perhaps because of – such intended broad inclusion in anti-trafficking discourses.

The Calgary-based chapter, in particular, initially maintained a broad participation of multiple and divergent perspectives that included harm reduction and sex worker rights advocates alongside exit-based and anti–sex industry advocates. However, proponents of the exit-based strategy that participated in the Calgary chapter of ACT Alberta initially refused to associate its mandate with the language of trafficking, but over time reframed its position as *the* anti-trafficking organization in the city. This occurred alongside national and local-ized shifts in funding mandates towards trafficking-centred dis-courses that excluded sex worker–serving organizations, resulting in a number of organizations rebranding as anti-trafficking groups and disassociating themselves from more diverse conversations about sex industries and labour trafficking (Clancey, Khushrushahi, and Ham 2014). Thus, in a broader context in which dominant discourses are guided by abolitionist narratives, an apolitical stance in effect repro-duces the dominant conflation of sex trafficking and sex work over time. This creates problematic challenges for coordinating bodies aiming to adopt an inclusive approach through perceived neutrality. As Byrd articulates (2011: xxiv) "rights struggles have often cathected liberal democracy as the best possible avenue to redress the historical violences of and exclusions from the state," whereby "scholars and activists committed to social justice have been left with impossible choices: to articulate freedom at the expense of another, to seek power and recognition in the hopes that we might avoid the syllogism of democracy created through colonialism" (Byrd xxiv). In settler colonial states, coordinating bodies can play beneficial roles in the identification of human rights infractions and service provision responses, while also reproducing and reinforcing the conditions and context in which such infractions emerge. In this, refusals to participate in anti-trafficking – including limited engagement with harm reduction, sex worker rights, and Indigenous rights groups – are an important perspective from which to examine resistance to rights-based modes of inclusion.

Nonetheless, in spite of its origins emphasizing trafficking of migrant women, the focus of ACT Alberta, and particularly the Calgary chapter of ACT, expanded to emphasize broader conceptions of trafficking. In Calgary, an emphasis on labour trafficking stemmed in part from ACT Alberta's efforts to raise awareness and educate about the barriers created by human trafficking myths, especially myths conflating sex work and sex trafficking. It further arose as an attempt to not duplicate existing services. As a representative of the Calgary-based chapter discussed,

> I think ACT, we have evolved into our own organization because we have seen that there is a need, but we are not a new organization that is going to set up an office and a shelter and all of that. We would rather work with those [organizations] that are here, and where there is a gap, for instance men who have been trafficked for labour exploitation ... What we get are people who want to start [an] organization to help women and children ... you end up competing for funds and duplicating efforts.

Thus, an emphasis on trafficking for the purpose of labour exploitation arose as an attempt to work "where there is a gap" without duplicating existing service provision. Particularly important for developing the typically underrepresented areas of labour trafficking was the provision of a conversational forum whereby multiple perspectives were shared. In the words of a frontline worker at an agency that provides supports to precarious status migrant workers,

> We didn't really realize we were handling human trafficking cases, until we were made aware that this is human trafficking, fits the definition of human trafficking … we deal with labour and workers. We were able to be aware of human trafficking only when ACT Alberta, the Action Coalition on Human Trafficking, started to keep in touch with us, and there's lots of agencies there, so that's why we started to attend the meetings. That's when we started to realize "oh yeah, we handled those cases before, we should have handled them as human trafficking.

As this participant discusses, the training provided by the Calgary chapter of ACT and conversations with other formal social service sectors led the agency to reconsider the experiences of migrant workers under the trafficking framework. A law enforcement representative furthers this perspective, indicating, "there's a lot of victim services in place for other crimes, and [ACT] essentially just takes these services that are already in place and trains them about trafficking." As this excerpt suggests, intervention and funding for the response is directed towards "victims of crime." Nonetheless, because services for individuals victimized by sexual assault and sexual exploitation as well as services for individuals engaged in sex work were more developed in Calgary than services for individuals experiencing other forms of labour abuses, the Calgary chapter of ACT emphasized developing response mechanisms for individuals victimized by labour trafficking while partnering with existing organizations in the areas of harm reduction, exit-based strategies, transitional housing, domestic violence, and others with respect to sex trafficking cases. In this context, sex trafficking remains conceptualized as distinct from labour trafficking in Alberta anti-trafficking discourses. Nonetheless, the dominant focus of the Calgary chapter at the time of this research was labour trafficking, although, similar to other cities in Western Canada, various discourses emerge when examining the construction of trafficking through internal and international conceptions.

Domestic versus International Anti-trafficking Discourses in Calgary

As did those in the other Western Canadian cities, anti-trafficking advocates in Calgary described a shift from international conceptions of human trafficking to understanding trafficking through a domestic or internal lens. However, the context of Calgary provides some unique insights about this transition given the awareness efforts that emphasized labour trafficking (defined separately from sex trafficking) and collaborative responses with organizations providing services to precarious status migrants. Despite the centrality of labour-related discourses, domestic trafficking remains predominately interpreted through discourses of sex trafficking. However, Calgary does provide the only instance in this research in which a domestic framework was used in relation to nonsexual labour trafficking. Nonetheless, in a context that prioritizes labour trafficking, the marginalization of labour in discourses emphasizing domestic trafficking further underscores the redefinition of anti-prostitution advocacy under the rhetoric of trafficking and modern-day slavery. A service provider highlights this transition towards internal representations: "Human trafficking is not just something that happens in other parts of the world, it happens in Canada as well. Traffickers recruit, transport, and control people by pushing or forcing them into selling sex or working for little or no pay ... It's up to all of us to do something about human trafficking. The first step is recognizing what human trafficking looks like in Canada."

As the representative indicates, conceptions of trafficking as something that "happens in Canada as well" emerged in relation to sex and labour trafficking. While this depiction enables a potential distinction between forced provision of sexual services and other forms of sex work, others conflate sex trafficking with sex work when describing domestic involvement. Along these lines, a representative of a faith-based organization describes a shift in emphasis from international to domestic as a means of responding to the sensationalized depictions of international trafficking:

> I mean it's pretty different if you are talking about human trafficking in Canada than if you are talking about the typical view of trafficking: "We need to go to Thailand and rescue these children from the brothel or whatever" ... I've had more exposure to that kind of mindset. Just because I was a pastor in a church before I worked here, and that was kind of a very religious institution and I kind of jumped on board with that whole thing. The more international scale of it. So I feel like I'm just learning the Canadian context.

Of significance, the representative notes the "rescue" mentality associated with religious institutions that "jumped on board" to respond to international human trafficking; however, similar critique is not extended to the growing emphasis on domestic trafficking. Rather, domestic trafficking is framed as a response to the overly sensational depictions of international trafficking and a means of overcoming bandwagon responses. Another service provider in the area of sexual violence indicates something similar: "I think there are a lot of things that people maybe wouldn't know … they just assume international human trafficking when we know there's a lot of human trafficking from like reserves into urban centres or from just from city to city, like the domestic human trafficking piece and I think people probably forget about that." Here again, the representative portrays domestic-trafficking discourses as an evolution of awareness. Movement here provides the central point of connection. In particular, the employment of movement connects domestic trafficking to movement from "reserves" to "urban centres" or from "city to city." In this context, domestic trafficking is interpreted in relation to "risky" movements, particularly of "at risk" populations – predominantly Indigenous youth.

Paralleling other discourses in a settler colonial context, the notion of moving for "a better life" is described as the primary factor in creating vulnerability to human trafficking. The construction of structured dispossession and restricted access to essential services for Indigenous communities remains concealed. Significantly, a criminal justice representative discussed the only mention of domestic labour trafficking in the context of a non–sex related industry; the representative draws on notions of "at risk" subjects to discuss the evidentiary struggles associated with proving domestic trafficking: "It's not that we don't accept that it can happen domestically, obviously; anywhere where there's vulnerable people or they've been moved, such as reserves where you've got the native population, which may be looking to better their lives, they're vulnerable as well, if they've got substance abuse issues, alcohol issues, they're liable to be exploited not only in the sex trade but in other forced labour as well."

In line with dominant depictions of trafficking, the representative distinguishes forced labour from sex work. Nonetheless, this does provide the only instance in which the dominant understanding of domestic sex trafficking is challenged. Given the resource-driven economy of Alberta and the emphasis on labour trafficking, domestic forms of trafficking are expanded in some instances to include varying forms of labour. At the same time, the continued emphasis on "at risk" subjects naturalizes particular bodies as "liable to be exploited," while the construction of vulnerabilities remains hidden.

In a context that emphasized labour trafficking, conceptual space was created to discuss different perspectives on the relationship between trafficking and sex work. Advocates of sex workers rights and abolitionists initially engaged in dialogue through both the Calgary Network on Prostitution (CNOP) and the Calgary chapter of ACT Alberta. As one sex worker–rights advocate suggested, "I know I speak frankly about sex work as work, but I do know there is an exploited side of that continuum." For this participant, human trafficking lies at the far end of the "exploited side" of the continuum, which provided context for engaging with abolition approaches to exit-based service provision. As the next chapter discusses in further detail, although initial discussions were depoliticized by distinguishing between sex work and sex trafficking, abolition-centred responses have since adopted the language of anti-trafficking as central to their mandate and thereby conduct their work in isolation from differing perspectives.

This shift from exit-based services for individuals wanting to leave sex industries to anti-trafficking is described by the following advocate of abolition: "So I've done that kind of work for several years … it's frankly not a big step from domestic sexual exploitation to trafficking." In this context, labour and sex trafficking were discursively separated into distinct issues. As the representative goes on to say,

I think that the experience is going to be different if the person is trafficked for labour as opposed to sex. I would describe sexual human trafficking as one of the most egregious forms of trauma that I know of … In a in a case of a domestic victim, where they have an extensive trauma history, they have serious mental health stuff onboard by the time they're trafficked, whereas in an international case they may have had a relatively stable life and then it all gets blown to hell. Then in the labour case, it's again different because it's not the same violation of the bodily integrity that you would have with repeated accounts of rape; however, it does involve exploitation, degradation, in the case of men, for example, there's a some stuff around you know a man who cannot feed his family and how that affects his sense of manhood, his self-esteem, the desperation that can drive him to stay in a trafficking situation, so there's a lot of pressures there. Certainly I think domestic trafficking in terms of mental health issues is probably the most complicated and then I would put international sex trafficking next, and then both labour – international and domestic labour trafficking next in terms of severity of trauma.

As this excerpt highlights, the separation of domestic versus international trafficking is read through the degrees of trauma experienced by trafficked persons. As with the law enforcement representative in British Colombia who discussed an overt emphasis on sex trafficking investigations based on perceived degrees of trauma, domestic *victims* in the above description are seen as already traumatized and thereby "vulnerable to exploitation," whereas international trafficked persons are read as "deceived" (i.e., as having a stable life before being trafficked). The gendered nature of anti-trafficking discourse is also revealed through this negotiation of domestic and international. Labour trafficking, in particular, is interpreted through representations of a man unable to "feed his family" and thereby meet the gendered expectations of the male breadwinner. Conversely, domestic (read as sex) trafficking is interpreted through the lens of sex work as exploitation and "repeated accounts of rape." This draws on feminist anti-prostitution discourses that characterize selling sex as commercialized sexual assault (see Farley et al. 1998). In turn, such discourses facilitate the conflation of trafficking and sex work and the removal of the possibility of consent based on the "previously traumatized" status of domestic victims.

Of note, in the area of labour trafficking, women typically only emerge in relation to live-in caregiving, and such representations are employed as a means of countering sensational sex trafficking images: "I think a lot of people forget about, like, nannies, or you know like that it [labour trafficking] does happen there as well, in that area, and I think that there needs to be more attention brought to that, for the public as well. I always forget about it too ... I immediately go to the sexual violence stuff. So I think that is something that's really important, just the idea that we always think of the worse-case scenario. I think there's a lot of myths around it."

The "sexual violence stuff" is again interpreted as far "worse" than labour trafficking, yet understandings of labour trafficking are believed to counter anti-trafficking myths. At the same time, labour trafficking narratives continue to rely on gendered notions of labour that emphasize the experiences of live-in caregivers (Macklin 1992). The resultant attention has further contributed to restrictive immigration policies that disproportionally target migrant women who are perceived as potentially "at risk," while, structural and material inequalities and the conditions of labour are reproduced.

Representations of trafficked persons in Calgary were especially divergent between service providers and sensational public awareness campaigns. Therefore, the broad aim of awareness was directed toward challenging public perceptions, rather than addressing systemic or structural factors that produce trafficking experiences. The general consensus among service providers was that a multifaceted response is needed. In the words of one frontline worker, "There is never going to be a one-size-fits-all stamp that you can place on anybody that has been trafficked, woman or man ... anybody who has done some kind of case management realizes that every situation is going to be so different." Significantly, this participant draws a distinction between the complex understandings of human trafficking associated with working directly with trafficked persons, as opposed to the sensationalized public representations of trafficked persons. Describing the gap between public and practitioner knowledge, the participant went on to say,

> I think there is a bit of disconnect there. But then I'm not really that experienced on how you get that kind of groundswell. Maybe with all sort of movements, if you want to call them that, maybe you had to go for the most gruesome, [the image of the] woman in a cage in the basement. You had to go for the images that would get people fired up ... And get them marching in the streets if that's what they want to do. Whereas on the other hand, you're always going to have the professionals and the practitioners, and they are going to be the ones to understand the nuances and complexities of what it takes to support someone who has been a victim of trafficking.

In a context of sensational awareness and myths, the intervention strategies of the "professionals" and "practitioners" are thereby framed as necessary to address the "nuances and complexities" of anti-trafficking, yet the highly gruesome, gendered (and often racialized) depictions that naturalize violence through images of women "caged in a basement" are still justified as creating the necessary "groundswell" for the anti-trafficking movement and professionalization of anti-trafficking responses. Similarly, a participant in a Calgary-based study discusses the challenge sensational images create for service providers: "it's easy to ignore, if you believe [human trafficking] is one thing and then you come into contact with someone [and] if you had the correct information, red flags would be going up, but you're thinking, 'no, it has to be this. This is what it is.' You're missing potential people who are at risk" (as cited in Kaye, Winterdyk, and Quarterman 2014: 10). Similar to this service provider's experience, provincial government and law enforcement representatives as well as frontline workers indicated they had come into contact with cases of human trafficking, but were unable to identify the cases as trafficking until they had received more realistic awareness than the predominant "gruesome" public messaging. Thus, the construction of "at risk" bodies is advanced through images of natu- ralized violence used in anti-trafficking awareness campaigns and anti- trafficking advocates are simultaneously produced as the interpreters of real trafficking experiences. In effect, such campaigns necessitate the reproduction of social intervention strategies in the lives of people who are deemed "at risk."

Another prominent discourse that emerges in the examination of international versus domestic constructions of trafficking in Calgary is the assumed benevolence of state-based practices in the domestic sphere compared with the international sphere, in which police and criminal justice actors are interpreted as potentially complicit in trafficking and subject to critique. In this way, anti-trafficking response provides a means with which to reinforce Canadian criminal justice systems while also exporting these systems under the pretext of controlling transna- tional criminal activity. A criminal justice representative discusses the relationship with police from an international and domestic lens and the perceived investigative challenges to proving cases of trafficking:

> Often [victims] just don't want to cooperate with the authorities because where they have come, from an international basis, they haven't had a good relationship with the police ... The reason why [domestic victims] can be exploited by the movers is because they have troubled back- grounds. It usually means they don't have a trust in authority, that's why they're vulnerable to the manipulation. So they're not typically going to want to give an interview to the police.

Police mistrust is interpreted as a limitation in both domestic and international cases. Internationally, however, the mistrust of Canadian enforcement is seen as a natural outcome of "where they have come from" in that law enforcement is deemed to be inherently untrust- worthy, whereas domestically, the lack of trust in law enforcement is believed to be a result of having "troubled backgrounds."

Similarly, a law enforcement representative argues, "when we talk international, that's one of the biggest things, that the police is corrupt in their country they don't think the police will help them here ... So those are some of the reasons why they don't want to cooperate with the police. Which are all valid reasons." Interestingly, police corruption is seen as problematic *over there*, which is perceived to validate mistrust of police in Canada. However, similar consideration is not extended to the mistrust of police by migrant and Indigenous women in Canada or concerns about the framing of Indigenous women as domestically trafficking from a crime control perspective. The following excerpt from a frontline worker in the field of sexual violence demonstrates this process:

> They don't want that person abusing them and hurting them and what-not, but the minute that the police are involved, they're swearing at the cops and not cooperating with the police and if we don't have an understanding about that, we're like "what the hell is going on?" like "we're here to help you!" And I think in my own job if I'm trying to help someone, sometimes they don't like my help and I think that's hard for people who are in a helping position to understand. ... especially in that moment that I'm coming from a good place of good intentions, like "why are you not cooperating, I'm here for you, to help you." I think that there would be a lot of the manipulation and the psychological torture type stuff.

Police mistrust in the domestic context is understood through the experience of being "manipulated" by a trafficker, rather than legitimized mistrust of law enforcement. Similarly, a discourse of manipulation emerges when the assistance provided by those in a "helping position" is not well-received by the recipient. In turn, this naturalizes the role of the helper and the police in processes of intervention on behalf of the "manipulated" while eliding the role of such interventions in the creation and reproduction of structural inequalities and violence faced through criminalization and other forms of formal intervention. Rather than removing the self-determination of individuals deemed "too manipulated" to know what is good for them or minimizing the structural, material, and psychological violence experienced by individuals, attentive examination of the reasons for police mistrust in a context of systemic inequality reveals that such inequality is both produced by state forms of intervention and upheld through ongoing state violence.

This negotiation of internal and international mistrust of police also provided a forum in which to suggest the exportation of Canadian anti-trafficking police practices. Interestingly, this suggestion was made in the context of a growing resource-extraction economy, which is of particular importance to the prosperity of Calgary. In this context, a former law enforcement representative indicates the following:

> We can have the best laws in the world, and I think we do, but if the perpetrator is in another country, as some of the criminal organizations are located abroad, then what do we do? That is why we need to have an expansion of organizations, so that we can coordinate and bring people who are participating in these types of crimes, international crimes, to the International Criminal Court to be held accountable at that level. But that is, again, incredibly expensive. And it means the notion of sovereignty … there needs to an international buy-in, that states can enact extra state enforcement and work collectively and in conjunction at a global level to address global crime. We are trying to address global crime within a domestically restrained jurisdiction in Canada, US, and the UK. If we are truly going to address issues of human trafficking we need to have the mechanisms and laws in place to deal with this at a global level, and I think that maybe that will come …
>
> I think if we are going to have true global economy we not only need laws for trade and commerce, but also those that address criminal activity … It's a long ways away, but as we become the true global village, the village needs a police department.

In the context of settler colonialism, anti-trafficking is framed as a mechanism of transnational crime control, and concerns about sovereignty are framed as an impediment to expanding a global police force. Moreover, the global police force is read as an expansion of *our* domestic police system: "the best laws in the world." Not only does such a conception naturalize the legislated dispossession of Indigenous persons in Canada, similar notions of sovereignty are elided in discourses of trafficking of Indigenous persons. In turn, anti-trafficking is seen as a transnational crime necessitating a global "police department." Emphasizing crime control further erases the global structural inequalities of a global capitalist economic system in the production of trafficking as well as the role reinforcing *our* systems of policing will play in reproducing the gendered, racialized, and national priorities and boundaries of the Western nation-state.

Negotiating Anti-trafficking in Western Canadian Cities

Overall, each of the three cities differentially negotiates conceptions of trafficking through domestic and international discourses. In Vancouver and Winnipeg, the negotiation was employed to reinforce conflations of sex work and sex trafficking. For Vancouver, this conflation occurs in a context that prides itself in multicultural inclusivity; however, such perceptions ignore the ongoing conditions of settler colonialism in which racialized exclusions and domestication of Indigenous bodies continue to be reproduced through anti-trafficking discourse. Moreover, the emphasis on trafficking as "prostitution" ignores continuities with racialized programs of migrant labour and the reproduction of institutional racism. In Winnipeg, the ongoing civilizing mission of domesticating Indigenous women is particularly evident in the conflation of children and women in anti-trafficking as a means of reinforcing formal interventions from law enforcement, government, and nongovernment sectors. In Calgary, sex trafficking and labour trafficking are discursively separated; however, the separation maintains gendered and racialized forms of domination and oppression that construct notions of "at-risk" bodies while reproducing material and social structures that create the conditions in which vulnerabilities emerge and necessitate the ongoing imperative of intervention and the reproduction of the Canadian nation-building project.

Chapter Four

Settler Colonialism, Sex Work, Criminalization, and Human Trafficking

Human Trafficking: "It's great for criminalization. That's a part of the history as well. That significant criminalization of a racialized group."
– Frontline service provider, Indigenous-led organization

The 2012 National Action Plan to Combat Human Trafficking (NAPCHT) consolidated national anti-trafficking efforts in Canada within a criminal justice framework. Premised on conceptions of human trafficking as a crime perpetrated by organized criminal networks and individuals, the plan confirms that trafficking occurs "within Canada's borders and internationally" (Public Safety Canada 2012a: 4). The NAPCHT further specifies that Aboriginal women and girls and "socially and economically disadvantaged" migrants, new immigrants, women, and children are at particular risk of being trafficked and sexually exploited in Canada. Given the discursive separation of domestic and international trafficking and the effect of such discourses on anti-trafficking articulations in different cities, this chapter examines the implications of this split for individuals working in sex industries who are directly affected by anti-trafficking responses.

Discourses in Vancouver and Winnipeg focused almost exclusively on human trafficking for the purpose of sexual exploitation. In Vancouver, this focus continues in spite of the reality that British Columbia, like Alberta, also hosts a number of temporary migrant workers and was identified in the NAPCHT (Public Safety Canada 2012a) as one of the three provinces where non-sexual forms of labour trafficking is problematic. Although this emphasis has shifted somewhat in British Columbia, the previous chapter reveals how enforcement responses to trafficking have placed more value on "the female victims of human trafficking in the sex trade" (law enforcement representative, Vancouver). In this context, misplaced attempts to rescue *victims* of sex trafficking have led to silencing and disciplining of sex workers, including criminalizations and deportations that work counter to the aims of the individuals involved. Moreover, contested areas of feminism and particularly Indigenous feminism differentially negotiate the relationship between women involved in sex industries and the resurgence of human trafficking discourses in a settler colonial context.

Anti-trafficking and Continued Criminalization

Criminalizing Sex Work through Anti-trafficking Raids

In Canada, sex work–establishment raids are depicted as a central means of implementing anti-trafficking legislation. In doing so, Canada reinforces a carceral approach that relies on rights-based and even feminist discourses in the criminalization of mostly women and gender-nonconforming persons working in sex industries. Such criminalization is evident in a prominent and recurring narrative informing representations of trafficked persons and responses to human trafficking in Vancouver. In particular, a failed attempt to carry out coordinated raids of massage parlours throughout the lower mainland of British Columbia in 2006 was a recurring theme underpinning anti-trafficking discourses in Vancouver. The effort involved multiple law enforcement agencies, including RCMP detachments in Coquitlam, Surrey, Richmond, and Burnaby; the Vancouver City Police; and the Integrated Border Enforcement Team (*National Post* 2006, December 9). The raid was an attempt to implement a "partnered" or "coordinated" response to human trafficking by involving the British Colombia Office to Combat Trafficking in Persons (BCOCTIP) and the nongovernment partnerships established by BCOCTIP.

On December 7, 2006, eighteen massage parlours were raided and, despite assurances to BCOCTIP and the nongovernment partners that the women working in the parlours would not be arrested, more than one hundred people were taken into custody. Of those taken into custody, seventy-eight were – at the time – suspected victims of human trafficking. The media was also notified of the raid and published images of women working in the massage parlours being handcuffed and arrested were widely distributed. These images served the dual purpose of reinforcing and naturalizing the criminalized position of migrant women involved in sex industries through the mechanism of anti-trafficking.

The following excerpt from a British Columbia government representative details the experience of partnering with law enforcement for this raid effort and the subsequent disillusion of the nongovernment partners:

> They had been doing an investigation for about eight months; we had been brought in probably at about the three-month point. And they told us little bits about the date they had selected, and they said that they would probably free one hundred trafficked women. They had located eighteen different brothels all over Vancouver, so we lined up quite a few of our partners, and we had beds available, and we had interpreters and other very large pieces of it. And we were attached to – we had divided ourselves – different RCMP detachments. And some detachments didn't know we were coming and some did, it was very badly coordinated. And the condition for the NGOs [nongovernment organizations] to become involved was that women were not to be arrested and not handcuffed. Both of those things happened, almost instantly. And they filmed it, they had let the media know and they were following them around. It was just a zoo. It was terrible ... *we didn't know any of that was going to happen.* They completely violated the conditions that we put forward for being involved. It was a big media circus. And absolutely no women were found to be trafficked and no charges were ever laid. It was terrible. So what we learned out of that was to keep it very small ... our role is really to coordinate.

Although critical research, as well as sex workers, have shown how individuals and especially migrants involved in sex industries are criminalized, the collaborative provincial model aimed to "free" trafficked women with a partnership between nongovernment and enforcement agencies. The interventionist standpoint neglects consideration of the role such interventions have played in the criminalization of racialized bodies. The statement "we didn't know any of that was going to happen" is only possible in a context that hides the civilizing role of early anti-trafficking efforts and ignores sustained critique of anti-trafficking as a means of criminalizing individuals working in sex industries. Nonetheless, the described shift away from service provision further discredited the province's response in the eyes of service providers.

Disengaging from service provision was a common theme emerging from the experience of this raid. In the words of a frontline worker,

> They found no trafficked persons. And I was kind of, to be honest, devastated. I was angry for two years ... and it wasn't that we had agreed on anything that calls into question the potential for those kinds of collaborations, they are necessary. But the very first thing I said, at the very first meeting, was that we don't support raiding and rescuing women. There are ways in which the community can work so that women can identify themselves if they need assistance and they are not stupid, they know when they need assistance and will let us know ... the fact that the women were violated and their pictures were in every little newspaper and what happened was that the women moved into even less safe places to work ... Coming out of that, I'm not doing a lot of direct service work.

While this participant maintains the importance of collaborative responses to human trafficking, the experience of this raid created significant mistrust between law enforcement and the provincial government and nongovernment efforts and attempts to re-establish partnerships became limited. However, rather than situating the experience within the broader context of racialized and national boundary-making, the mistrust was interpreted through a lens of power imbalance between law enforcement and service providers. The representative qualifies, "we don't support raiding and rescuing women," yet collaborating in raid-and-rescue was seen as a necessary part of engaging in anti-trafficking response. In this, the continuous cultivation of the settler colonial state is seen to naturalize exclusion and the boundaries created by citizenship through the criminalization of migrant women.

In the context of this mistrust, the law enforcement approach was described by a provincial government representative as a "top-down" model, with limited ability to develop effective partnerships: "There just wasn't an appetite to formalize a relationship at the RCMP, so it just wasn't going anywhere. That's the imbalance; unless they wrote it and controlled it and put us into the picture instead of doing it jointly, they weren't interested ... I think that would be a key part of a plan of action, formal relationships between all the partners. But we just couldn't make it happen ... very one sided." It is important to note that government, service providers, and law enforcement representatives all reinforce the importance of cross-sector collaboration in responding to human trafficking. However, as the coordinated raid experience in British Columbia reveals, in the absence of addressing the structural inequalities and roles these institutions play in the criminalization of racialized persons through rescue efforts, such collaborations reproduce the structural vulnerabilities faced by migrant women.

It was due to a perception of security risk that the raid led to significant criminalization of migrant women. As Aradau (2004) theorizes, "at risk" subjects are intertwined with "risky" subjects in anti-trafficking discourses. Citing Cpl. Norm Massie, Canwest News Service reported, "some of the potential victims were handcuffed by police during the raids, which he said had to be done to secure the scenes and ensure officer safety" (*National Post* 2006, December 6). This occurred in a context whereby both nongovernment and law enforcement officials noted that ensuring the cooperation of trafficked individuals required levels of trust that can be irreparably damaged by such enforcement-based tactics. In fact, gaining the trust and cooperation of trafficked persons is one of the primary challenges identified by law enforcement in proceeding with human trafficking charges. The following excerpt reflects law enforcement's need for collaboration as well as a possible lack of appreciation regarding the degree and legitimacy of distrust with its nongovernment partners:

> I like the partnerships we have with a lot of our NGOs. Traditionally the police and NGOs haven't gotten along, which makes no sense to me. I think once we explain to them and show them that we really do care about these victims, then they're much more on board. They're still quite guarded with us, but we need them to help us with our investigations. If a victim goes to an NGO and nongovernment organization, they're seeking help … our number one priority is the safety of the victim, and also we want to charge people.

While the respondent recognizes the importance of responding to the needs of victimized individuals, it is also clear, and not surprising, that obtaining a criminal charge is a key priority for law enforcement. Yet, the idea that police *need* NGOs for help in implementing legislation is presented as a novel reality produced by anti-trafficking. In actuality, such interdependencies of formal intervention are clearly evident in the foundational role of the settler colonial nation-state, including the role of anti-trafficking in processes of state formation. Nonetheless, as the raid demonstrates, in the absence of critical reflection, anti-trafficking legislation serves little more than an alternate means of prostitution control and reinforces existing power structures that make way for the disciplining of migrant women. In the end, this failed collaborative effort continues to shape politicized discourses about what constitutes human trafficking in Vancouver.

The experience also raises questions about the representation of trafficked persons that led to the raid in the first place; namely, in continuity with white slavery discourses, the assumption that women, primarily of Asian descent, working in massage parlours are likely to be victims of human trafficking. Although law enforcement and service provider representatives attested that no *victims* were found through the raids, migrant women were publically criminalized in conjunction with anti-trafficking efforts in the minds of Canadians. Much like with other anti-trafficking efforts, migrant women were victimized by state and social interventions in a context of ongoing structural and systemic inequality.

Anti-trafficking and Ongoing Criminalization of Indigenous Communities

Alongside direct criminalization of individuals working in sex industries, anti-trafficking discourses emphasize intergenerational forms of exploitation. Such discourses are discussed predominately in relation to domestic trafficking of Indigenous women. For example, advocates emphasize scenarios of "mothers putting their daughters out [for sale for sex]" in the context of intergenerational colonial legacies. Far from emphasizing the context in which such forms of exploitation occur, anti-trafficking emphasizes criminalizing those who profit from the prostitution of women and girls. In turn, this potentially means further criminalizing families of the victimized individuals. As a frontline worker in Calgary indicates, "the bulk of the survival sex workers are Aboriginal. I don't have specific numbers, but I had over 1000 client contacts and quite a few of those, the street level workers, are Aboriginal ... when I hear about trafficking with Aboriginal groups, I hear about family members trafficking, taking them out of the reserve and into the city. So like Grandma pimping."

On the one hand, such representations reinforce stereotypical depictions of Indigenous persons as perpetrators of crime. In various anti-violence campaigns, the federal government has invested in the narrative that Indigenous persons, particularly Indigenous men but also Indigenous women, are responsible for the disproportionate rates of violence against Indigenous women and girls in Canada. While lacking solid basis in statistical evidence, such claims successfully naturalize the ongoing oppression of Indigenous people through overrepresentation as both victimized and incarcerated figures while concealing the role of the state in perpetuating violence against Indigenous people. On the other hand, when cases of intergenerational trafficking emerges, criminalizing those who profit from the sale of sexual services perpetuates an ongoing cycle of state apprehension, as the Native Women's Association of Canada (NWAC) notes, including "residential schools, foster homes, group homes, and *prisons*" (2012; emphasis added). Discussing the first charge of human trafficking in Manitoba, which was laid in Winnipeg on September 23, 2010, a frontline worker from an Indigenous-led organization indicated the following:

> The first person who has been charged with trafficking is an Aboriginal woman. And we know stories about them, we hear it a lot, families who ran out of money, addiction is a big part of it, and they send their child out on the street. Basically it's street level, it's not escort level of sexual exploitation or prostitution. So we are vulnerable to the charges that come with those kinds of new laws … It's great for criminalization. That's a part of the history as well. That significant criminalization of a racialized group. And then it really is a kind of perfect crime, where you engage in a colonial process to create a population that is so highly vulnerable … any population, it doesn't matter, any group that you keep in historic oppression is going to manifest behaviours like indigenous people have manifested, like suicide and chronic health, criminalization. So it is pretty created, the environmental conditions, social and environmental conditions where people are behaving in such a way that verifies, confirms the stereotypes that took them there in the first place. It's like the perfect crime … We can't have people saving us anymore, look at where that has gotten us. That's a very false notion to, very misplaced, but it is part of the ideology of the dominant culture, the white man's burden.

In the Winnipeg case, the Aboriginal woman charged had no familial relation to the alleged trafficked woman and, in the end, the Crown prosecutor dropped the human trafficking charges after meeting with the alleged victim. Nonetheless, as this excerpt highlights, criminalizing mothers and grandmothers does little to address the historically constructed cycles of poverty and violence in Aboriginal communities; rather, it continues the process of state apprehension.

Significantly, it is in this context that Public Safety Canada issued a request for proposals to tender research that explores "how Aboriginal family members play a role in human trafficking." The proposal omitted any reference to colonization or other broader contextual factors. Such a funding mandate confirms the concerns of some participants of this research who feared anti-trafficking legislation would build on previous legal precedents that aim to "civilize" Indigenous communities through measures of criminalization.[1] While the effects of patriarchy should not be discounted, a broader lens that considers ongoing settler colonial relations of oppression underscores the complex experiences of individuals posited as internally trafficked, which demands that response models address the broad-ranging structural and material inequalities underlying cyclical experiences of poverty and violence.

Reproducing Structures of Intervention and Control

Organizations that facilitated early nation-building civilizing missions continue to advocate for and profit from moral interventions premised on the ongoing marginalization and sexual violences experienced by Indigenous women while erasing their role in facilitating colonial dispossession. Faith-based organizations, in particular, were mandated with intervening in, promoting, and lobbying for the anti-trafficking cause as an extension of responses to sexual exploitation. As one representative of a faith-based organization in Winnipeg discusses,

> I kinda got chosen because of my background in sexual exploitation, prostitution, so we've been running those types of programs for quite some time. So there was a natural affinity there ... It was really left up to [faith-based organization] to go and find out what organizations, NGOs, faith groups were doing – not only awareness of human trafficking – but also to assist victims potentially as well as prevent it, which they weren't as good at, and do some lobbying too ... if I could take away the term human trafficking, I think I would get rid of that whole term because it's exploitation, period. And it's different forms of exploitation.

This becomes particularly troubling in the context of ongoing settler colonialism whereby lobby efforts continue to promote legislative interventions that disproportionately affect individuals working in sex industries as well as facilitate the ongoing apprehension of children into state-based systems of welfare. Further discussing the role of faith-based organizations in taking on anti-trafficking work in Winnipeg, the following exchange took place:

> SARAH: The Salvation Army won [a] tender to be basically the lead on distributing the funding, millions and millions of dollars to the rest of the country for the [United States], for dollars to be to be spent on that, so the Army down in the States has been really sort of proactive and very well structured in that way for those things.
> MARY: Well this is also a good fit way back to Catherine Booth's vision and she focused on this {SARAH: Oh ya, for sure} back in the 1800s.
> SARAH: And it also fits really well with, you know, raising the age of consent and all of those things too right like cause it's almost a...
> MARY: One of the most highest profile stuff that the Salvation Army did at the very beginning.
> SARAH: Mm hm, ya, ya. So it certainly fits and hence the reason why we really focus on human sex trafficking because it does fit with our mission we, other than the shelters, there really isn't the connectivity with the community and I think the history of working with really seriously marginalized people and that that seems to be where it's at right now so ... And this is just a provincial [response], it doesn't fit under the territorial, the Canadian stuff. This is just the Salvation Army partnership with Manitoba Police and a bunch of other, Winnipeg Police, and a bunch of other folks really getting together every few months and talking about human trafficking.

As the advocates discuss, anti-trafficking work can be seen as a continuous effort stemming from the early interventions of the Salvation Army and their nation-building role in "civilizing" and "saving" "marginalized people." The role of Catherine Booth, in particular, provides an important continuity, since she has been upheld as a central evangelical advocate for women's rights. As identified in *Christianity Today* (2008) "she founded her argument on the absolute equality of men and women before God." In doing so, Catherine Booth paved the way for women to work in Christian ministry, alongside fulfilling their domestic labours, as well as play a corresponding role in prohibition and civilizing campaigns that contributed to the legal dispossession of Indigenous women in the formation of the Canadian state. Along with her husband William Booth, Catherine Booth advocated for the militarization of civilizing processes: "If you can't get them in by civil measures, use military measures. Go and COMPEL them to come in ... let them have no peace until they submit to God and get their souls saved" (as cited in Fischer-Tiné 2011: 130). In direct connection with the civilizing mission and Imperial expansion, Fischer-Tiné (2011: 130) analyses, "It was precisely the high degree of organization and discipline achieved through this 'militarism' that transformed the former 'Christian mission' into an authoritarian 'imperial structure' able to 'overcome, conquer, subdue [and compel] all nations." Thus, it is noteworthy that anti-trafficking advocates reference the continuities of their work to Catherine Booth's vision, particularly considering such campaigns continue to contribute to ongoing interventions in the lives of colonial subjects, including the removing of Indigenous children into state-based care and the criminalization of Indigenous women in Manitoba. In this context, it is noteworthy that the RCMP and the Salvation Army lead the provincial anti-trafficking response team.

In agreement with faith-based approaches, the provincial anti-trafficking strategy in Manitoba forefronts criminal justice and child welfare interventions, including expanded child welfare mandates through the adoption of later phases of the strategy. Discussing the new standards for child welfare workers throughout Manitoba, one government representative indicates, "[the] unit has really expanded and we are able to do a lot more exploitation and trafficking case consultations or policy consults with child welfare or people who are doing placement or programming for children. So we are able to do a lot more of that than we have in the past." As the representative further indicates, the expanded role included the development of specialized training for child welfare workers "to identify kids being exploited, and deal with kids being exploited":

> They were seen as uncooperative. And are often missing from places, either because someone has trafficked them to another residence and are keeping them there, or cause they are not fitting into mainstream society, regular programs. So how do workers deal with that? What are some of the types of resources they can look at? What are best models or theories of treatments for the kids? ... What is going on in the sex trade? How do you deal with people who are being trafficked or exploited, cause they do have to deal with lots of different issues.
>
> In Manitoba we have changed our Child and Family Services Act to include exploitation as abuse, and we expect all child youth care workers to react in the exact same way that we would respond to another type of third party or familial sexual abuse. So investigations need to be

launched, those types of things. So that that training gives workers a better sense ... how do you do the investigations, what are you looking for, where does this go under the Criminal Code? Where does it fall under the [Child and Family Services Act]? When we first started training we were primarily training child welfare and youth care workers, but after a few years we started a larger response from law enforcement. So now I would say it's half and half. Whenever we run the training we have RCMP or local police, depending on where we are running the training cause it's moving all around Manitoba ... Again, just because we recognize that it's not a child welfare issue or justice issue, it's both. And how do our systems both work together, because we have very differing needs. So it helps to identify that for people.

Anti-trafficking reinforces the ongoing apprehension of Indigenous children and youth in a settler colonial context. In particular, trafficking is interpreted as both a matter of child welfare and law enforcement. Anti-trafficking initiatives claim to address colonial legacies by moving beyond colonial-derived assumptions that depict Indigenous youth as merely "uncooperative." However, it does so by strengthening the very state-based mechanisms that functioned and continue to function towards the dispossession of Indigenous communities, while concealing the role of these state-based mechanisms in naturalizing dispossession. Such approaches elide possibilities for transformative change and decolonial praxis.

Sex Work and Human Trafficking: Ongoing Conflict and Resistance among Indigenous Feminisms

Human trafficking discourses were most openly contested in Vancouver. In fact, anti-trafficking discourses in Vancouver are driven by undertones of violence and hatred between proponents of decriminalization, who advocate for decriminalizing the sale and purchase of sexual services, and abolitionists, who generally argue for the adoption of the Nordic or Swedish model that decriminalizes "the prostituted person" while criminalizing purchasing sexual services or profiting off the sexual services of others (Waltman 2011: 450).[2] As one provincial government official reveals, "It was much more violent than I thought. And these women are dealing with violence against women and they are so violent towards each other. It's stunning, and I have never gotten over that and it's never improved." Advocates on both sides of this debate described themes of violence, emotionally charged interchanges, and even emotional and physical abuse.[3] One self-proclaimed abolitionist social service provider described personal threats – including death threats – she had received to vacate the city. In another instance, a sex worker–rights advocate expressed her anger towards abolitionist approaches, which have jeopardized her personal safety as well as the safety of her friends and colleagues. She also discussed personal threats she has received for advocating on behalf of sex workers rights: "[T]he abolitionists, in the end, all they care about are their own personal goals of eliminating prostitution and the only way that's going to happen is if they kill us, which has happened. [Many] of my friends are dead ...and it's [all been] so sensational people were making death threats against me."

The intensity of the conflict is further exemplified by the use of war metaphors, including descriptors such as "minefield" and "allies" versus "enemies" that were alluded to in multiple interviews. For example, a provincial government official described the debate as: "a minefield ... so NGOs, they can kill each other; they are brutal, nasty to each other." A social service provider in Vancouver indicated that "we have created allies through our identity as abolitionists, so through our political beliefs and our trust in each other." Others try to distance themselves from the violence among advocates by aligning themselves with individuals involved in the sex trade: "[I]t took time to get someone to understand that we were just allies of mainly the women and we are not judgmental" (frontline worker, Vancouver). As this quote suggests, much of the anti-trafficking discourse draws on varying perspectives of how ideology and morality intersect with sexuality, which often invokes morally charged discourses and, at times, moral panic.

By focusing anti-trafficking on "female victims in the sex trade," sex workers who fail to identify as a "victim" as well as those who are discriminated against based on intersecting oppressions of gendered, racial, and national identities are likely to be overlooked or silenced, even when their experiences involve the forms of violence and exploitation that provide the rallying point for anti-trafficking advocates. In Vancouver, in spite of a context of idealized representations of trafficked women advanced in highly publicized campaigns and the stated emphasis on female victims, those victimized by Robert Pickton were left to mobilize and defend themselves in the face of clear patterns of predatory violence. Sex workers had been calling for action for years in a legislative context that increased insecurities for street-level workers before Pickton was charged in 2002 for the deaths of seven of the sixty-seven women confirmed missing from Vancouver's Downtown Eastside, the majority of whom were Indigenous women. Within this context of material and physical violence, Indigenous feminists differentially negotiate and resist ongoing forms of oppression. Anti-trafficking discourses increasingly form a fissure in such discussions.

In this climate of fear and mistrust, the mobilization of sex workers to advocate on behalf of their own rights challenges the ability of cross-sector anti-trafficking partnerships to address the complex and interrelated forms of exploitation without reproducing structural inequalities. As an abolition-focused service provider indicates, "I just didn't know that there would be so much suspicion between NGOs and cops ... a couple weeks ago [in the Downtown Eastside] there was a case of police brutality against a prostituted women. That stuff you can't believe happens anymore. You think, 'are you kidding me?'"

The acknowledgment of not believing this "stuff ... happens anymore," points to an overarching position that aims to address colonial legacies by mobilizing enforcement and criminal justice–based responses in overcoming their failure to respond to violence against Indigenous women. In particular, such approaches aim to criminalize perpetrators of violence against Indigenous women. Yet by narrowly defining perpetrators as "pimps and johns," the law enforcement and formal service providers are reinforced as the agents of rescue and change. This elides the role of these agencies in the reproduction of settler colonial violence, including the stark overrepresentation of Indigenous women incarcerated in Canada as well as experiences of direct and targeted police violence.

Responding to Colonial Legacies and Canadian Apathy

The documented apathy and failure of law enforcement and the controversial public inquiry into the investigation of missing and murdered women by both Vancouver City Police and the RCMP contributed to a context of further mistrust between law enforcement, service provision sectors, and individuals involved in sex industries. The public inquiry was fiercely protested from the outset until the day it ended. Protesters dismissed the inquiry as "unfair, incomplete and above all, unable to truly answer why the justice system failed ... [F]amilies of Pickton's victims remain unconvinced their voices have been heard and listened to, although their complaints have grown louder with each passing day of the hearings and the families now condemn the hearings as a complete failure" (*Vancouver Sun* 2012, June 6).

In spite of clear and highly controversial limitations, the final report by the British Columbia Missing Women Commission of Inquiry (2012) points to widespread inequality in the treatment of the missing women. In particular, the report identifies "systemic police failures"[4] in response to the targeted patterns of violence: "the initiation and conduct of the missing and murdered women investigations were a blatant failure" (Volume IIA: 3). In spite of idealized notions of enforcement-driven rescue of women enslaved in the sex trade, when clear patterns of violence were apparent, notions of rescue and protection were not extended to Indigenous and sex workers bodies, which inhibited adequate response to complex systems of exploitation. It should be noted, the aim here is not to conflate the experiences of missing and murdered Indigenous women with human trafficking, but to examine the employment of anti-trafficking discourse in the contested space of Indigenous feminist theories about ongoing forms of structural and material violence.

Missing and Murdered Indigenous Women and Conflations of Sex work and Human Trafficking

Significantly, NWAC initially advanced the position that human trafficking should be maintained as a separate matter from missing and murdered Indigenous women. In line with Sikka's (2009) conclusion, NWAC (2010) suggested the experiences of missing women – particularly Aboriginal women – was a serious matter that warranted attention in its own right. In other words, such experiences should not be conflated with human trafficking. Although this stance has changed, the experiences of ongoing targeted violence against disappeared women (Dean 2015) bring to light how anti-trafficking narratives have failed to address ongoing systems of violence embedded in settler colonial realities while claiming to address the *legacies* of colonialism. As the 2010 report documenting the research findings from the Sisters in Spirit initiative indicates, "[b]ased on what is known from cases of women who were missing and later found murdered, human trafficking has not emerged as a significant factor in the disappearance of Aboriginal women ... trying to fit cases of missing and murdered Aboriginal women into the trafficking box, we serve only to diminish or hide what we know to be true about their experiences." Despite these claims, two years later NWAC formally adopted anti-trafficking discourses in their discussions about sex trade industries, including women that have gone missing or been murdered while working in the sex trade.[5] After years of advocacy to bring the experiences of missing and murdered Indigenous women to light, including the *Stolen Sisters* report produced in collaboration with Amnesty International,[6] NWAC's discursive shift took place at a time when the Canadian government moved to restrict NWAC from using the name *Stolen Sisters* (March 2011) and reduced funding to support their database of missing and murdered Indigenous women (Million 2013). Nonetheless, from a clearly abolitionist framework, NWAC's resolution in support of the abolition of prostitution was adopted in November 2012. The organization's (2012) position on prostitution states the following:

> Aboriginal women are grossly overrepresented in prostitution and among the women who have been murdered in prostitution. It is not helpful to divide women in prostitution into those who "choose" and those who are "forced" into prostitution. In most cases, Aboriginal women are recruited for prostitution as girls and/or feel they have no other option due to poverty and abuse. *It is the sex industry that encourages women to view prostitution as their chosen identity* ... Supporters of decriminalizing johns and pimps claim that women will be safer if they are prostituted in legalized brothels and massage parlours. We know that Aboriginal women will mostly remain on the street because racism and poverty selects them for the most exploitative forms of prostitution, wherever they occur. But the more important point is that brothels and massage parlours are *not acceptable spaces* for Aboriginal women and girls. The state has pushed Aboriginal women from one institution to another – residential schools, foster homes, group homes, and prisons, to name a few. NWAC refuses to accept brothels as the new official institution for Aboriginal women and girls and we refuse to accept that prostitution is the solution to addressing women's poverty.

In advancement of this position, NWAC became a member of the Women's Coalition for the Abolition of Prostitution, which obtained intervener status in the Bedford v. Canada case. In alignment with a postcolonial perspective, NWAC emphasizes their concern for reclaiming the power, authority, and autonomy that was lost through the imposition of patriarchal systems of colonial rule, including systems of prostitution. In this way, as Ferris (2015: 136) points out, they "foreground the role of state-sanctioned racism and colonial violence in populating the survival sex industry." Prostitution in this context is interpreted as an "unacceptable space" for Indigenous women. NWAC (2012) further states, "prostitution is not a traditional activity of Aboriginal women." In direct response to discourses of empowerment, NWAC's position unapologetically stigmatizes sex workers for occupying this "unacceptable space" and promoting what they perceive as the illusion of choice among Indigenous girls and women involved in sex industries. In doing so, NWAC suggests that the claims of sex worker–rights advocates have failed to address the intersectional forms of racism and poverty experienced by Indigenous women. Therefore, the abolition of prostitution is perceived to be tied to the fulfilment of treaty agreements and the rights of Aboriginal women "to live lives free from violence, poverty and to meet their physical, cultural, and spiritual needs" (NWAC 2012). The emerging standpoint on abolition provided space for the mobilization of anti-trafficking discourses, which similarly attribute Indigenous experiences of sex trafficking, equated with prostitution, to colonial legacies of patriarchy, domination, and exploitation.

This response was established in reaction to the general apathy of Canadians in the violence experienced by Indigenous women and lack of response to missing and murdered Indigenous women. Tina Beads, for example, is an activist with the Aboriginal Women's Action Network (AWAN) in British Colombia who discusses her emergence into political activism around what she perceives as the "inherent violence" of prostitution: "And then the missing women stuff started coming up a bit, right. And the lack of outrage from society at large was really pissing me off, so that's when I decided I needed to get more organized in my political activism" (Beads and Kuokkanen 2007). The network's "Statement Opposing Legalized Prostitution And Total Decriminalization Of Prostitution" (AWAN 2007) further demands that "Aboriginal women have the opportunity to raise our families within our Traditional values of having a respected position for women and children in our societies."

Building on discourses of the "inherent violence" and "unacceptable space" occupied by Indigenous women overrepresented in the most dangerous, street involved parts of the sex industry, in 2014, NWAC prepared a report for the Canadian Women's Foundation (CWF), *Sexual Exploitation and Trafficking of Aboriginal Women and Girls*. The report fully conflates sex trafficking with all forms of sexual labour: "NWAC maintains that all sex acts performed for an exchange of money, services, for pimps, johns, in brothels or on the streets, even when the person is of the age of consent, is a form of sexual exploitation and may be deemed sex trafficked (NWAC 2014: 5)." In this way, the goals of abolition intersect with the unique spaces carved by some Indigenous feminists that aim to reclaim the power Indigenous women, allowing Indigenous voices to inform the overrepresentation of Indigenous women in Canadian systems of prostitution. As one frontline worker in Vancouver states, "We see prostitution as a form of violence against women. It has been the main issue that we've been dealing with, but of course that branches out into child apprehension and the foster care systems, and the Indian Act, and all those other issues they're all so interconnected, but prostitution is the main issue … we definitely see prostitution really is one and the same as sex trafficking. We know that demand fuels them both." From a violence against women standpoint, this respondent goes on to echo NWAC's resolution by discussing her organization's support of abolition and the Swedish model of criminalizing those who purchase sexual services or profit from the sale of sexual services.

Given this standpoint, some Aboriginal women, particularly national Aboriginal women's leadership, work alongside social conservatives and radical feminists in the interest of the abolition of prostitution in the county. Discussing this alliance, the respondent went on to say,

> It can be a tricky one, but what I like to think is that you know the kind of white, middle class, feminist organizations that are supporting abolition are actually the ones that listen to Aboriginal women. They're listening to what we want and they're accepting the responsibility to do something about it and sure there's mistakes made and things go wrong and there's educating that needs to be done but at least I know that white, middle class, feminist organizations aren't going to sell my ass. They're not going to abandon me for their own sake and I think when you have the pro-prostitution – we call them the "pro-pimps" – when you have the "pro-pimp" camp arguing for that, I get left out of that equation … A lot of people say a lot of things to try and discredit abolition and when those criticisms are lobbed it's like well 'what about us? Are you saying we're stupid, we don't know that, we're just these little puppets being driven by a white women's agenda, you know, how racist is that? We actually do know, we actually are smart and you know we're going to go for it with them or not and we're grateful for women willing to stand with us.

A complex dynamic of stratified relationships emerges whereby sex worker–rights advocates criticize abolitionists for silencing the realities of their lived experiences and their right to safe working conditions. Meanwhile, in the context of legacies of colonization, some Aboriginal women suggest that efforts to decriminalize prostitution fail to listen to Aboriginal voices and address the experiences of Aboriginal women who, as NWAC (2012) stated, "will mostly remain on the street." Further, such advocacy is connected to critiques of the state for pushing Aboriginal women "from one institution to another," including brothels, and suggests that decriminalizing sex industries will result in re-institutionalization in brothels. Interestingly, such advocacy pivots on the inclusion of Indigenous women through the addition of state-based enforcement of sex industries where Indigenous women are overrepresented. In turn, such criminalization fails to counter settler colonialism and, rather, reproduces state-based criminalization of Indigenous bodies while also further restricting sex workers access to indoor working environments.

Anti-Colonial Resistance among Indigenous Sex Workers

In light of this incapacity to challenge settler colonial reproduction of colonial power relations, such perspectives are contested among anti-colonial Indigenous feminists who highlight the ongoing stigmatizing effects of abolition on Indigenous women and the way in which it undermines their autonomy, particularly their bodily autonomy. Hunt (2013), for example, broadens the narrow focus on legacies of patriarchy: "If our streets, workplaces and our homes are all shaped by patriarchal colonialism, I see no reason to support abolishing sex work without arguing for the abolition of every other gendered activity in which we are violated. Instead, it seems more useful to agree that colonialism structures our lives as Indigenous women and then choose to centre our agency, choice, mobility and *relationships in resistance* to this structure in all aspects of our lives." Hunt's argument is particularly relevant in a context where the state forms a primary site of colonial gender violence that relies on gender oppression to conceive notions of national belonging. As Monture-Angus (2005: 59) depicts, "every oppression that Aboriginal people have survived has been delivered up to us through Canadian law." Like the legal system and other colonial systems, sex industries comprise a space where colonialism is both reproduced and resisted. However, sex workers are particularly stigmatized in their embodied resistance of colonial violence and blamed for perpetuating gender violence. Rather than argue for the removal of harmful legislations, anti-trafficking is mobilized to reproduce the structures of colonial dispossession and naturalize violence experienced by "at risk" subjects.

Far from centring "relationships in resistance," as sex workers organized to respond to violence, their voices were contested by readings of prostitution as domestic trafficking. In turn, sex worker advocacy for the need for safer and better working environments have come into conflict with anti-trafficking discourses shaped by abolitionist perspectives. But as Ferris (2015: 144) highlights, questions regarding the historical and everyday expressions of systemic racism and colonialism "are rarely addressed directly by sex worker activist groups." In this gap, some Indigenous feminists involved in sex industries have contested the ongoing stigmatization of sex workers and the omission of the significant role sex workers have played in anti-violence movements in Canada. The following is a statement from the Indigenous Sex Sovereignty Collective:

> Organizations that stigmatize or criminalize sex workers' lives are not safe or welcoming for sex workers. For sex worker voices to be truly heard, communities need to build environments in which people who have previously or are currently trading or selling sex are respected, valued and seen as experts in their own lives. This means addressing the stigma against sex work and creating stronger relationships among sex workers, their families and wider communities. We believe that this community based anti-stigma and relationship-building work is in keeping Indigenous teachings and values regarding respect and inclusion. We must adopt responses that support individuals where they are at without further stigmatizing their choices or lifestyles. We must not forget that people in the sex trade, sex industries and street economies and their families and allies have been integral to anti-violence movements across Turtle Island …
>
> In anti-violence organizing, we have observed that state-led responses (new laws, increased policing, and social services) are frequently seen as the best or the only way to create change. We instead call for solutions that address personal violence, such as targeted murders and disappearances, as well as systemic and legal violence, such as that perpetrated through the actions of police, social workers, and the judiciary in maintaining colonial power relations. We call for solutions that move away from protectionist or rescue oriented policies and practices adopted by colonial governments. We must begin to support communities and their unique

needs in addressing violence against Indigenous peoples. Some immediate solutions and support includes access to housing and transportation, and community safety plans that do not rely on increased criminalization of our lives and work when industry surrounding our communities increases. This is necessary in order to address all forms of violence together, and to ensure self-determination is available for all members of our Indigenous communities, including sex workers. At a personal level, self-determination means the ability to choose how to identify one's experience, sovereignty over one's body, and respect for the decisions a person makes over their own lives today.

Here the idea of safety is necessarily decoupled from criminalizing approaches, and self-determination is rooted where Indigenous people are currently located within the context of settler colonialism and ongoing forms of colonial gender violence. Sovereignty, from this perspective, means respecting lives as they are today, rather than aiming to "fix" or "rescue" in the name of tradition. As Million (2013) argues, "Native peoples become marked as national wounds requiring healing rather than as nations requiring decolonization" (as discussed by Smith 2014: 98). By focusing on respect and meaningful inclusion, the emphasis shifts from "rescuing poor bodies" – which reinforces colonial forms of intervention – to fostering Indigenous sovereignties and the self-determination of Indigenous people. Discussing the work of Danforth (2013) and the Native Youth Sexual Health Network (NYSHN), Smith (2014: 98) says, "[T]he success of the anti-violence movement in addressing gender violence looks much less successful if we centre the experiences of sex workers. In addition, if we build movements based on these places, then we are more likely to build movements that address the intersecting forms of violence people face."

Along these lines, Indigenous activism centring self-determination, including bodily self-determination, has initiated partnerships with anti-violence and sex worker rights organizing. For example, WISH Drop-In Centre Society in Vancouver provides an Aboriginal health and safety project in partnership with Vancouver Native Health and Vancouver Coastal Health (Ferris 2015), including a cultural reclamation program with Indigenous women involved in sex industries. The NYSHN has also partnered with Maggie's in Toronto, an organization run by and for local sex workers, to provide the Aboriginal Sex Work Education and Outreach Project – a project run by and for Indigenous people in the sex trade (Maggie's Toronto Sex Workers Action Project

2012). Given the nation-building role of anti-prostitution laws in Canada, it is not surprising that standpoints regarding the sex industries remain highly contested among Indigenous feminists and anticolonial gender-based organizing.

Of note, although Indigenous feminist expressions of abolition aim to counteract legacies of colonization and the ongoing violence experienced by Indigenous women, they do so by maintaining a hegemonic discourse of blame and stigma that excludes sex workers from potential solidarity in decolonial engagements. From a moralizing standpoint of what it means to be a "traditional" Indigenous woman, such approaches emphasize prostitution as harmful to society by foregrounding the social harms of patriarchy, objectification of women, and associated violence against women. Meanwhile, other structures of violence remain underexamined or naturalized, including state-based violence, legal systems, and rescue efforts underpinning overrepresentation in positions of marginalization in the context of settler colonialism. As Suchland (2015) highlights, the assumption of trafficking under the framework of violence against women alienated anti-trafficking, distancing it from anticolonial, antiracist, and critical perspectives of development. Silencing nuanced discussion about national harms and foundational gender and racial formations, such advocates instead emphasize their opposition to what they refer to as the "pro-prostitution" or "pimp lobby." By restricting the conversation to polarities between the "oppression" and "empowerment" frameworks, "the discourses of both sides *construct* the 'other.' In this space, voices go unheard, ideas and intentions are judged out of context, and the arguments of others weighing into the debate are distorted and caricaturized" (Benoit and Shaver 2006: 249). In turn, nuanced considerations of national, racial, and gendered inequalities are removed from the discussion – as are the voices and experiences of Indigenous women involved in sex industries.

Meanwhile, with the exception of the partnerships discussed above, sex worker–rights organizing that does prioritize an "empowerment" framework similarly omits nuanced consideration of the way colonialism differentially shapes Indigenous sex workers experiences. In other words, in the context of settler colonialism, anti-trafficking in particular and some sex worker rights-based narratives have demonstrated limited applicability in mobilizing anti-violence in decolonial ways of addressing systemic violences without compromising the agency and self-determination of Indigenous women and racialized bodies. As noted by the Indigenous Sex Sovereignty Collective (2016), however, ensuring self-determination for all Indigenous women requires safe and destig-matizing spaces that include the lives and experiences of Indigenous sex workers. Such spaces are not possible within hegemonic narratives that emphasize sex work as a form of social harm and blame sex work-ers for perpetuating gender inequality.

Silencing and Disciplining through Anti-trafficking

Sex Work versus Sex Trafficking: Battling for Voice in Vancouver

The discourse in Vancouver is severely polarized over the rights of sex workers (to safety, dignity, and labour protection) and efforts to abolish sex industries. Advocates of each standpoint draw on human rights discourses, particularly the rights of women as well as the pro-tection of trafficked persons, to justify their respective standpoints. Yet, there are significant power dynamics shaping the adoption of certain discourses above others. Many sex worker–rights advocates who mobilized in the interest of self-protection draw on experiential knowledge and, therefore, indicate they are silenced by abolitionist representations, which they perceive as top-down approaches driven by moralizing agendas. In the words of a frontline worker and expe-riential representative, "[y]ou know it has a huge impact on the sex workers human rights movement when all sex work comes to be seen as just another form of slavery. You know, how do you argue for your human rights when if you are sort of in my camp, you're seen as suf-fering from false consciousness at best and at worst you're the devil … and it's really difficult as a feminist, it's quite painful. You know I can usually agree to disagree with just about anyone, but I don't even get an opportunity to do that with [abolitionists] because they won't talk to me." Elaborating on the concept of false consciousness, this participant went on to say the following:

> I'm a former sex worker, I'm a former IV [intravenous] drug addict and that makes me a survival sex worker, although I was primarily able to work in my own home…I don't feel I was particularly harmed by doing sex work, I was particularly harmed by being a drug addict and the con-sequences of that made me make some bad choices about clients. Prior to my addiction getting crazy, I never made bad choices about clients. So my thing is just that sex work has to be an option, it can't be a means

to survival. But in order to change that we have to be able to offer survival sex workers real options out and we're not able to do that. And so while we're working toward the ideal world I just really feel we need to decriminalize it, we need to find a way to support street level sex workers to work more safely.

This representative and other representatives of sex workers' rights express concern for the experiences of survival sex workers, especially women victimized through trafficking, as well as a desire to eradicate forced sexual labour. However, from a sex worker–rights perspective, the rights of sex workers should not be violated in the development of a response to sex trafficking; rather, the voices of experiential workers should inform the response:

> We've always maintained that exploitation is critical, experiences of exploitation are critical and we want to make sure that we're filling the gaps that allow it to happen. However, the experiences of people making those choices and not being hurt are also critical. If only they would acknowledge that some people are making a choice … and, ya, we have to protect kids, but no you can't control me or force me to work at McDonalds or maybe I should go work in the fields? So to me, it's oppressive. Economically independent, strong women keep us from making choices that would empower us, whether they believe it would or not. It's not up to them to decide what's right … And in communities where sex work takes place on the street, those women need to feel safe too. How can we work on making sure everyone in the community is safe if we can't talk to one another and we're still stuck in this type of thinking that we're this voiceless, abused, no capacity group of people.

As this excerpt suggests, abolitionist anti-trafficking discourses are perceived to disempower sex workers by framing their experiences in terms of disenfranchised victims incapable of choice or, worse, blaming sex workers for ongoing violence against women. The representative further points to class distinctions whereby "economically independent" women impose morally conservative ideals that limit the capacity of women facing poverty and working in sex industries. Other sex worker–rights advocates and experiential workers similarly express deep concern about the victimization of children as well as trafficked individuals, and would like to be partners in developing effective prevention strategies and response mechanisms; however, they also expressed a desire for recognition that sex work can be a chosen profession and that most sex workers are not victims of sexual exploitation. From a service provision standpoint, such advocates offer similar recommendations to those of some abolitionist approaches (e.g., housing, social support, income equality, safe detoxification), yet tend to adopt a harm reduction approach that assumes self-determination within the contexts in which people reside. From a policy perspective, however, sex workers rights advocates diverge significantly from abolitionists, arguing for the decriminalization of sex work with the aim of creating safer working conditions and the ability to advocate for labour standards within sex industries.

Similar to sex worker–rights advocates, abolitionists also draw on discourses of gender inequality and the protection of trafficked persons to advocate for their perspective. As one self-proclaimed abolitionist indicates, "By putting women in the centre of what she wants to happen, [anti-trafficking] is absolutely centred on her and what she wants to do … The fact is women come from all different kinds of situations and all with very specific kinds of needs. And there is this myth out there of this "one case," with one clear, clean "victim A," and you have the saviour organizations over here. And we haven't seen that to be true. So what we do is ask the women 'what do you want?' and she can choose." In this way, the frontline worker asserts the complexity of experiences that fall under definitions of human trafficking as well as distinctions within abolitionist approaches in an effort to distance the adopted standpoint from those of "saviour organizations" and forefront the choice of women victimized by human trafficking in anti-trafficking responses. At the same time, this frontline worker went on to discuss "the ways trafficking and prostitution are related and all driven by the male demand for paid sex":

I think there is this refusal to see prostitution and the sex industry as violence against women. And there is this notion that people are going to differentiate between willing and unwilling. But I don't know any man going to buy a woman and saying, "hey honey, are you here because you want to be?" And that's essentially what they want, women are told to speak and act innocent because [men] want to have a situation where they have more power and control. And we know that men want these young and innocent girls, who are not the women who are going to be in prostitution, they will be forced into prostitution. So there is this unwillingness to look at the demand side, and how you wouldn't have supply if there wasn't this demand.

From this perspective, the frontline worker foregrounds the perception of sex industries as inherently violent and suggests there is very little distinction between prostitution and human trafficking. Therefore, while advocating for similar services as proponents of decriminalization, the policy recommendations of abolitionists focus on the adoption of the Swedish law, which perceives prostitution as a form of male violence against women and children and thereby decriminalizes the sale of sex and criminalizes the purchase of sex.

While the focus of this book is not legislative debate, the research does point to some key ways anti-trafficking discourses have shaped this debate and, conversely, how this debate has shaped anti-trafficking responses. In particular, the dichotomous and even violent undertones directing anti-trafficking discourses reflect an ongoing struggle to control the human trafficking narrative, a conflict that finds its origin in the initial construction of definitions of human trafficking as a mechanism of assimilation and control as well as ongoing politicized notions at the international level. Because the international community was unable to reach consensus, the battle continues over the right to control the relationship between prostitution legislation and anti-trafficking responses at the national level. In the contested space of anti-trafficking, collaborative efforts and cross-sector initiatives reinforce criminalization and silencing, while anti-trafficking initiatives develop disjointed and ideologically driven niches of response. However, in Vancouver, the reality of contested definitions reflects a context in which women working in sex industries have mobilized and created solidarities to resist the imposition of external labels and to represent their own experiences, rather than having their voices and experiences suppressed by dominant anti-trafficking representations calling for abolition.

Discipline and Silence in Winnipeg

Conflating anti-trafficking with sex work reproduced structures of criminalization in each of the three cities examined here. However, in Winnipeg, equating human trafficking with sexual exploitation to represent the varying and complex narratives of children, youth, and adults in sex trade industries further compounded the disciplining and silencing of experiences and narratives that do not conform to the dominant anti-trafficking discourse. As a frontline worker in Winnipeg describes,

> I know several ladies who were hired to talk and they are told what to say: "say it in this way." And I can think of three right off hand, for instance, they all got physically sick because they were talking about stuff that wasn't quite their experience. So after a while, each one of them, and these are at a different times, would say, "I don't want to do it this way, I'd rather talk about it from my experience." And each one was told "then we don't need you." So if you're not going to demean and degrade and talk about how much of a victim you were, then you can't talk about it. I think that's part of the problem and *why I can't speak openly* ... because there is so much politics in it. The people that banter around this terminology have the ear of the government, they have strong allies, and so they make it hard for people to talk openly about it. Even for the clients, they are told what to say. You are not going to get from some of these agencies, they will screen them first to make sure they know the banter. And some of the women have said to me, "it's just like having a john, the john tells you what he wants to hear, and you say it. And if I need some money, to work for these agencies, I do the same thing" ... But a lot of them, like I say, after a while they start feeling ill. To come out of the sex trade and not feeling like you are a victim and, for some, even feeling empowered because they get to choose who, when and where and how much. So that experience gets changed around, people start feeling ill. Is this a healthy thing to do? Certainly there are the victims out there, but not everybody is, and that's the problem, painting everybody with the same brush stroke. It is dishonouring people. (emphasis added)

The statement "why I can't speak openly" echoes other frontline workers' concerns about speaking freely against the dominant discourse, fearing job loss or funding cuts to their programming. The statement further reveals an experience echoed by experiential voices that women who fail to identify with the victim narrative by presenting themselves as sex-trafficked are disciplined or discarded from the public sphere because their experience does not fall in line with the dominant anti-trafficking narrative. Individuals identifying as formerly trafficked further reinforced this statement through shared experiences of being constrained in what they were permitted to share in public speaking venues.

In addition to creating insecurity for women whose experiences deviate from the dominant narrative, another frontline worker suggests that by placing specific experiential voices on a "pedestal," dominant discourses also create insecurity for women who, in the absence of adequate support structures, fail to live up to the expected image:

> We find a golden child or woman who has made it, who has gotten out of the sex trade, quit drugs, and lives in a stable apartment or even in a youth serving agency … and then put them up on a pedestal, and they are the ones who will speak when they need to put together a panel when they need to decide on what is going to happen with one of the Manitoba strategies. Of course we want the people that have been or are currently in that place to inform us and let us know what to do. I'm a firm believer in having experiential voices at the table all the time. But if you ask someone to go up and speak, I need to make sure I have the proper supports in place for that women … [s]hould she fall off that pedestal, and end up back on the street or back to using, or whatever the case may be. And I certainly have seen some agencies do that to people … so they were asked to [share] their pain and then the doors close, and they are told to go home, when they may not even have a home to go to. And that feels even shittier … we have this thing of using experiential women, hiring them and using them in our work.

As this quote suggests, advancing experiential voices to inform public discourses, policies, and response strategies is key to developing an effective understanding of the complexities of lived experiences. However, instead of providing a safe space for self-determined voices to influence policies, too often such approaches rely on experiential narratives to confirm preconceived notions of intervention. Representation, in this way, reinforces settler colonial conditions rather than a meaningful inclusion of lived experiences. Moreover, when a dominant or hegemonic narrative disciplines and screens experiential voices, they come to represent little more than the structures of power dictating the narrative; in this case, the anti-trafficking discourse adopted by the provincial government.

In the end, the actual voices of experiential workers and trafficked persons are silenced, whether directly or out of fear of such disciplining:

> And here's the thing about me, is that I am experiential. And not a single person would I tell that to, because as much as they say they wouldn't,

I would be looked down upon. Held up on a pedestal for certain things, but for other things, they would be looking: "Is she late for work? Does she drink with her friends on the weekend? Is she competent to do this work? Should she get a promotion?" Rather than just keeping it at the status quo … [So] I choose not to divulge that info to anybody that I work with. So, I guess that goes to say that, yes, voices are silenced … when the policies and responses are silencing, what's really going on, then that's challenging … it's not that people aren't doing things with the best of intentions. But the best of intentions can create things that actually cause more suffering for the people they were actually trying to help in the first place. Because there is just a lack of understanding.

As this excerpt suggests, anti-trafficking discourses that conflate human trafficking with sexual exploitation and sex work represent a single, dominant narrative that silences the experiential voices of women in sex industries as well as the complex experiences of trafficked persons. Thus, while anti-trafficking discourses claim to reduce the stigmatization and criminalization of women in sex industries (i.e., good intentions), such discourses are vulnerable to the manipulation of a variety of political agendas, such as the abolition of sex trade industries, that fail to recognize the varying and divergent experiences being represented by a single, dominant narrative. Similarly, another frontline worker describes how, despite aiming to address the effects of colonization, the adoption of a dominant victim narrative and the corresponding rescue response results in intervention models rooted in colonial ideology:

We don't see people as problems to be fixed. So that's the main difference … I worked in a mainstream organization and they almost killed me over there because they treated people as problems. They were polite enough, but confused politeness with respect. But if you can't see people as powerful, then you don't see them. So if you only see people with their problems and I'm going to fix their problems, because you can't fix anybody's problem, first of all. It is really a false notion, also of themselves … I just thought that was so dishonest and oppressive. I would leave at night sick, sick to my stomach and it goes on. It goes on and on. That is colonization. To me a fully engaged act – full on colonization – and it just goes on from there. And they don't even know it. They are unaware of it. And it's racist, it's classist, and oppressive. And if you call them on it, oh my god, they get so fucking offended. They cannot handle it.

Similar to the experience of other frontline workers, the excerpt suggests that any discourse that contradicts the dominant anti-trafficking narrative is met with great offence. This also points to problematic reactions progressive and liberal voices emit when faced with a politics of refusal. As Flowers (2015: 35) highlights, "solidarity means decentering ourselves, in order to engage productively in the unknown and 'in-between' spaces of resistance, and confronting the impulse to claim to know or have authority over a struggle." The anger that is too often induced by such refusal negates the responsibly of settler rights advocates in relation to Indigenous claims of self-determination and sovereignty.

In this context, frontline workers and trafficked persons suggest that anti-trafficking discourses are demeaning for women working in sex industries and create more insecurity by limiting their ability to report experiences of abuse and exploitation. As one frontline worker indicates,

> The argument of "you're going into a dangerous profession and we need to save you from that" is demeaning: "You poor weak thing, we need to save you from all the predators." And there are predators and evil men out there. And pedophiles and child molesters and those people need to be looked at. But what is going to make it more likely for women to come forward and say, "this man raped me?"… And what is going to make it possible to get [these men] off the streets? And that would be giving people respect. And respect is calling them what they want to be called. Whether that is sexually exploited or a person involved in the sex trade … As you can guess, it's not a popular [point of view] and I don't want my name attached to it.

By assuming human trafficking and sex work are interchangeable, and emphasizing the victim status of trafficked women, the provincial government in Manitoba aims to eliminate stigmatization of women in sex industries; however, when the lived experiences of some women in sex industries conflicts with the dominant anti-trafficking narrative, they experience greater insecurity because they are unable to access protections afforded to victims of sexual exploitation and violence. Meanwhile, models of state and formal social intervention are reinforced, further increasing the likelihood of individuals in sex industries experiencing criminalization and discipline.

Open Dialogue, Missing Voices in Calgary

While service providers in Calgary engaged in cross-sector and inter-political dialogue and collaboration in response to human trafficking, there was a significant absence of experiential voices, including formerly trafficked persons as well as sex workers and migrant workers informing this dialogue. In the words of one frontline worker: "I feel like in a lot of ways we are speaking on behalf of the victims of trafficking without ever asking them ... I think if we did [consult victims] what would end up happening is that we would get a couple voices. And then we would say, 'check, consulted with victims of human trafficking.'" Similar to the experience of frontline workers in Winnipeg, this representative raises concern about the advancement of a few nonrepresentative narratives at the expense of the array of experiences that fall under or are politically debated under the human trafficking label in Canada.[7]

At the time of the interviews in Calgary, anti-trafficking discourses were far less politicized than in Vancouver and, unlike in Winnipeg, representatives of multiple standpoints engaged in dialogue that recognized the need for services that emphasize both abolition and exit strategies as well as sex worker–rights and harm reduction approaches. As one representative of a harm reduction and sex worker–rights organization suggests, organizations holding dichotomous perspectives distinguish between approaches, but work together from their distinct mandates:

> Well the [abolitionist organization] is a very structured program, they have different levels of participation as opposed to us, where we do one-on-one, we see people as they come. With the [abolitionist organization] they generally have clients live in that environment and then they will do school and that's a requirement. So we have a relationship with them to the extent that I would do a referral and have done referrals in the past given that the client has identified that they need some serious structure in their lives. The [abolitionist organization] is strictly exit-based so they have to be in that mindset and be ready and wanting to exit and change their lifestyle basically. We do sit on the Calgary Network on Prostitution (CNOP) and the [abolitionist organization] shares a seat there as well. So I mean we do try to collaborate with them in the community. We have differing views on sex work certainly, but we try to work together as best we can.

While the harm reduction mandate of this organization would require offering a referral to the more structured, abolitionist organization, it is clear from the research that the abolitionist agency would be unlikely to consider a referral in the other direction (i.e., for harm reduction supports). The abolitionist standpoint that all forms of prostitution constitute sexual exploitation/assault specifically restricts the relationship from flowing in this direction.[8]

In part, this can be attributed to the absence of mobilizing forces in Calgary, such as those amassed during the public inquiry into the missing women killed by Robert Pickton or the international attention sex trafficking garnered leading up to the Vancouver 2010 Olympics. In the absence of defining narratives leading to a mobilization of experiential sex worker rights or former victims of sex trafficking advocates, the discourses are dominated by the service-provision sector. Although service providers in Calgary may hold divergent political views, the discourses do not reveal the emotionally charged representations that have occurred between sex workers–rights advocates and abolitionists in other cities. Therefore, while Calgary permits open dialogue between abolitionists and sex workers rights advocates, there is a stark absence of experiential voices from both perspectives. Meanwhile, by adopting a harm reduction approach, advocates of sex workers' rights can be more flexible from a service-provision standpoint. This flexible approach can account for the complex and intersecting experiences of sex trafficking, sexual exploitation, and sex work. However, from a policy standpoint, divisions between decriminalization and proponents of the Nordic model are more explicit.

In the absence of sex worker and migrant rights perspectives and the widespread shift in abolition responses to prostitution adopting anti-trafficking discourses, coordination increasingly emphasizes and reproduces dominant anti-trafficking narratives. In the case of ACT Alberta, funding mandates from federal bodies increasingly shape the discourses employed by the provincial response. For instance, ACT Alberta initially maintained a substantial focus on labour trafficking; however, labour trafficking was placed in opposition to sex trafficking. Therefore, while claiming to adopt a neutral standpoint, the coordinating body nonetheless promotes assumptions that individuals trafficked for sex are somehow different from individuals trafficked for other forms of labour. Moreover, and further challenging the possibilities of apolitical positioning in anti-trafficking work, ACT Alberta has also been shaped by dominant funding mandates and the reproduction of discourses enabled by such resourcing. For instance, funded by SWC and the CWF, ACT Alberta released the Community Action Plan to Prevent and Reduce Sex Trafficking in Edmonton. Although ACT Alberta seeks to maintain a conception of human trafficking that accounts for a variety of labour sites, the release of the report was accompanied by statements identifying "women, minors, aboriginal people and new immigrants" as "particularly vulnerable" (CBC News 2015, November 3). In doing so, the reproduction of gendered and racialized "at risk" bodies provide the basis for further intervention towards the aim of reducing and preventing violence; however, the structures in which such violence is produced remain largely intact.

Overall, the contested discourses of human trafficking claim to counter the legacy of colonization; however, without situating trafficking in the context of settler colonial continuities, such rights-based mobilizing only reproduces the structures of criminalization, discipline, and control that were foundational to the colonial civilizing mission and formed, in part, by early conceptions of trafficking. As a result, anti-trafficking efforts fail to disrupt and continue in many ways to recreate the national, racial, and sexual priorities of the nation-state that is premised on the dispossession of Indigenous women, migrants, and sex workers.

Chapter Five

Anti-trafficking and Border Secularization: Reproducing the Citizen–Subject through Restrictive Measures and Potential Threats

Anti-trafficking "is also equally about immigration and the policing and shaping of citizenry, both in terms of the potential victims who are given the opportunity to become legal residents and citizens and in terms of the construction of the [citizen-subject] who helps combat trafficking through gendered and racialized terms.

– Julietta Hua, *Trafficking Women's Human Rights*

Like early nation-building endeavours, anti-trafficking in Canada continues to reify national entitlements through uneven mechanisms of inclusion and exclusion. Whiteness, civility, and purity comprised the reference point for early exclusions of racialized Others from access to the nation-state while also establishing Indigenous communities as an internal Other. In both instances, the white settler was produced and reified as the sovereign national body. As a nation-building project, anti-trafficking provides a particular site to examine how Canada consolidates national entitlements and the citizen–subject against migrant workers and gendered and racialized migratory movements, while simultaneously and discursively rendering Indigenous nations and communities as domestic dependents.

The politicized conflation of trafficking with migrant smuggling as well as efforts to place migrant smuggling in opposition to trafficking produce categories of "deserving victims" and "complicit criminals." In doing so, Canadian approaches to anti-trafficking have led to direct forms of criminalization, including arrests, detentions, and deportations, as well as overt silencing and disciplining of narratives that do not conform to dominant anti-trafficking conceptions. Trafficking and smuggling conflations and distinctions now both work to consolidate the Canadian security state. From a transnational crime perspective, and due to corresponding concerns over threats to the nation-state, human trafficking has been viewed as a highly profitable, low risk, criminal enterprise (United Nations Office on Drugs and Crime [UNODC] 2008) carried out by "criminally sophisticated, transnational organized crime groups" (Lee 2011: 24; Williams and Masika 2002).[1] At the same time and in spite of recurring conflations, the UNODC has consistently drawn definitional distinctions between migrant smuggling and human trafficking. Migrant smuggling, according to UNODC (2000), involves a contractual agreement to help facilitate the illegal movement of persons across borders for financial or other forms of material gain.[2] Conversely, human trafficking is characterized by an overarching purpose (exploitation) and involves the use of threat, force, coercion, abduction, fraud, deception, abuse of power, or bribes (UNODC 2000).

In theory, Canadian responses to trafficking distinguish between migrant smuggling and human trafficking, drawing on UNODC's (2009) three points of distinction: consent, exploitation, and transnationality (Public Safety Canada 2012a). According to UNODC (2009) smuggling and trafficking are distinct because 1) migrant smuggling involves consent whereas trafficked persons either never consented or their consent was obtained through deceptive or coercive means; 2) the relationship with a human smuggler ends upon arrival at the country of destination whereas human trafficking occurs when the trafficked individual is not free to end the transaction, terminate employment, or generally leave the situation; and 3) migrant smuggling is a transnational activity by nature whereas human trafficking can occur both between and within nation-states (UNODC 2009). Critical literature has troubled the binary discourse of coercion/consent and freedom/unfreedom, and, in practice, frontline workers and law enforcement representatives also highlight significant challenges to drawing strict distinctions between the concepts.[3] As one frontline worker indicates, there are considerable "gaps between the legislation and the realities."

As well as the international/domestic binary and its role in naturalizing settler colonial forms of intervention, this chapter examines the way in which anti-trafficking discourses shaped reforms to the Immigration and Refugee Protection Act (IRPA), resulting in increasingly restrictive immigration policies and heightened border securitization. Specifically, anti-trafficking discourse produces and manages racialized concepts that influence the relationship between gender, migration, and the state in a way that has directly restricted the migratory options available to women, migrant workers – including migrant sex workers –and asylum claimants. This chapter examines trafficking discourses emphasizing perceptions of "risk" and "potential vulnerability," which led to the dismantling of the exotic dancer visa under the Temporary Foreign Worker Program (TFWP). Other policy amendments drawing on anti-trafficking focus on criminalization and deportation, including the criminalization of some temporary migrant workers whose experiences align with trafficking definitions as well as other forms of labour exploitation in a context of political and socioeconomic constraints. As Suchland (2015) points out, human trafficking has garnered substantial attention that has been misdirected towards activities that are symptomatic of broader systems of exploitation while simultaneously obscuring systemic forms of violence.

Moreover, reminiscent of the exclusionary and racialized immigration policies that governed the Komogatu Maru incident of 1914, the arrival of two boats off the coast of British Columbia in 2009 and 2010 elicited anti-trafficking discourses that emphasized perceived threats to national security, leading to "moral panic" and further exclusionary responses. In particular, politicized oversimplifications of the relationship between human trafficking and migrant smuggling provided the discursive framework for the adoption of restrictive immigration policies that have created more insecurity for trafficked persons alongside migrants, refugees, and asylum claimants. In turn, such policies reproduce notions of national sovereignty and the citizen–subject while criminalizing gendered and racialized bodies moving between nation-states among the complexities of a global capitalist economic system. Although such complexities are not new, anti-trafficking discourses underscore the appropriation of rights-based discourses that maintain existing boundaries through border securitization; moreover, such discourses are rooted in the foundational narrative of the settler colonial nation-state. Therefore, while enhanced security appears to be an appropriate solution to address human trafficking and can potentially facilitate the identification of trafficked individuals, such securitization reproduces the gendered and racialized nature of immigration controls and naturalizes the settler colonial state's definition of who is considered domestic and who is seen as a racialized "other," and thereby excluded from "national" belonging.

Anti-trafficking, Potential Threats, and Pre-emptive Exclusion

Anti-trafficking discourses informed policy changes enacted through clauses in the 2012 omnibus crime bill (Bill C-10) and the budget bill (Bill C-38). Under the leadership of the conservative government in Canada, this enabled the withdrawal and refusal of visas issued to exotic dancers under the Temporary Foreign Worker Program (TFWP) and, at the discretion of immigration officials, the pre-emptive restriction of foreign nationals from working in Canada if they were *believed to be at risk* of exploitation. Although the restrictive measures can theoretically be applied to other temporary employment sectors where there have been documented cases of trafficking, such as live-in caregivers or construction workers, restrictive measures have, at the time of writing, only been applied to curb sex industries. As of July 14, 2012, work permit applications are no longer processed for foreign nationals seeking employment in strip club, escort services, or massage parlours, and such businesses no longer qualify to hire temporary foreign workers (TFWs). In addition, foreign nationals holding open work permits are restricted from working in sex industries. As the following analysis documents, amendments to the exotic dancer visa program further illustrate the use of anti-trafficking discourses to shape exclusionary immigration policies. Given the gendered and racialized nature of the visa program, the elimination of the program reflects how anti-trafficking discourses are shaping the relationship between the state, migration, gender, and sexuality.

Since the implementation of the temporary work permit process in Canada in 1978, "foreign exotic dancers" have participated in the cross-border movements facilitated by the program (Macklin 2003). Typically, applicants are required to obtain temporary work permits overseas by providing evidence of a job offer and a validation of the offer by Human Resources and Development Canada (HRDC).[4] Temporary employment offers were validated when employers obtained a positive labour market opinion by reasonably demonstrating a shortage of qualified Canadians or permanent residents to recruit, train, and fill the position. However, in the case of migrant dancers, the requirement of obtaining a work permit overseas and the employment validation from HRDC was exempted.[5] The exemption was implemented because the initial cross-border movements in the 1970s and 1980s primarily involved "Canadian and U.S. women engaging in an informal stripper exchange program" (Macklin 2003: 467). However, in the early 1990s, migrant dancers increasingly arrived in Canada from countries in Eastern Europe and Asia.[6] It was in this context that concerns of human trafficking entered the public dialogue: anti-trafficking discourses suggesting the special exemption of the exotic dancer program reflected the state's complicity in facilitating human trafficking. Significantly, reflections on state complicity from this rights-based framework supports the restriction and criminalization of migratory movements while neglecting the role of anti-trafficking in the production and reproduction of structural inequalities within and between nation-states. Regardless, such concerns resulted in public discussions about restricting the program.

Alongside the shift in exotic dancers' countries of arrival, workplace standards were also changing in the 1990s with the institutionalization of lap dancing as an industry standard.[7] This resulted in a declining supply of Canadian dancers, which facilitated industry claims of labour shortages (Macklin 2003). As a result, in 1998, the minister of HRDC, Pierre Pettigrew, classified foreign dancing as a job to be monitored for shortages, which, in effect, eliminated the need for individual labour market opinions.[8] While in appearance this facilitated a streamlined entry of migrant dancers into Canada "to serve the economic interests of the private sector," Citizenship and Immigration Canada (CIC) relied on legal devices to restrict the movements of exotic dancers (Macklin 2003). Specifically, CIC denied employment authorizations based on the qualifications presented by the applicants. For instance, as Macklin (2003: 478) highlights, the Federal Court of Canada upheld a CIC decision that an applicant who "only had experience topless dancing" lacked the necessary qualifications for "nude dancing" in Toronto (see Silion v. Canada 1999). Applicants were also rejected based on the assumption they would only enter the exotic dancing industry in Canada if their life circumstances overseas were extremely dire, which meant they would pose a risk of not wanting to return to their home countries – a violation of the temporary design of the program.

Despite the already constrained flow of exotic dancers to Canada, a political scandal led to further calls to cancel the exotic dancer visa program. In 2004, Immigration Minister Judy Sgro was alleged to have a conflict of interest over an exotic dancer visa issued to an individual that worked on her re-election campaign (Hughes 2005; CBC News 2005, June 21).[9] The scandal led to the resignation of Minister Sgro and to a renewal of criticism surrounding the visa program and its implications for the role of the state in human trafficking (Hughes 2005; *Globe and Mail* 2004, December 3). As a result, the requirement to have the job offer validated was applied to the exotic dancer program and the number of work permits issued and extended dramatically declined: 342 permits and extensions were granted in 2004 while only six were granted or extended in 2010 (Library of Parliament 2012). Measures to further restrict and/or eliminate the program were proposed between 2007 and 2010;[10] however, they gained little footing until a Progressive Conservative majority was attained in May 2011.

Introduced on September 20, 2011, and receiving Royal Assent on March 13, 2012, the omnibus crime bill, Bill C-10, amended the Immigration and Refugee Protection Act with the stated intention of addressing international forms of human trafficking. Specifically, in an earlier announcement of the provisions in the bill, Rona Ambrose, the Minister of Public Works and Government Services Canada and Minster of the Status of Women Canada, indicated, "the bill should help to preclude situations in which women *might be* exploited or become victims of human trafficking" and the legislative changes will "help close the doors to the dangerous victimization of girls and women" (Library of Parliament 2012: 146; emphasis added). To this end, the bill enabled the pre-emptive exclusion of overseas visa applicants on the basis that they could *potentially* be exploited once they arrive in Canada. In particular, clauses 205–8 of Bill C-10 "[gave] immigration officers discretion to refuse to authorize foreign nationals to work in Canada if, *in the opinion of the officers*, the foreign nationals are *at risk* of being victims of exploitation or abuse" (Library of Parliament 2012: 146; emphasis added). The discretionary power granted to border security officials presupposed the benevolence of state enforcement mechanisms as well as an understanding of what constitutes human trafficking and exploitation. However, law enforcement officials in this study suggest border security officials have been markedly underequipped and uniformed in the identification of human trafficking in Canada and play a central role in the criminalization and deportation of trafficked persons as well as others affected by the implementation of restrictive modes of border securitization. Moreover, the bill proposes to address the problem of human trafficking by excluding the migratory movements of the visa applicants. In doing so, the measure restricts freedom of movement without addressing the root cause of the presupposed *risk* or the motivating factors leading to the visa request. Thus, while the policy potentially limits cases of trafficking through this specific visa program, it expands other forms of insecurity where "at risk" individuals use or are forced to use alternate, often criminalized routes of entry.

In addition to Bill C-10, further measures to eliminate the exotic dancer visa program were implemented with the passing of Bill C-38, the omnibus budget that received royal assent on June 29, 2012. Building on the program restrictions implemented in 2004, provisions in Bill C-38 drew on anti-trafficking discourses to grant immigration officials the power to invalidate existing visas issued to exotic dancers, refuse new applications to the program, and prohibit individuals with open work visas from working in the adult entertainment industry. Announcing the new measures, Diane Finley, minister of human resources and skills development indicated, "Through collaborative partnerships and preventive action, these new measures will further strengthen Canada's National Action Plan to Combat Human Trafficking" (Employment and Social Development Canada 2012). The measures are, in fact, in step with the National Action Plan to Combat Human Trafficking (NAPCHT); however, as some frontline workers who were engaged in the limited consultation underlying the formulation of the plan indicate, certain recommendations are out of step with the realities: "One of the [proposed] recommendations was that we should have more stringent immigration procedures and policies *for women entering Canada alone*. It was totally uninformed, it was just like 'this will fix it' and we were just like 'we would like to state our concern with this' and I don't know if it has been revised ... my concern is that people go 'oh yeah, that will do, we are dealing with it: pass.' It is kind of frightening if something like that can even get in there" (emphasis added).

In the end, the NAPCHT does emphasize some exclusionary measures aimed at restricting the migratory movements of girls and women, including voluntary movements.[11] The plan states, "[T]hose who are likely to be at-risk [of trafficking] include ... girls and women, who may be lured to large urban centres or *who move or migrate there voluntarily*" (Public Safety Canada 2012a: 6; emphasis added). By including women's voluntary movements and migrations under the category of "at risk," the NAPCHT creates a rationale for restricting women's movements through measures, such as Bill C-38, and, in doing so, reinforces the power of the state to discipline and control migration.

The minister of CIC, Jason Kenney, further announced measures to be implemented with the passing of Bill C-38, building on this discourse of suspected risk and, as previously discussed, framing the issue as a matter of integrity for the immigration system:

> The government cannot in good conscience continue to admit temporary foreign workers to work in businesses in sectors where there are reasonable grounds to *suspect a risk* of sexual exploitation ... I think we could all agree that Canada's immigration system should not be used or abused to exploit vulnerable people ...
>
> I should also point out that today the Safe Streets and Communities Act, known as Bill C-10, comes into force, and that as well gives me as the Minister of Immigration the authority to issue instructions to our visa officers around the world – which I will be doing – instructing them that if they have evidence that an applicant for a work permit abroad is likely to face degrading or humiliated treatment in Canada, that they can and should refuse the visa ... we will no longer issue work permits in [sex trade] sectors. (CIC 2012b, July 4; emphasis added)

Significantly, the emphasis on not allowing the Canadian immigration system to "exploit vulnerable people" is consistent with early forms of colonial immigration controls devised to protect the emerging national identity from "undesirable" (gendered and racialized) migrants in the name of protecting women from "degrading" circumstances. In this, the ongoing role of immigration in concealing the dispossession of Indigenous communities as well as the concurrent values of capitalist societies built on white supremacy are reproduced by omitting troubling bodies. Nonetheless, as the former minister suggests, the new measures augment ministerial power to pre-emptively restrict migratory movements on the basis of perceived risk, a power that has been extended to restrict the migration of sex workers. Kenney further pointed to a 2010 RCMP report to justify the amendments:

> We have good reason to believe that temporary foreign workers entering Canada to work in sex-related businesses are often at high level of risk. In a 2010 report on human trafficking from the RCMP, it said that "human trafficking for the purpose of sexual exploitation has been mostly associated to organized prostitution. Specifically, human trafficking has been found to occur discretely behind prostitution fronts like escort agencies and residential brothels ... and possibly in massage and escort services." (CIC 2012b, July 4)

The RCMP (2010) report points to the involvement of organized crime with connections to convicted traffickers in facilitating the entry of women from the former Soviet states to Canada to work in massage and escort services. Specifically, the RCMP threat assessment associated strip clubs with human trafficking of foreign nationals to Canada, citing "investigations conducted in the 1990s" which found "strong indications that women were recruited from Eastern European countries for nonsexual work but were later forced to dance in strip clubs and even provide sexual services" (RCMP 2010: 18). Since human trafficking legislation was not in place at the time of the investigations, the RCMP (2010) argued that anecdotal stories alongside investigations pointing to circumstances consistent with human trafficking should be considered in lieu of numerical data.

However, the report goes on to contradict discourses connecting human trafficking with the exploitation of foreign nationals in exotic dancing industries. Specifically, according to the report, more recent investigations in Ontario, Quebec, and the Atlantic regions all concluded that in clubs offering sexual services "human trafficking complaints were mostly unfounded ... though foreign workers were indeed located in the clubs, investigations determined that these subjects were engaged *voluntarily* as exotic dancers" (RCMP 2010: 19; emphasis added).[12] As a result, the report concluded, "Overall, investigations so far have not been able to substantiate the trafficking of foreign nationals in exotic dance clubs but this possibility has not been ruled out" (RCMP 2010: 20). Conversely, the report suggests that interprovincial (domestic) trafficking of Canadian citizens is an "increasing trend" (RCMP 2010: 20).

Of note, similar confusion exists among municipal police officers. Consider, for instance, the following statements issued by vice officers in two different Western Canadian cities: "I work in the vice unit, so mainly we deal with prostitution-related offenses. So we deal with a lot of bawdy houses, and then we try to get the girls off the street, and get them out of the sex trade if we can. That's mainly our goal ... We haven't seen a whole lot of human trafficking ... most of the places we go, the women certainly aren't being forced to stay there." However, another vice officer indicates, "In all our investigations of bawdy houses ... they all have parts of human trafficking, they all have those indicators that say [human trafficking] is happening here." As these excerpts suggest, perceptions of sex industries and enforcement-based approaches vary across the country. Nonetheless, federal approaches clearly delineate a perceived risk of exploitation. Yet by connecting the migratory movements of women, including voluntary migrations, to the risk of human trafficking, anti-trafficking discourses inform restrictive measures as a preventive strategy to address the victimization of foreign nationals potentially exploited in exotic dancing industries. In turn, such measures enable ongoing victimization and reproduce structural and material insecurities.

In spite of scarce evidence connecting human trafficking to the exotic dancer visa program, abolishing the program has, in effect, prevented *potential* cases of international human trafficking from occurring through the specific use of exotic dancer visas. However, in doing so, the restrictive measures reinforce gendered and racialized forms of exclusion by limiting the legal migratory options for predominantly women dancers; criminalize the experiences of dancers that continue to work when their visas are declared invalid; and, in the name of protection, fail to address the core issues identified by migrant women. In particular, excluding women from accessing legal migratory options fails to address the socioeconomic realities of the migrants, the motivations behind their migrations, and mobility rights in general. In doing so, these measures contradict the already restricted purpose of the UN Trafficking Protocol: "to protect and assist the victims of trafficking, with full respect for their human rights" (UNODC 2000). Moreover, such restrictions reproduce early constructions of racialized bodies as a threat to the purity and benevolence underpinning the national identity. Far from increasing mobility rights, restrictive measures reinforce national settler colonial boundaries on the basis of gendered, economic, and racialized exclusion.

In spite of such criminalization, migrant and sex worker–rights organizations, such as SWAN in Vancouver (SWAN 2015) and Butterfly in Toronto (Lam 2016), have resisted the harmful effects of anti-trafficking and the restrictions imposed through anti-trafficking discourses. In this context, structural and material violence, including institutionalized racism, are identified as particularly harmful for migrants, and especially Asian, sex workers. As Butterfly states, the main challenges migrant sex workers face are "challenge[s] with the criminalization of sex work and the immigration status. They are marginalized and isolated because of race, language and [the] stigmatization of sex work and their legal status" (Global Network of Sex Work Projects [NSWP] 2014a). Given the targeted effects of anti-trafficking for migrant, and especially Asian, sex workers, Butterfly collaborated with the Migrant Sex Workers Project, Maggie's, Canadian HIV/AIDS Legal Network, STRUT, and No One Is Illegal on a joint endeavour, "Stop the Harm from Anti-Trafficking Policies and Campaigns." Jointly, the group of sex workers (both migrant and not) and sex workers' organizations and allies argue that anti-trafficking legislations "are not only being used to control and limit migration; these laws prohibit migrant involvement in the sex industry, even for those who are allowed to work in Canada and freely choose to be sex workers … These measures limit sex workers' safe migration, and increase their risk of exploitation." In light of this stance, the collective aims to counter the gendered and racialized effects of anti-trafficking by advocating the following:

1) Recognize that sex work is work and eliminate discrimination against sex workers. Support sex workers' rights, and justice, and the right not to be "rescued."
2) Support peer-led models so that the sex work community can connect with others and assist in cases of exploitation and abuse. Stop using criminal laws to address sex workers' migration and review anti-trafficking policies with sex workers' organizations to develop measures that are rights-based and supportive to the community.
3) Urge the federal government to repeal the Protection of Communities and Exploited Persons Act (PCEPA), which endangers sex workers' lives, health, and safety.
4) Urge the government to stop raids, detentions, and deportations of sex workers. [Canada Border Services Agency] should never be involved in anti-trafficking investigations. (Butterfly 2015)

Similarly, in Vancouver, SWAN provides "non-judgemental support and services to newcomer, migrant and immigrant women who do indoor sex work." In spite of this work, organizations like SWAN have been alienated from anti-trafficking funding because they refuse to adopt an anti-prostitution framework (Clancey, Khushrushahi, and Ham 2014). The harmful effects of anti-trafficking for migrant and racialized sex workers in the SWAN report *Im/Migrant Sex Workers, Myths and Misconceptions: Realities of the Anti-Trafficked*. Drawing on experiences of migrant sex workers, the report documents the racializing work of anti-trafficking. As one focus group participant quoted in the report said, "I think racism does come into play because police go into massage parlors where they know Asian women are working expecting to find migrants that are illegal" (SWAN Vancouver Society 2015). Similar to the Indigenous Sex Sovereignty Collective (2016), migrant sex worker rights advocates argue the harmful effects of criminalizing racialized bodies in a context of colonial gender violence wherein institutionalized racism was foundational to the nation-building narrative and, in spite of claims to multicultural inclusion, migrants continue to experience gendered and racialized mechanisms of exclusion, such as those advanced through anti-trafficking in Canada.

Temporary Insecurity: Migrant Worker Programs in Canada

The intersection between anti-trafficking discourses, human rights, including the rights of migrants, and boundaries of inclusion and exclusion are particularly apparent when examining the experiences of low-skill TFWs in Canada. On the one hand, despite the stated aims of the program to meet temporary labour shortages,[13] TFWs have been incorporated into the fabric of the Canadian labour market and the proportion of low-skilled migrant workers with temporary and precarious status has been on the rise.[14] Since 2006, the number of TFWs entering Canada has consistently surpassed the number of economic immigrants that received permanent resident status, with the majority of this growth occurring in the low-wage sectors.[15]

On the other hand, despite inclusion through legal entry points into Canadian society and being extended the same rights and legal protections afforded to Canadian workers, low-skilled TFWs lack substantive access to actualize these rights. Precarious status and restricted access to permanent residency and citizenship for low-skilled migrants naturalizes exclusion within the boundaries of the state where low-skilled migrant workers are disadvantaged in relation to high-skilled migrants and Canadian citizens.[16] Such restrictions reinforce settler colonial dominance over state boundaries and controlled access over the land. In addition to restricting access to citizenship and inclusion in Canadian society, low-skill workers are often limited to a single employer, job, and location, which further limits substantive access to employment rights and protections.[17] As Hanley et al. (2012: 245) point out, the racialized and gendered nature of the Seasonal Agricultural Worker Program (SAWP) and the Live-in Caregiver Program (LCP) "have placed migrant workers in situations vulnerable to exploitation and, at best, inequality with other workers." Moreover, as reliance increases on low-skill labour associated with employers using the Pilot Project for Occupations Requiring Lower Levels of Formal Training (PPORLLFT), researchers and advocates suggest "a new wave of workers from the global South [are] simply joining the ranks of their LCP and SAWP predecessors in terms of vulnerability to exploitation and categorization as 'less than equal'" (Hanley et al. 2012: 245). Along these lines, the precarity and structural insecurities legislated through the low-skill TFW program have provided a context in which some employers rely on limited access to actualize legal protections and restrictive immigration policies to exploit the labour of low-skill TFWs in the country and, at times, this precariousness has led to instances of trafficking.[18]

While the labour of low-skill TFWs falls within the bounds of national conceptions of inclusion, the rights of TFWs have fallen outside such boundaries, creating insecurity for TFWs and their families. At the same time, discourses of human trafficking have also created an exclusionary boundary by garnering significant attention through representations of extreme forms of exploitation, organized criminal networks, and the associated need to "crack down" on migrants that would "exploit the system." In turn, such representations exclude the broader-ranging insecurities of low-skill migrant workers living and working in Canada under conditions of authorized inequality.[19]

One of the primary constraints frontline workers and law enforcement representatives – particularly from Alberta and British Columbia[20] – identify when describing their perception of the relationship between low-skilled TFWs and human trafficking is the ability of TFWs to report their experiences of trafficking as well as other forms of labour exploitation. Specifically, given the restrictive nature of work permits for low-skill migrant workers, fraudulent recruitment by some employers in Canada facilitates exploitation by placing the worker in legal violation of their visa requirements. In the words of a national law enforcement official,

> There are so many temporary foreign workers in the province of Alberta and they are exploited quite heavily … In Alberta, in particular, it's dealing with foreign workers and them being brought into the country under fraudulent pretences and being exploited … in hotels, fast food industry, live-in caregiver industry, construction. So what will happen is that they are supposed to come and work for Quiznos and instead they will make them work at Tim Hortons. So they are in violation, they are working without a permit, and they can be removed from the country. So they are working at Tim's for longer hours and less pay than

everybody else. And so it will be within the fast food industry: "I need a body here, don't tell immigration, we will get the paper work for you and get it sorted out, it's fine." So sort of the same [type of work] but within that industry itself ... the exploitation happens and a lot of head offices don't know it's going on. [As soon as they are in violation of the Act] they can be deported and removed, just by working in some place you are not supposed to be working: "we'll tell immigration if you don't [comply]."

As this excerpt suggests, TFWs victimized through the use of fraud, threats, or coercion have been criminalized and deported because they are in violation of the TFW work permit requirements. Despite law enforcement claims that such experiences of exploitation are frequent in nature, border security officials implement the restrictive nature of the permit, which reproduces racialized exclusion and naturalizes border securitization. At the same time, the government relies on anti-trafficking to justify more restrictive immigration that penalizes illegalized or "out of status" migrants. However, it is noteworthy that anti-trafficking has not led to substantial calls for bans on migrant labour in industries, such as construction or welding, where documented cases of trafficking have emerged. Rather, workers in these industries are perceived to assume the *risks* associated with temporary, insecure employment while workers in sex industries are declared "at risk."

Even when no initial violation of the work permit occurs, reporting instances of trafficking or other exploitative practices of an employer can result in job loss, which can also jeopardize the low-skill TFW's legal status in the country. Specifically, in many instances, temporary migrant workers are placed in situations of dependence on their employers because they are only authorized to work for that specific employer, who obtains a particular labour market opinion (LMO) for the occupation listed on the work permit. As one frontline worker argues,

Within the temporary foreign worker population is a lot of potentially trafficked people ... so there is a lot of human rights that have been violated with just some of the policies ... they are getting the work visas that designate them to the workplace that applied for them to come. So if there are any problems then they are in a very bad position. If I am not satisfied with the job that was promised versus the reality I have no other options.

Cause if I to work for this employer, automatically my visa isn't valid and I can be deported or asked to leave ... Yeah, you are at the mercy of your employer.

As this excerpt suggests, to leave an exploitative employer and remain in the country legally, a low-skill TFW must "find another employer who is willing to go through the lengthy process to apply for and receive an LMO [labour market opinion] to hire them and who is then willing to wait again until the migrant worker is able to apply for and receive an amended work permit" (Faraday 2012: 77). As a result, changing jobs or employers can result in months of unemployment, which many low-skilled TFWs cannot afford, especially if their work in Canada is tied to remittance obligations in their home countries. Yet, any work done in the absence of the amended work permit violates the TFW program and can result in deportation. Thus, given the risks associated with reporting incidences of trafficking and other forms of abuse, frontline workers indicate that many TFWs choose to endure the abuse. In the words of one frontline worker,

[Temporary foreign workers] would choose not to file a complaint for fear of being sent home and not being able to find a job because of the nature of the work permit, which is restrictive. So if they will complain, then the huge possibility of being out of a job is just so huge that they can't have that ... they don't want to come out, no matter how much we tell them. Even the foreign workers who come to our door and admit that they are being abused, at the end of the day they still have to want to file a complaint because it has to be done with their consent, and they will just say no. So what can you do? Because they are afraid of losing their job ... they would rather endure it.

As this excerpt highlights, structural constraints, including job loss and possible deportation, prevents low-skill temporary migrant workers from reporting experiences of labour trafficking as well as broader forms of exploitation. Anti-trafficking advocates have aimed to mediate the potential of deportation through temporary resident permits (TRPs); however, this has had limited effect. And even when granted, the TRP similarly reproduces an insecure status.

Temporary resident permits were created with the stated aim of preventing trafficked persons from being criminalized and deported when reporting experiences of human trafficking by granting temporary legal immigration status in Canada. However, frontline workers indicate the TRP has been decidedly limited in its ability to offer real protection to trafficked persons. As one frontline worker summarizes,

> We don't see [the TRP] as a very useful tool. One specific attorney we work with doesn't recommend using them. I mean, they only get you six months and you have to come to the attention of law enforcement and immigration to get one. And you just go, there's no dedicated person or anything, you just show up at the office and say, "Hey, I have a trafficking case." So it can be up to anyone's discretion on how they evaluate that case. And there is an immediate consultation if you go with law enforcement ... It's for six months, but you can get an extension, but that is absolutely subjective ... yeah, that six months would be great to have, but then what is going to happen next? They can be deported ... but we do have several women who have been trafficked and do have a legitimate refugee claim. And so that's how they end up staying, they make a refugee claim.

As this excerpt highlights, the process for applying for a TRP necessitates having the case evaluated by the CIC, which is required to report the evaluation to the RCMP. Yet, alongside a mistrust of police and authorities, many applicants have reasonable concerns about de facto reporting to enforcement agencies. Significantly, in sex trafficking cases, inclusion in state and enforcement-based responses is supported by many working in anti-trafficking, yet the harms of the potential for criminalization are more readily acknowledged with respect to non-sexual labour contexts.

Further, the suggestion that trafficked persons opt for alternate means of obtaining protections instead of relying on the TRP offers insight to discussions about whether anti-trafficking legislation produces victims of trafficking. In particular, some evidence suggests undocumented migrants might identify as victims of trafficking to secure legal protections, such as the TRP, and possibly obtain permanent immigration status. For instance, in a human trafficking case involving allegations of domestic servitude in British Columbia, the Supreme Court Justice ruled to acquit the accused of all charges:

> I wish to emphasize that this is not a case in which I am left with only a reasonable doubt about whether the offences occurred ... I am left, rather, with the conviction that the allegations made by [the complainant] are

improbable. On the evidence before me, it appears far more likely that the complainant took advantage of [the accused's] generosity in order to come to Canada then took advantage of an opportunity she saw to remain in this country, showing a callous disregard for her benefactor and the truth in the process. (CTV News 2013, November 22)

Although such cases raise important questions about the role of trafficking legislation in the construction of human trafficking environments, frontline workers suggest the stringent regulations around reporting trafficking to law enforcement, the challenges associated with obtaining a TRP, and associated fears of criminalization and deportation excludes, rather than creates, trafficking cases. Thus, by opting to "make a refugee claim," the limitations of anti-trafficking protections potentially also construct other forms of seeking to obtain asylum. In turn, agents of social intervention are reaffirmed as those who promote anti-trafficking mechanisms and negotiate the implementation of such mechanisms by mediating the relationship with law enforcement.

The risk of job loss and potential deportation is further exacerbated for low-skill TFWs who are constrained by the dependency of families and governments relying on their labour in the form of remittance payments (Preibisch 2012). The need to supply remittances to family members and dependent public sectors of home countries, alongside the restrictive policies governing TFW programs, were identified by frontline service providers and law enforcement representatives as another key form of insecurity faced by TFWs, leading some to persist in exploitative work situations rather than report possible experiences of trafficking. For instance, one frontline worker details a case where despite explicit abuse – including both sexual abuse and labour violations – by an employer, the low-skill TFW refused to report the abuse until it compromised her ability to provide remittances: "She only came to complain because she was not receiving her salary and so we probed further and came to know that she was being sexually abused by her employer. But then had the employer not been paying – she is a cleaner, so she cleans maybe one office to another – so that's only when she told us that she was sexually abused, but she told us that pay is more important to her because by that she will be able to send money home."

As this excerpt suggests, the socioeconomic constraints of maintaining remittance payments prevented this TFW from reporting the abuse of her employer, until the violence threatened to compromise her ability to make the remittances. On the one hand, the narrative of this TFW challenges notions of an "ideal victim" (particularly images portraying sexually exploited women in need of rescue), as her primary concern was the labour violation and her ability to maintain remittance payments to her home country rather than her experience of sexual abuse perpetrated by her employer. On the other hand, her experience points to the insecurity faced by low-skill TFWs who are constrained by socioeconomic obligations to their home countries, yet dependent on specific employers for their legal inclusion in the host country. In the end, she was unable to recover the pay and she left the employer; however, since her status in Canada was dependent on the labour market opinion obtained by this employer, she was subsequently deported: "[She] was sent home because there was no other labour market opinion for her. So if she doesn't have any labour market opinion, she can't have a work permit. If she doesn't have the work permit, then she doesn't have the legal status to stay here, so she had to leave the country." In this way, the legal constraints of the TFW program create a context of insecurity for migrant workers who are tied to specific employers and are limited by their need to make remittance payments in continued contexts of structural inequality.

The socioeconomic context that framed the demand for low-skill TFW programs in Canada – namely, the perceived need for cheap, flexible labour – creates a context conducive to the exploitation of low-skilled migrant workers who migrate with the aim of maintaining remittance payments, thereby facilitating the continuation of a two-tier, racialized labour market that discriminates against migrant workers through lower forms of compensation and precarious working conditions. The prevalence of this problem is further suggested in the following excerpt from a law enforcement representative:

> They [TFWs] come for a job, the job doesn't exist. "Okay go here, you know you are now working without a permit, we are going to tell immigration if you stop." So what will happen is that the people who have status are paid one wage and the people who don't have status are paid another wage. And that just seems to be common knowledge and accepted practice. People tolerate it and put up with it because they can still get enough money and send money to support their family back home.

The statement "that just seems to be common knowledge and accepted practice" aligns with findings of a study in Alberta examining the working and living conditions of migrant workers in the province. The report concludes: "There is still widespread occurrence of employers abusing foreign workers' rights at work" (Byl 2009: 1).

Given such abuse, temporary migrant workers have mobilized rights-based organizing in an effort to improve their treatment in Canada, particularly to pressure the state towards greater levels of inclusion. Drawing on community organizing with migrant workers, Hanley et al. argue, "the time has come to devote organizing resources to sustained and united pressure for a reorientation of Canadian immigration policy – one that demonstrates a shift away from programs conferring precarious immigration status upon foreign workers and toward programs that offer full equality for migrants to Canada" (2012: 246). Thus, *inclusion* within the nation-state provides a means with which migrant workers resist the racialized policing of borders. However, in a context of settler colonialism, such inclusion also holds the potential for reinforcing state boundaries and rendering invisible Indigenous sovereignties. An extended focus on the role of national priorities that are produced and maintained through anti-trafficking discourses and practices reveals the colonial imperative of domiciling Indigeneity while restricting entry to other racialized bodies.

Nonetheless, anti-trafficking discourses have restricted the movements of some migrant workers on the basis of perceived risk, preventing entry into the country through policies of exclusion, while other low-skill migrant workers endure situations of exploitation within the country in order to avoid the penalties of restrictive immigration and deportation out of the country. On both counts do restrictive measures are exacerbate the insecurities faced by trafficked persons in particular and migrants in general while reinforcing settler colonial notions of national inclusion.

Contested Territory: Human Smuggling, Human Trafficking, and the Rights of Migrants

By redefining human trafficking as a transnational criminal activity, the UN Trafficking Protocol focused international anti-trafficking initiatives on law enforcement responses and anti-trafficking policies on national security and border controls. This, combined with definitional ambiguities, has created a context in which anti-trafficking discourses are subject to a variety of competing political agendas. As discussed, domestic anti-trafficking discourses that focus on policy struggles aim to redefine the relationship between human trafficking and anti-prostitution laws in Canada; meanwhile, anti-trafficking discourses targeting international forms of human trafficking have placed restrictions on migrant workers, especially those with precarious status. Similarly, Canadian anti-trafficking discourses emphasize the relationship between human trafficking and human or migrant smuggling. Human trafficking and migrant smuggling are theoretically distinct concepts, yet, in practice, law enforcement personnel and frontline workers identify significant challenges in clearly distinguishing the concepts. Moreover, although not necessarily discernable at the border, the concepts themselves can, at times, overlap when a migrant-smuggling transaction becomes human trafficking. Although practical experiences often fall into a conceptual grey area, conflating anti-trafficking policies and initiatives with enforcement-based migration controls designed to address migrant smuggling has created insecurity for trafficked persons and other migrants to Canada while reinforcing state-based conceptions of who is permitted inclusion into settler colonial notions of Canadian citizenship.

The definitional complexity of migrant smuggling and international forms of human trafficking is compounded by the "diverse motivations and messy realities of migration" (Lee 2011: 149). In particular, parallel to the continuum discussed in relation to sexual labour experiences (empowerment through to oppression), migrant experiences can include voluntary movements as well as varying forms of exploitation and coercion at multiple junctures in the process, regardless of whether the means of crossing the border were deemed legal or illicit. Moreover, polarized distinctions between "deserving victim" and "complicit criminal" (O'Connell Davidson 2013) ignore migrant self-determination and conceal the variety of motivations that underpin movement, such as a flight from conflict, persecution, environmental factors, gender discrimination, ability to access education, desire to ameliorate economic or political circumstances, or simply a desire to move (Sassen 2002; Agustín 2007). As one frontline worker reveals,

> Just to try to find the distinction between [human trafficking and human smuggling] ... it is very confusing because if you look at the definitions in the law, they are really quite different from the realities of frontline work ... it's difficult for a lot of the frontline workers because it's the people who are trying to get out of their country of persecution. They don't have other options and they are paying these fees and yet once they get here they

figure they are going to have the human rights perspective, but then they are taken and detained and don't have access to services.

This excerpt points to a disjuncture between the "messy realities" of migratory experiences and the legislations designed to control cross-border movements. It further points to response mechanisms that criminalize the experiences of refugee and asylum seekers (see Morrison and Crosland 2001). For now, it is important to recognize that migrant rights are too often jeopardized when anti-trafficking and smuggling laws (which are by nature black and white) meet the complex (inherently grey) experiences of migrants, particularly when they intersect at a single point in the migratory trajectory (i.e., the border).

The relationship between human trafficking and migrant smuggling is further distorted in cases in which migrant smuggling becomes exploitative upon arrival in the country of destination and shifts in definition to human trafficking. In these cases, human trafficking may not be identified as such because the trafficked person appears to border security officials as a smuggled migrant and is therefore intercepted at the point of human smuggling. As one former law enforcement representative highlights, "there's the legal distinction between a person who is smuggled and trafficked, but in my experience, with a person who is trafficked, often the victimization begins with someone who is smuggled." In light of this, a logical argument can be made for relying on anti-migrant smuggling legislation, such as mechanisms of border security for the prevention of human trafficking. While logical from an enforcement perspective, such restrictive policies increase the insecurity faced by migrants in general and trafficked persons in particular. For instance, the very nature of the coercion involved in some human trafficking experiences can prevent a readily identifiable distinction between human trafficking and migrant smuggling: "If they were smuggled or trafficked then there is also the family back home they have to worry about," said a frontline worker. "If they paid large fees, and if those fees aren't coming in there is the potential to hurt the family back home. So there is that hesitation coming forth with that type of information. It is really difficult to determine if they were trafficked or smuggled. There is really a fine line."

As this quote shows, threats issued to individuals and their families can serve as a significant deterrent to self-reporting experiences of trafficking or other forms of exploitation. These threats are further compounded in situations in which trafficked persons risk criminalization and possible deportation, such as the penalties associated with criminalized forms of migration. In this way, mechanisms designed to deter migrant smuggling and address human trafficking can be used as a tool to coerce or threaten migrants. Anti-trafficking policies aimed at preventing the exploitative practices of human trafficking also serve to reinforce existing boundaries of inclusion and exclusion by strengthening the ability of nation-states to secure their borders vis-à-vis a migrant "other."

Overall, the ambiguous nature of the relationship between human trafficking and migrant smuggling has created space for politicized discourse that connects anti-trafficking initiatives to a variety of forms of border securitization. In particular, as Lee (2011: 149) highlights, discourses that connect human trafficking to criminalized forms of migration enable officials to "state a commitment to combat abuse and exploitation of trafficked victims while at the same time setting in place stricter border controls, deportation for those who migrate outside migration laws, and detention in immigration detention centers and prisons that intensify the suffering of migrants and curtail their right to freedom of movement and the right to personal liberty."

Meanwhile, anti-trafficking discourses aiming to delineate clear distinctions between human trafficking and human smuggling separate cross-border migrations into "deserving victims" and "complicit criminals" when, in reality, the experiences are far more complex than such dialectic categories express. In continuity with previous settler colonial forms of boundary maintenance, the arrival of two migrant ships off the coast of British Columbia propelled anti-trafficking discourses in Canada to contribute to debates about migrant smuggling and existing boundaries of inclusion and exclusion, including the adoption of more restrictive immigration policies in the country.

Migrant Ships and Moral Panics: Human Rights versus National Security

In October 2009, the M.V. Ocean Lady was seized off the coast of British Columbia after arriving to Canada with 76 refugee claimants from Sri Lanka on board (CBC News 2012, March 29). The second boat, the M.V. Sun Sea, arrived in Victoria, British Columbia in August 2010 with 492 Tamil migrants on board. The arrival of the boats signalled a heightened discursive battle regarding the relationship between migrant rights and national security,[21] including drawing discursive connections between "illegal" (i.e., criminalized) migration and human trafficking.

The debate resulted in a number of legal challenges as well as policy discussions and amendments, such as the adoption of more restrictive immigration policies in Canada and corresponding legal challenges to the legislative amendments.[22]

This arrival is not the first time boats carrying smuggled migrants have been intercepted by authorities in Canada; however, it is the first known mass arrival since the adoption of the UN Trafficking Protocol that connected human trafficking to transnational criminal activity and the inclusion of counter-trafficking legislation in the IRPA and the Criminal Code of Canada. In addition to the previously discussed 1914 Komagata Maru experience driven by racialized conceptions of purity that were perceived to be threatened by "foreign" contamination, in the summer of 1999, four boats and one shipping container arrived carrying close to 600 migrants smuggled from the Fujian Province on the southeast coast of mainland China, representing the largest group of refugee claimants detained in recent Canadian history and subsequently, in the spring of 2000, the largest mass deportation (*Vancouver Sun* 2009, October 20; Mountz 2004). Similar to the more recent 2009 and 2010 arrivals from Sri Lanka, the 1999 boats triggered an intense public debate over the strength and sovereignty of the nation-state and the rights of migrants. According to Mountz (2004: 324), media discourses and the federal government portrayed the "migrant ships as a threat to the nation-state, presented the migrants as a threat to public health, and thus contributed to fears regarding the porosity of international borders, the integrity of Canada's refugee program, and the vulnerability of the nation-state more broadly." Meanwhile, the federal government "presented public images of authorities in control of the situation" (Mountz 2004: 325) through depictions of containment and detention.

Similarly, in 2009 and 2010, the federal government responded to the arrival of the migrant ships by detaining the migrants on board and, in the case of the latter, issuing public statements connecting the migrants to the threat of terrorism associated with the Liberation Tigers of Tamil Eelam (LTTE or Tamil Tigers), a declared terrorist organization by the Canadian government. In doing so, the government reaffirmed the autonomy of the nation-state to secure its borders and the priority of national security. Specifically, in response to the arrival of the ships, the prime minister at the time, Steven Harper, issued the following statement: "Canadians are pretty concerned when a whole boat of people comes – not through any normal application process, not through any normal arrival channel – and just simply lands ... We are responsible for the security of our borders, and the ability to welcome people, or not welcome people, when they come ... we'll take whatever steps are necessary going forward (*Globe and Mail* 2010, August 17).[23]

Although there are arguably important reasons for discouraging the arrival of migrant ships, including the safety of the migrants on board, such declarations neglect the complex reasons why migrants engage in "risky" cross-border movements and the reality that, by nature, refugee and asylum claims often deviate from regularized immigration processes delineating the boundaries of the nation-state.[24] Nonetheless, in its statement, the government reaffirmed the priority of national security and its role in enforcing such state-centric boundaries. The prime minister further affirmed that the federal government would "not hesitate to strengthen the laws if we have to" (*Globe and Mail* 2010, August 17). As will be seen, consistent with this "tough on crime" and "tough on smuggling" approach, anti-trafficking discourses played a role in shaping discussions about the arrival of the boats, migrant rights, and the eventual strengthening of laws targeting border securitization.

Discussing the complex relationship between human trafficking, migrant smuggling, and national security in relation to the arrival of the MV Ocean Lady and the MV Sun Sea, the following excerpt from a former law enforcement official suggests that an overemphasis on national security and the conflicts posed by the complexity of migratory experiences, in which trafficking and other forms of exploitation are erased by a "black and white" approach to boundary maintenance that emphasizes clear-cut cases of migrant smuggling:

When I was working as an investigator I saw everything in black and white. There were those who violated the law and those who didn't and I had the assumption that everybody makes the rational choice to break the law. There was some rational decision that resulted in the person using the services of a smuggler to get from wherever they were to Canada. I didn't recognize that smuggling could turn into trafficking and that often, trafficked people originally sought out the services of a smuggler. I think to find that line – we saw the Sun Sea provides an excellent example, in that there are allegations that in the Sun Sea – which were Tamil migrants – that there were members of the LTTE, therefore the LTTE is a listed terrorist organization with the *Canada Gazette*. Therefore, any member of the LTTE is a threat to Canadian security and a terrorist. We haven't taken a look at, in my opinion, the fact of what capacity of the LTTE were they a member of? Were they coerced or threaten to become a member of the LTTE? ... They don't always have the ability to make what we would see

as a rational choice … so to apply the law on the notion that someone
has made a rational choice is erroneous, and navigating that tricky line
between the threat to society and the victims comes down to taking the
time to examine what it is that led this person to be in the system. Often …
there isn't that time taken because it takes a long time, expensive, requires
highly educated individuals.

The excerpt suggests the problematic placement of migrants into clear-
cut categories of "those who follow the rules" and "those who break
the rules" emphasizes enforcement-based priorities yet limits detailed
investigation into the unique experiences of individual migrants and the
structurally unequal context in which complex intersections between
human trafficking and human smuggling are negotiated. In situations of
restrictive asylum policies, this results in wide-ranging criminalization,
including the criminalization of asylum claimants, potential refugees,
and trafficked persons. Of note, in a context of national securitization,
the representative is arguing for increased investigative capacity, even
while pointing to how, in addition to detaining the migrants, the government allegedly placed the migrants at greater risk by emphasizing
the threat they posed and the "illegal" nature of their arrival. The compounding circumstances – connecting the migrant ships to the possible
racialized threat of terrorism and the associated insecurity created by
the label of "terrorist" for the migrants in their origin country of Sri
Lanka, including possible torture – created sufficient grounds for one
of the migrants on board the ship to claim refugee status irrespective of
the perceived validity of his initial claim (CTV BC 2012, September 21).
In particular, the Federal Court of Canada ruled that publically associating the ship with the LTTE was sufficient grounds for the Immigration
and Refugee Board to accept a refugee claim made by one of the Ocean
Lady migrants.[25]

By stirring up moral sentiments and fear through discourses of
human trafficking, illegality, terrorist connections, and "cue jumpers,"
the government justified the immediate detainment of the migrants
upon arrival and their treatment as potential criminals. As one frontline
worker said, "When the Sun Sea vessel arrived, it took them two weeks
to get the legal aid number in to those folks … lack of [language sup-
ports], lack of access to counsel, lack of info about the process they are
in and lack of info about their rights, as having arrived on this based on
previous jurisprudence. The rules are never stated [for the detained] so
folks learn by trial and error." In addition the racialized framing of the
migrants as "criminals threatening border security," the migrants were

also considered potential victims of human trafficking. Specifically, in the detention hearings, where the onus is on the state to justify the reason for the detention, the *potential* threat of human trafficking was cited as a reason for detaining the migrants. As said one frontline worker from an international organization,

> I don't know that anyone thinks that any of those people were trafficked per say. Clearly there were smugglers involved, no evidence of trafficking. What is interesting though is that the CBSA at many of the detention reviews is suggesting that passengers from the second ship who are in detention are unlikely to appear because they have debts that they owe to the smugglers and would therefore be vulnerable to the smugglers and be forced to disappear to pay off the debts, which can cross over into trafficking.

In this way, state protection from the potential risk of human trafficking is cited as a valid reason for criminalization and detention, such that response to the arrival of the boats draws attention to the "intersection between detention and smuggling and trafficking." In a context of national securitization and reinforcement of settler colonial state controls, some participants of this study suggested that such an overemphasis on national security and enforcement-based responses alongside discourses conflating human trafficking and migrant smuggling created a context of "moral panic." In the words of one frontline worker, "This [human trafficking] conversation is off the rails and it's turned into an almost hyperbolic moral panic to call into question in an unprecedented way the rights of people migrating to us." Despite the relative rarity of migrants arriving to Canada by ship, migrant ships produce substantial public attention though images of mass arrival (Mountz 2010). This attention provided a context within which discursive connections between migrant smuggling and human trafficking that supported controversial immigration reforms could be drawn.

Anti-trafficking Discourses and Restrictive Immigration Laws

"Cracking Down" on Human Smuggling: Protecting Canada's Immigration System Act

Shortly after the arrival of the migrant ships off the coast of British Columbia, then public safety minister Vic Toews announced a partnership between the RCMP and Crime Stoppers, "Blue Blindfold," to raise public awareness about human trafficking in Canada and to provide a means for members of the public to report suspected incidences of human trafficking (CBC News 2010, September 7). Describing the campaign, one law enforcement representative indicated "[Blue Blindfold] puts the Crime Stoppers phone number on all the awareness material ... so Public Safety, the RCMP, and Crime Stoppers partnered to start a campaign for the public. That one is just for the public." By focusing on public reporting of human trafficking incidents, the Blue Blindfold campaign suggests that human trafficking is occurring in plain sight and is directly identifiable by an aware public, while simultaneously placing human trafficking in relation to criminalized migration and migrant smuggling.

In addition to an emphasis on raising public awareness of human trafficking, the initial announcement of the Blue Blindfold campaign tied human trafficking to issues of migration, migrant smuggling, and national security, suggesting human trafficking poses a security threat for Canadian citizens and foreign nationals. In an interview to launch the awareness campaign, Toews gave the following response to the question of how serious the problem of human trafficking is in Canada:

> I think it's an issue that has come to the forefront as we welcome more and more people to Canada – as also, at the same time, individuals take advantage of Canada. We are a democracy, we have – generally speaking – very open polices towards people coming in and there are individuals who are taking advantage of this particular situation. The trafficking issue, of course, is a much more significant one than smuggling in terms of the day to day impact on people here in Canada. Trafficking, of course, essentially leaves people in servitude, in fact, modern day slavery, and *these are situations that are occurring around us.* (CBC News 2010, September 7; emphasis added)

Of note, although the question centred on human trafficking, the response discursively emphasized the role of "individuals" who take "advantage of Canada." In doing so, the minister reinforced the perception that Canadian borders required protection in the form of border securitization. Moreover, by indicating that human trafficking is "occurring around us" the minister connected the publicized threat posed by the arrival of the migrant ships, including the threat of terrorism associated with the Tamil Tigers, to the day-to-day realities of the general public. Such discourses reinforce colonial notions of Canadians as welcoming, inclusive, and caring, while constructing racialized migrants as a threat. This, in turn, elides the ongoing threat settler colonialism poses for Indigenous sovereignties and for migrants experiencing ongoing precarity.

Further, in response to the question of whether new laws are needed to address human trafficking and migrant smuggling, Minister Toews asserted, "I think we have to be responsive to new kinds of threats to our security" (CBC News 2010, September 7). Minister Toews made specific note of the potential connection between migrant smuggling and human trafficking when he announced the federal government believed the Sun Sea was a "test ship" to assess the Canadian's government's response, and that new laws were being considered in light of the mass arrival (CBC News 2010, September 7). In this context, the federal government framed restrictive immigration reforms as a means of enhancing national security and border integrity while protecting individuals victimized by human trafficking.

On October 7, 2010, CIC minister Jason Kenney and public safety minister Vic Toews jointly announced Bill C-49, Preventing Human Smugglers from Abusing Canada's Immigration System Act. Announcing the bill by standing in front of the Ocean Lady at the Port of Vancouver, Toews declared, "[O]ur government is cracking down on those criminals who would abuse our generous immigration system … human smuggling is a despicable crime and *jumping the line* is fundamentally unfair" (CBC News 2010, October 21; emphasis added). Such an approach underscores the hegemonic perspective that a key function of the nation-state is to regulate, restrict, and discipline migrants that deviate from "normal" asylum procedures – in other words, to discipline those who "jump the line." In doing so, the announcement reinforced the prime minister's earlier statement, suggesting there are "regular" (i.e., fair) and "irregular" (i.e., criminal and unfair) channels for claiming refuge and asylum. The new bill would enable the citizenship and immigration minister to designate a new category of foreign national called the "designated foreign national" based on an "irregular arrival" and a new detention regime associated with the designation (Library of Parliament 2010). Further, the bill aimed to add "trafficking in persons" as an aggravating factor to be considered by the court when sentencing a human smuggling case.

In response to the announcement, some representatives in this study expressed frustration over the connections made between human trafficking and the proposed restrictive measures: "Every time there is a boat that arrives off our coast it gets all mixed up: smuggling;

trafficking … like the public safety minister Vic Toews, talking about human smuggling and immediately talks about trafficking" (provincial government representative, British Columbia). Frontline workers suggested the bill would create more insecurity for trafficked persons and other migrants by criminalizing their experiences and creating grounds for their deportation. Similarly, a former law enforcement representative indicates: "the most recent bill [C-49], the anti-smuggling, I think it was a knee-jerk reaction to the arrival of the Sun Sea, and I don't agree with that because it criminalizes those who use the services of a smuggler." Expressing similar concerns about criminalization, another frontline worker suggests the bill inaccurately draws on anti-trafficking discourses to propose measures aimed at the securitization of borders:

> When the Tamil ship showed up [and the concern was] like "we have got to make sure that there is no human trafficking and smuggling, and we must create a new bill on smuggling and trafficking." Really? One is a crime against the state and the other is a crime against the individual. So is this one piece of legislation really going to cover them both and are we not criminalizing them under the same umbrella anyways? … So it's almost like the tag on now and it's because it gets the human rights perspective, but what they are actually dealing with is national security and border integrity.

This excerpt also points to the ways in which anti-trafficking discourses are relied upon to justify varying political agendas, especially when conflated with border securitization. It also points to the role of non-government interveners in interpreting the appropriate distinction between migrant smuggling and human trafficking. As can be seen, however, such interpretations reinforce those of the state by creating neatly bound categories: smuggling involves perpetrators against the state and trafficking impacts individual victims. Both of these designations elide the structural conditions in which such movements are produced and continued powers of Bourgeois citizen subjects in controlling the movements of racialized migrants. On the one hand, anti-trafficking discourses were drawn upon to support claims of the need for more restrictive immigration policies. On the other hand, given the complex relationship between human trafficking and migrant smuggling, some frontline workers challenged the proposed policies, which they believed risked creating more insecurity for trafficked persons by criminalizing all smuggled migrants, particularly in instances where smuggled migrants become trafficked persons. As this former law enforcement representative discusses,

> So those who are not here lawfully in Canada or any other country contrary to that nation's immigration law, they become the immigrant other and there is a moral panic that exists that if someone is an illegal immigrant, then they must pose a threat to society and then they have to be dealt with in the same manner that we deal with other law violators. We use the criminal justice model to address what is really a human tragedy as long as we don't distinguish between the victims and the smugglers, because technically everybody is in violation of the law.

By reinforcing divisions between "victim" and "illegal," the excerpt suggests simplistic enforcement approaches that reinforce state boundaries to exclude certain types of migrants on the basis of perceived threat. Significantly, this type of concern about restricting migration and criminalization was not present in enforcement or service provider anti-trafficking discourses relating to sex industries. On the one hand, this highlights the insecurity created by restrictive immigration controls that broadly criminalize migrant experiences by failing to recognize the nuances of *why* a migrant might be in violation of the law and the structural and material conditions in which migrants come into contact with the settler colonial state and enforcement-based boundary controls. On the other hand, the notion that clear distinctions can be drawn between victims and smugglers is equally problematic. In an attempt to challenge images of an "ideal victim" by suggesting persons victimized by human trafficking might appear to border security officials as an "illegal immigrant" or "threat to society," anti-trafficking advocacy reinforces the role of national securitization. The following excerpt from a frontline worker questions the detention practices outlined in the proposed legislation while reiterating the importance of border control response mechanisms:

> And with their new anti-smuggling legislations, parts of it are very good. You want to prosecute and you want to penalize the smugglers. But what a lot of people don't see is the other part of what the government isn't telling you about, how they are victimizing the victims. They can be detained for a minimum of a year without any type of judicial review … The whole process to have their hearing is long, could be five years or longer. With the Tamils, there is still a large number of men, women, and children who are still in detention.

From this frontline worker's perspective, the proposed legislation would create a context in which the government plays a role in revictimizing potential refugees, smuggled migrants, and trafficked persons; however, the representative elides the role of the state in producing such context for victimization while reinforcing the necessity of state intervention in criminalizing migrant smuggling.

In the context of a minority government, Bill C-49 was unable to withstand opposition. In particular, political opponents rejected the enhanced discretionary powers the bill would afford to the citizenship and immigration minister and argued the proposed legislation would create a two-tiered refugee system based on the means of arrival to the country. For example, in response to the bill, Justin Trudeau, who was then the official opposition critic for citizenship and immigration, argued the following:

> Bill C-49 is a terrible piece of legislation but a very effective announcement. It is effective because the government gets to talk about getting tough on vile human smugglers who criminally take advantage of extraordinarily vulnerable people fleeing persecution and oppression. It is always effective to be able to stand up and talk about defeating the evildoers while protecting the innocent and the just. The problem is that is all this is, talk. This legislation actually does very little to go after the evildoers, and far from protecting the vulnerable, actually goes after and punishes asylum seekers … We have good reason to be concerned about this bill. I – we – understand that the problem of human trafficking needs to be dealt with, but the Conservatives' approach lacks refinement, subtlety and respect for the Canadian Charter of Rights and Freedoms. They are classifying people not according to the dangers they face at home, but according to how they get to Canada. (Parliament of Canada 2010, October 28)

While the Opposition Critic is similarly conflating human trafficking and migrant smuggling in this excerpt, his reaction expresses the concern of Bill C-49's opponents, namely that the bill oversimplifies complex migratory movements into "black and white" or "evildoers versus innocent" categories. Despite his critique, the opposition critic similarly creates an ideal category of "evildoers," neglecting the reality that in a context of restrictive border controls, migrant smugglers, at times, offer a valuable service to would-be refugees and asylum claimants. Nonetheless, the standpoint that the bill risks criminalizing asylum seekers despite claiming to protect the rights of migrants is supported by the perceptions of frontline workers.

In this context, lack of political support prevented the bill from being adopted into legislation. However, on June 16, 2012, the proposed legislation was reintroduced as Bill C-4 and then subsumed under the omnibus Bill C-31, An Act to Amend the Immigration and Refugee Protection Act, the Balanced Refugee Reform Act, the Marine Transportation Security Act and the Department of Citizenship and Immigration Act or, for short, Protecting Canada's Immigration System Act (Parliament of Canada 2012). Although it is beyond the scope of this book to describe the numerous clauses outlined in the omnibus bill, it is important to note that Bill C-31 contained most of the provisions that were in Bill C-4.[26] Bill C-31 received Royal Assent on June 28, 2012.[27] Of note, there are no direct provisions in the legislation that address human trafficking; nonetheless, anti-trafficking discourses and a prominent case of human trafficking informed the discussions, leading to the adoption of the legislation.

Overlapping the discussions about the proposed restrictive measures, criminal charges were laid in Canada's largest human trafficking case to-date. On October 6, 2010, the RCMP laid nine charges of human trafficking and fraud following a ten-month investigation that was initiated through the self-reported experience of a Hungarian refugee claimant in Hamilton, Ontario (RCMP 2010) An additional nine charges associated with the case were laid on September 7, 2012. According to the RCMP, the trafficked individuals were all men and were recruited from Hungry to work with promises of "steady work, good pay and a better life" (RCMP 2010). However, upon arrival, the trafficked individuals had their documents withheld and were told to sleep on the basement floor with a number of other hired workers (Victim Impact Statement 2009; *Globe and Mail* 2012, April 2). Significantly, the trafficked men were "coached to file false Refugee Claims as well as social assistance," benefits that would eventually be appropriated by the traffickers (RCMP 2010). Based on this, anti-trafficking discourses suggested cases like this one could be prevented through immigration reforms, such as those proposed by Bill C-31. However, as will be discussed, the legislation has also created insecurity for at least one of the trafficked individuals directly involved in the case.

The case provided a context for anti-trafficking discourses to inform debates over the right to claim asylum and the perceived threat of asylum seekers abusing the refugee system in Canada. According to the *National Post*, then Minister of Citizenship and Immigration, Jason

Kenney, said, "The government has tried but so far failed to stem the tide of Roma coming into Canada and abusing its refugee system...the flood of asylum-seekers is 'highly organized' and not at all spontane-ous. More worrisome is the evidence of human trafficking involved in these cases" (*National Post* 2012, April 22).[28]

By connecting the influx of Roma refugee claimants to the abuses of the refugee system (i.e. against state boundaries) and the "highly orga-nized" criminal network responsible for the Hamilton human traffick-ing case, Kenney effectively presents human trafficking as a racialized threat to national security and the integrity of the immigration system. Further, when sharing a news article detailing how the Hamilton case puts a "spotlight on the refugee system" (*Hamilton Spectator* 2012, January 12) by stating on Twitter: "Hungarian human trafficking rings exploiting Canada's asylum system" (@jkenney 2012, January 12). From this per-spective, it is the "asylum system" that is being exploited[29] and human trafficking is represented as a threat to the integrity of the system. Restrictive immigration policies and reinforcing the boundaries of the settler colonial state, in turn, are effectively framed as an appropriate response.

Criminalizing Trafficked Persons: Deporting the Problem

Before the implementation of the more restrictive border control mea-sures in Canada, frontline workers participating in this research – along-side law enforcement personnel and past and current border security officials – were already suggesting an overemphasis on the securitiza-tion of national boundaries at the expense of the rights of migrants and trafficked persons, and many feared the newly proposed, more restric-tive, laws would lead to further criminalization of migrant experiences. Because the Canada Border Services Agency (CBSA) is responsible for the monitoring, control, and enforcement of border security, partici-pants were especially critical of the role it played in ongoing criminal-ization by focusing efforts on the border control strategies of detention and deportation.

Far from increasing migrant rights and in spite of anti-trafficking advocacy, frontline service providers, law enforcement representatives, and government officials all suggest an unwillingness or incapacity on the part of the CBSA to recognize the experiences of trafficked persons and to consider the nuanced circumstances that can lead trafficked per-sons and other criminalized migrants to be in violation of immigration laws. For example, as one provincial government representative in British Columbia suggests, "The [CBSA] don't want to admit that we have got trafficking in this country. They see everybody as trying to break in illegally, cue jumping, and that kind of stuff, so they never have taken this issue seriously, they will tell you differently in Ottawa, but they just want to deport. So that's really unfortunate because they are huge gate keepers and could make a huge difference." Anti-trafficking, in this way, both critiques border control mechanisms while also advocating for border security to appropriate an anti-trafficking lens in order to become more effective "gatekeepers." While some, like the above excerpt suggests, believe the CBSA is unaware of, or unwilling to consider, the experiences of trafficked persons, others indicate that the CBSA is aware of human trafficking, but is led by an enforcement-based approach that prevents a more nuanced examination of the narratives of individuals in violation of immigration policies. In the words of one frontline service provider in Vancouver, "[The] CBSA is aware of trafficking, but they are probably less intent on prosecuting it because their approach is to detain, interview, deport. They don't even get to what is the story of this person." Further, in the words of a law enforcement official, such detailed investigations are necessary for accurate identification of human trafficking at the border: "The problem is what looks like one thing isn't always what it is, so sometimes things look like trafficking and the turn out not to be. Sometimes they aren't trafficking, but they start to turn out to be or there are some elements of trafficking. So it kind of goes both ways." In this way, using enforcement approaches that have the capacity to examine the complexity of migrant experiences is seen as necessary to balance the conflict between national security and the rights of migrants. As a national law enforcement officer further suggests, "If you have the staff to enforce it, you can be a little bit more facilitative on the entry." Although such approaches could potentially benefit the ability of individual enforcement officials to identify and perhaps protect the rights of trafficked individuals, it also presumes state neutrality and state benevolence in the protection of migrant rights. As the above excerpts suggest, though, state interest in Canada is securely rooted in national security and the maintenance of existing settler colonial boundaries. In turn, anti-trafficking discourses provide an additional mechanism of securitizing relations between *us* and *them* and naturalizing nationalist conceptions of Canadianness while ignoring the ongoing context of settler colonial domination.

In this context, former and current law enforcement personnel involved in border security acknowledge that the CBSA emphasizes exclusionary practices to the extent that border securitization is creating more insecurity for trafficked persons. As the following excerpt from a former law enforcement official suggests, border security is prioritized above the rights of trafficked persons, in particular, and migrant rights, in general:

> We would look at them as being in violation of the act, overstaying, mis-representing the purpose of why they are here, then take them into cus-tody and proceed with removal processes. Then we would physically deport them back to their country of origin. I have never received, in the 14 years that I was with the CBSA, I never received any formal training on what constituted human trafficking ... and I think what happens with law enforcement officers is that we go look at the individual, more so look at the person who is in violation of the act, we don't look at the nuances of why they are in violation of the act. Technically, yes they are in violation of the act, but why are they in violation of the act? ... Our resources, our training, our ability to conduct investigations was limited, we just didn't have enough investigators. We didn't have enough training, didn't have enough education of what to look for. Unfortunately, these people really fell through the crack. I know personally for myself, I am responsible for removing dozens upon dozens of people that were victims of trafficking and we dealt with them as immigration violators and removed them.

Of note, the official is only discussing cases that narrowly fit within a trafficking framework, which has further implications for the criminal-ization of individuals that fall outside such victim labels. According to a law enforcement representative, training and awareness have improved among frontline border security officials; however, the emphasis on enforcement approaches above migrant rights persists: "Do you send people home? Are they victims? Or are they breaking the law? And I don't know if [the CBSA] has found a happy balance yet. They are aware of the issue [of human trafficking], but how they handle it hasn't progressed. Perhaps it leans more on the [enforcement] side of the bal-ance ... but some [officers] are really good."

Again, state benevolence towards migrants is assumed and anti-trafficking is interpreted as a reason for reinforcing the capacity of border security agents of investigation. Similar to evaluations of indi-vidual officers investigating missing and murdered Indigenous women in Vancouver, the quote highlights that some border security officers aim to adopt a more nuanced approach to the complex experiences of migrants, but the structural conditions of exclusion persist and the adoption of more restrictive policies in Canada has created greater emphasis on the criminalization and discipline of increasingly illegalized migrants.

There are far too many examples of migrant women and individuals working in sex industries experiencing criminalization and deportation as a result of anti-trafficking responses.[30] However, the following example demonstrates how restrictive measures that are reinforced through anti-trafficking intervention violate the rights of migrants even in clear-cut instances that meet the criminal definitions of trafficking in persons. As a particularly stark example, following the adoption of the more restrictive measures discussed in the previous section, such constraints led to the deportation of a trafficked person's family, despite concerns of significant risk posed by the trafficking network in the family's country of origin. As the following narrative will exemplify, notions of perceived risk are unidirectional. In other words, such notions are employed to restrict migration into Canada, yet are not similarly adopted when removal orders are concerned.

Tibor Baranyai was a key witness in the Hamilton human trafficking case. The case was in direct alignment with the prototypical representations of human trafficking that emphasize transnational crime activities. It involved a large-scale organized crime operation, including widespread criminal and fraud schemes, as well as the use of significant threats and violence in efforts of coercion. Moreover, compared with other identified cases of trafficking, the willingness of the trafficked individuals to cooperate with police and the availability of physical evidence provided exceptional support to proceed with criminal charges and, ultimately, criminal convictions under the anti-trafficking legislation of the Criminal Code.

Anti-trafficking discourses cited the experience of the Hungarian labourers, including Mr. Baranyai, as justification for the adoption of more restrictive immigration policies; yet, the adoption of these polices led to the deportation of Mr. Baranyai's family, despite fears they would be targeted for reprisals. According to a victim impact statement, at least one of the families of an individual victimized by the case had previously been subjected to threats and intimidation by the network affiliated with the traffickers:

My family has been threatened many times in Hungary. They promised them money if they tell them where I was. My family suffered a lot because of it. I have so much guilt because of what they did to my family, and because of what happened to my family back home. [They] visited my family home in Hungary many times, they surrounded my family and they intimidated them so they would tell them where I was. My parents' wouldn't allow my siblings to go to school because they were afraid for their safety. My father couldn't fall asleep because he was afraid that [they] will break-in in the middle of the night, and that something serious will happen to my family members. Every night he tried to sleep with a huge piece of metal next to his bed, for protection, in case someone do break in … If for some reason me and my family have to go back to Hungary one day I am sure that we are going to be harmed seriously, in short period of time." (Victim Impact Statement 2009)

Despite reasonable fears of family members becoming targets for reprisals, Mr. Baranyai's wife and stepdaughter were deported. Before the passing of Bill C-31, individuals in Canada who had been issued a pre-removal order would rarely be removed from Canada without being given the opportunity to receive a pre-removal risk assessment (PRRA).[31] However, as of July 1, 2012, failed refugee claimants have a one-year waiting period before being eligible for a PRRA[32] and are likely to be deported from Canada within that year, making the PRRA effectively unavailable to refugee claimants that have received a negative decision (CIC 2012c). Because Mr. Baranyai's wife and stepdaughter had been issued a failed refugee claim before the marriage, there remained limited legal options for considering the evolving narrative of the claimants. Thus, despite the changing circumstances and potential risk created for the family of this trafficked individual, they were deported back to Hungary. This occurred in spite of law enforcement officers suggesting that such risk assessments are an important part of the investigative procedure, particularly in cases involving human trafficking. For example, as one law enforcement representative suggests, "Navigating that tricky line between the threat to society and the victim comes down to taking the time to examine what it is that led this person to be in the system … You would need to have a team within the federal government that does risk assessment for these people." Here again, enhanced border security capacity is interpreted as the means of navigating "threats" versus "victims." Nonetheless, in the absence of a risk assessment and a recognition of the potential danger faced by the family members of a key witness in this trafficking case, the family was deported, which, according to Mr. Baranyai meant he was victimized not only by the traffickers, but also by the criminal justice system in Canada: "I want to say I feel used. The traffickers used me for my labour, Canada used me as a witness to get a prosecution. But both Canada and the traffickers would deny me the basic thing I need as a human – to be loved, to love, and be supported by a family that I can see and touch. You would deny those I love safety" (*Globe and Mail* 2012, October 18).

The PRRA clause offers one example of how the new restrictive measures under Bill C-31 has created more insecurity, but such enforcement driven approaches to reinforce national boundaries pre-dated the arrival of Bill C-31. Nonetheless, as the above cases delineates, federal anti-trafficking policies have encouraged a more restrictive border securitization approach that prioritizes state autonomy at the expense of migrants facing heightened grounds for exclusion and deportation.

By reinforcing national boundaries and emphasizing exclusion-based policies, anti-trafficking efforts become a mechanism of crime control and further border securitization. As a result, a number of frontline service providers conclude that policies claiming to prevent or respond to human trafficking are creating more insecurity for trafficked persons: "I think the main concern tends to be that these laws were not written with the victim at the core. The purpose is to address the crime. It's crime oriented, it's to stop trafficking. It's not to provide a remedy to those who have been trafficked and are in a difficult situation. And I don't know if that's going to change anytime soon" (frontline worker, international organization). By adopting anti-trafficking discourses, the state strengthens perceptions of its benevolence towards victims, yet erases the constructed purpose of such laws that disproportionately act against racialized persons. In turn, tough on crime policies of securitization further create significant challenges for some temporary migrant workers in Canada who, in a context of restrictive policies and precarious immigration status, endure exploitative practices, rather than risk job loss or deportation, which can accompany reporting abusive experiences.

Constructed Insecurity

Although Canadian anti-trafficking discourses claim to protect "at risk" migrants and vulnerable individuals from possible trafficking experiences, restrictive immigration policies and enforcement-based measures have created other forms of insecurities for trafficked persons and other individuals migrating in a globalizing workforce. As this chapter documents, even the prototypical case of labour trafficking in Canada that lent support to the adoption of more restrictive immigration policies was not exempt from the negative effects of the policies, namely the deportation of one trafficked person's family. Thus, immigration controls have led to criminalization and deportation in specific trafficking cases; at the same time, broader experiences of exploitation, criminalization, and deportation affect low-skill migrants. In a context of global structural inequality and ongoing settler colonial nation-building, the TFW program continues to supply labour for a low-skilled, racialized service economy without providing adequate access to rights and mobility for individuals working in these sectors. While targeted experiences of abuse have occurred in these sectors, anti-trafficking discourses have emphasized the exclusion of "vulnerable" migrant women deemed potentially "at risk", omitting broader consideration of the structural conditions of insecurity legislated under low-skilled migrant worker programs in Canada.

In turn, migrant workers and rights advocates mobilize for inclusion in citizenship rights as a means of addressing the criminalized status imposed upon them by the state. Yet, as part of such politics of inclusion, their experiences are adopted by the nation-building project as a mechanism to further naturalize the dominance of the settler colonial nation-state through Canadian conceptions of multiculturalism and inclusiveness. In this inclusion the ongoing deflection of Indigenous sovereignties resurfaces. This is not to undermine migrant efforts to attain safety and security free from precarious conditions, but to point to the challenge of transformative anticolonial relations in a context of ongoing settler colonial domination and the way anti-trafficking elides potential solidarity movements of the perceived "contaminants" of national identity and the continuation of the white, settler colonial nation-building project.

Conclusion

The considerable attention afforded to human trafficking and anti-trafficking responses in Canada shows no signs of decline. Since the inception of this project, new national and international policies, response models, networks, and advocacy groups have emerged. In continuity with white slavery discourses and their role in the nation-building project of naturalized colonialism in Canada, anti-trafficking discourses frame a number of contested policy agendas that have created more insecurity for trafficked persons alongside individuals working in sex industries, low-skill migrant workers, refugees, asylum claimants, and Indigenous communities and nations. Beyond merely demonstrating the appropriation of rights-based discourses for alternate agendas, contextualizing Canadian anti-trafficking initiatives within ongoing settler colonialism troubles the role of anti-trafficking in Canada and reveals the reproduction of the national, racial, and gender priorities of the nation-state through rights-based mobilizing and criminal justice interventions. This points to the restricted possibilities for transformative change involving settler societies characterized by ongoing structural and material domination. As detailed, anti-trafficking forms a site that positions low skilled migrant workers, Indigenous communities, sex workers, and gendered and racialized bodies in ways that reproduce state-based claims to sovereignty and naturalize mechanism of securitizing state boundaries. In doing so, anti-trafficking works to produce and maintain the domestication of Indigenous people and the consolidation of national policies and citizen-subjects against migrant workers and racialized "others."

National identity in Canada is premised on multicultural and humanitarian ideals of inclusion, which render invisible settler colonial structures of national, racial, and gender domination and legitimize settler interventions that continue to reproduce the systems and structures settlers claim, and often aim, to be addressing through rights-based mobilization.[1] As Dhamoon (2015: 30) identifies, in the context of settler colonialism, we are all "systemically (even if unintentionally) operating within, across, and through a matrix of interrelated forms and degrees of penalty and privilege." In this, anti-trafficking efforts, alongside other rights-based and anti-violence interventions, remain unreflective of the spaces of privilege they occupy within a persistent "matrix of domination" (Collins 2000). In particular, efforts are discursively conceived as mechanisms of inclusion, such as through the warranting of temporary status or as domestic efforts to address the disregarded gendered and racialized legacies of colonization in Canada.

In doing so, such efforts discount the ongoing conditions of violence upon which Canadian society is built, including the dispossession of gendered and racialized bodies that reinforce structural and material forms of deprivation. In the words of Arvin, Tuck, and Morrill (2013: 12), settler colonialism "cannot be reduced to, as many nationalist ideologies would have it, the merely unfortunate birth pangs of its establishment that remain in the distant past; settler colonialism and patriarchy are structures, not events" (see Wolfe 1999). Anti-trafficking discourses contributed to the establishment of settler colonial structures and anti-trafficking interventions appear to continue to reproduce settler colonial relations of dispossession. Far from addressing structural and material conditions of colonial gender violence, anti-trafficking in Canada has too often served to naturalize and reinforce the persistent structure of settler colonialism, which is part of a long history of exploitation against Indigenous, racialized, gendered, and illegalized bodies that are constructed as both "at risk" (vulnerable) within the nation-state and "risky" (threatening) to the nation-state.[2] Although anticolonial resistance continues from multiple spheres of struggle, such mobilization remains in opposition to settler rights-based mobilizing. Meanwhile, the possibility of reciprocal relations, respect for Indigenous sovereignties, and the self-determination and autonomy of Indigenous, migrant, and sex working communities remain untenable within settler colonial nation-states.

Definitions of human trafficking espoused in international agreements point directly to the obscured foundations of the Canadian nation-state. Canada, alongside other settler colonial nations, was premised on forced movement, coerced labour, fraudulent dislocation, sexualized violence, and varying forms of abuses of power and exploitation legislated through the Indian Act, the Immigration and Refugee Protection Act (IRPA), and Canadian criminal law. Early legislative frameworks reinforced these goals, including anti-trafficking legislations promoted by purity campaigns to rid the emerging national identity of "contaminates" to the burgeoning national identity: the foreigner, the prostitute, and the Indigenous woman. Thus, interventions designed to eradicate the "Indian problem" and assimilate the foreigner – especially the *problem* Indigenous and migrant women posed for establishing patriarchal, white-supremacist, capitalist dominion. As Ikebuchi (2015: 31) shows, settlement "was about creating and maintaining a hierarchy of race that solidified white settlers' rights to the land." In this way, control of Indigenous lands is naturalized alongside Canadian state sovereignty and securitization. In turn, ongoing mobilization and solidarities among Indigenous, migrant, and sex worker communities are disrupted by politicized interventions and state mechanisms of control.

The differential employment of discourses of domestic and international anti-trafficking reveals how colonial constructions operate in a context in which "different colonialism[s], arrivals, and displacements" interact (Byrd 2011: 67). In this context, rights based mobilization in the area of migrant worker rights have the potential to both reproduce structural inequalities by naturalizing the sovereignty of the settler colonial state while also experiencing the ongoing gendered and racialized effects of restrictive immigration policies. As Suchland (2015: 9) identifies, "when sex trafficking became an example of violence against women, it lost political connection to antiracist, anticolonial, and critical development perspectives that saw historical and racial formations and neoimperialism as key to understanding exploitation and violence." In this, anti-trafficking discourses function to deny citizenship and restrict and control movement in a way that reinforces notions of settler sovereignty and posits migrant women as "at-risk" and "risky foreigners," while simultaneously depicting Indigenous women as domestic subjects and sex workers as problems, both to be controlled, disciplined, and silenced.

In this context, anti-trafficking discourses have been employed to restrict the right to free movement of women across borders by drawing on discourses of *potential* exploitation and the *possibility* of trafficking. Here, border securitization is reinforced, as policies justified by anti-trafficking discourses have granted authority to immigration officials to pre-emptively restrict the movements of women and girls into Canada.

Such restrictions culminated in the dismantling of the exotic dancer visa program, granting power to immigration officials to invalidate existing visas to exotic dancers. In doing so, the policy specifically disciplines women migrating in sex industries for their "risky" (i.e., at risk) behaviour.[3] Similarly, the National Action Plan to Combat Human Trafficking (NAPCHT) represents persons *at risk* of human trafficking to include the voluntary movements of women and girls. Thus, interpreted alongside the NAPCHT, the dismantling of the exotic dancer visa program is seen as part of a broader agenda to discipline and constrain the cross-border migration of women in the context of unequal gendered labour markets that depend on the remittances provided by such migrations.

By redefining human trafficking under the auspices of transnational criminal activity, the international framework for responding to human trafficking emphasizes border control and securitization. Framing human trafficking as a violation of human rights that involves a threat to national security and existing systems of immigration reinforces dichotomous categories of "deserving victim" and "complicit criminal." As O'Connell Davidson (2010: 245) traces, "In place of efforts to build political alliances between different groups of migrants, as well as between migrants and non-migrants who share a common interest in transforming existing social and political relations, 'trafficking as modern slavery' discourse inspires and legitimates efforts that divide a small number of 'deserving victims' from the masses that remain 'undeserving' of rights and freedoms."

Similarly, Canadian anti-trafficking discourses reinforce the sovereignty (hegemony) of the nation-state to protect the rights of individuals identified as victims while pre-emptively restricting and/or criminalizing the experiences of migrants who fall outside the bounds of a legitimized "victim" narrative, including refugee claimants, asylum seekers, irregular migrants, and forced labourers or trafficked persons that deviate from constructed representations. Thus, protective measures continue to exacerbate insecurities for some trafficked persons and others affected by the immigration reforms. Meanwhile, by prioritizing the securitization of borders, anti-trafficking discourses premised on existing conceptions of settler colonial state sovereignty and citizenship reinforce a citizenship gap whereby the experiences of some trafficked persons migrating according to global patterns of mobility have fallen outside the very boundaries of protection established in their name.

At the same time, the narrow, yet highly sensational, construction of the wide-ranging problem of human trafficking has created an exclusionary framework that neglects wider-ranging experiences of structural inequality and associated forms of precarity and labour exploitation that occurs in the absence of legal and citizenship rights. As Suchland (2015: 17) rightly warns, "the immense attention to trafficking may turn out to be a perverse obsession in the midst of widespread exploitation." In such a context, temporary migrant workers in Canada have faced significant risk when reporting experiences of labour abuse and exploitation, including job loss and the associated inability to provide remittance support to families in home communities, loss of accommodation and possible homelessness, and potential criminalization and deportation. As a result, temporary migrant workers frequently endure exploitative working conditions or opt to leave their employers for better working conditions; however, in doing so, they lose any protective space carved out for them under the constraints of neatly bounded national identities. Similar to discourses surrounding sex trafficking in Canada and the erasure of space for sex workers, the emphasis on securitization has created another boundary of exclusion whereby the definition of trafficking limits conceptual space for the existence of widespread precarity experienced among migrants. In both instances, precarity is experienced and reinforced in conditions of labour as well as in relation to the law and heightened policing powers warranted to enforcement authorities.

As increasing numbers of migrants fall under the umbrella of economic refugees, and in conjunction with a growing dependence on low-skilled labour provided by migrant workers, anti-trafficking discourses are relied upon to shape restrictive immigration reforms. In response to the arrival of two migrant ships off the coast of British Columbia, the Canadian government justified criminalizing and detaining the passengers on board by drawing on anti-trafficking discourses alongside other panic-raising sentiments, such as references to terrorism, cue jumping, and other possible abuses of the existing system and threats to national security. By failing to place movements within the broader contributory context in which they occur – including international labour migration trends and the unequal limitations on flows of labour from countries of the Global South to the Global North, particularly to service the tertiary industries in Northern economies and to support families and economies in home communities through remittance payments – reactive anti-trafficking approaches prove incapable of accounting for the messy realities and complex motivations underpinning cross-border movements, which are unlikely to subside as migratory experiences continue to challenge conceptions of national boundaries. In turn, rights-based articulations are directed towards the reproduction of settler colonial sovereignty claims and corresponding forms of border construction and migrant regulation.

In spite of established critiques of the neocolonial role anti-trafficking has played in the lives of migrant workers, especially migrant sex workers,[4] the framework of domestic trafficking was nonetheless promoted in reaction to sensational depictions of international trafficking and the state's failure to include Indigenous women in anti-trafficking strategies. In this way, the inclusion of Indigenous women in dominant anti-trafficking agendas alongside the prioritization of "risky" migrants occurs within a context of nationalist projects that continue to construct Indigenous, racialized, and gendered bodies as *problems* to be solved, thereby reproducing assimilation and domestication efforts evident in colonial civilizing missions. Drawing on connections between bodies constructed as vulnerable, anti-trafficking elides this construction of vulnerability and the connection between settler colonialism, racial and gendered oppressions, and anti-immigrant and anti-sex work sentiments. In this, we see the framing of "Indigenous nations as dysfunctional people" requiring intervention, rather than fostering decolonial solidarities and supports (Million 2013, as discussed in The 18 Year Plan to End Global Oppression 2014). Such missions constructed the legislative context of dispossession and criminalization that continue to disproportionately incarcerate Indigenous bodies and remove Indigenous children from their families and communities as well as the corresponding insecurities, criminalizations, and deportations affecting migrant worker communities.

Moreover, in this context, discursive anti-trafficking representations of domestic trafficking have come to mean anti-sex work. Domestic trafficking is further conflated with Indigenous women and youth working in sex industries, an outlook that is employed to justify ongoing state-based and social service interventions and apprehensions at the expense of self-determination and decolonial praxis. Meanwhile, international anti-trafficking strategies targeting sex industries critique the role of the state in enabling exploitation as a justification for restricting the migratory movements of "risky" women. However, criminal justice and transnational crime-based initiatives further reinforce the securitization of national boundaries and settler colonial state sovereignty. In turn, other industries, including sectors with documented trafficking cases, have escaped the settler colonial gaze. In this, precarious status and other potentially exploitative conditions of migrant labour reproduce capitalist labour production in areas that are perceived to benefit Canada's position in the global market. As Tuck and Yang (2012) identify, "dispossessed people are brought onto seized Indigenous land through other colonial projects." The state is constructed as a "savior," rescuing Indigenous women from colonial legacies by including Indigenous women in rights-based anti-trafficking discourses and interventions while also pre-emptively restricting "risky" migrants "for their own protection." Yet, the state is also constructed as an "oppressor" in anti-trafficking discourses that conflate sex work and sex trafficking, particularly in facilitating "risky" entry into Canada. In both anti-trafficking constructions – state as "saviour" and "oppressor" – the role of the settler colonial state and associated settler interventions are reinforced and the structural conditions of trafficking continue.

In this context, contested spaces of Indigenous feminist thought differentially aim to address colonial legacies while negotiating ongoing conditions of settler colonial gender violence. Thus, abolitionists draw on discourses of deception, coercion, and manipulation that undermine the agency of women working in sex industries who fail to conform to dominant anti-trafficking narratives (including Indigenous women who claim a space of agency in sex work). On the other hand, some sex worker rights advocates have similarly drawn on discourses of manipulation and deception to discount the experiences of Indigenous women who align with abolitionists to address the disproportionate violence experienced by Indigenous women based on intersections of race, class, and gender and to reclaim positions of autonomy and power held before colonization and the imposition of European forms of patriarchy. In this, settler feminists discount Indigenous women's experiences by ignoring broader processes of colonization when advocating for the downfall of Western cultural systems of patriarchy: "What you call patriarchy, I call one aspect of colonization" (Lucashenko 1994: 22). Yet, Indigenous feminism remains contested and efforts to address colonial legacies by reproducing the structures of settler colonialism have been critiqued for their role in reinforcing ongoing methods of state intervention, especially the criminalization of women in sex industries or the promotion of legislative responses that create more insecurity for sex workers. In turn, such criminalization works counter to the aims of both sex worker rights and abolitionist advocates by perpetuating ongoing cycles of violence against women and reproducing structural forms of violence and inequality.

Alongside contested discussions of human trafficking and the glaring omission of the complexity of experiences discursively represented by varying conceptions of trafficking, equally destructive are hegemonic discourses that elevate a singular "victim" narrative. As we have seen, a dominant discourse of sexualized violence underpinning trafficking representations in Winnipeg in the absence, and even suppression, of diverse voices and experiences has created more insecurity for individuals who do not fit the image of such idealized "victims." In particular, women were subjected to disciplining and silencing when their experiences deviated from the dominant discourse adopted by the Government of Manitoba. In some cases, even when women did reflected the image of the ideal "victim" of trafficking in the province, their experiences were monopolized by an awareness-raising system that had little regard for providing adequate supports or resources to women caught in a self-reinforcing circuit of awareness. By disciplining or screening experiential narratives, the very voices that should be the central focus of anti-trafficking initiatives – those of sex workers, migrant workers, and Indigenous, anticolonial women – come to comprise little more than a singular, dominant discourse that reinforces the prevailing structures of power, including funding mandates and response models that depend on melodramatic victim narratives to reproduce and justify awareness-raising mandates.

Anti-Trafficking: A Way Forward?

For conceptions of human trafficking to have any transformative ability, they must first take up "critical reflection and a commitment toward structural change." This necessitates thoughtful examination of the ongoing logics of colonialism and the gendered and racialized imposition of the nation-state. In this, the usefulness of the trafficking construct is restricted so long as it is not employed to examine the role of the state-building practices of force, fraud, and coercion shaping Canadian relations with Indigenous people and the disciplinary boundary-making strategies affecting the lives of migrants seeking to enter Canada. In this, I remain unconvinced the trafficking framework, as currently constructed, provides a salvageable paradigm for moving forward. This is not to say that individuals victimized by human trafficking and other forms of exploitative practices have not received important, even essential, forms of assistance in response to their experiences from anti-trafficking responses. It is, however, necessary to situate the continued working of rights-based discourses and interventions, especially anti-trafficking, in the context of settler colonialism and to trouble the ways such discourse reproduce the national, racial, and sexual priorities of the settler colonial nation-state that privileges some at the expense of gendered and racialized "others." Given the ways anti-trafficking has been politicized and co-opted, the inability of associated discourse to address the root problems associated with the term, and the employment of anti-trafficking efforts in the reproduction of structural inequalities, there is little ability for anti-trafficking to address such inequalities. Yet, it is within this confined space that the alteration of rights-based discourses requires sustained engagement with transformative justice movements.

Cross-sector collaboration continues to be constructed as imperative to anti-trafficking intervention; however, in negotiating the power dynamics of such interventions, the lives and experiences of persons constructed as *objects* of intervention are hidden by the ongoing appropriation of settler colonial logic. In particular, nongovernment organizations (NGOs) are presented as the less powerful interloper in collaborative responses and must thereby negotiate on behalf of "vulnerable" subjects and provide a critique of the power brokers (i.e., the state representatives) while simultaneously reinforcing the imperative of state-based intervention. Such negotiations are informed by efforts to address the legacies of colonialism in Canada in a context of constraint wherein NGOs typically face their own financial restrictions, including limited human resources, making it difficult to maintain an equal footing in collaborations with government and law enforcement agencies. In this, the possibilities for reducing harms while also building transformative solidarities are restricted. Even more problematic are occasions when NGOs receive government funding that is attached to the mandates of the funding body.

For example, Action Coalition on Human Trafficking (ACT) Alberta receives funding from the Victim of Crimes Fund and, more recently, federal funds to help "women and girls" who are "victims of trafficking for sexual exploitation, or are at risk of becoming victims" (Status of Women Canada 2013). By adopting the mandate put forth by the state, ACT strategies, similar to British Colombia Office to Combat Trafficking in Persons (BCOCTIP), intend to adopt a depoliticized approach. But by restricting its ability to challenge the dominant anti-trafficking discourse and the wider systems that reproduce structural inequalities, such responses maintain the potential to reinforce dominant constructions of trafficking and are restricted in their ability to create transformative solidarities. Vancouver further reproduced interventionist strategies in spite of stark disillusionment of service providers following the criminalizing effects of anti-trafficking raids. Rather than take seriously the critiques of intervention strategies and seek partnerships with transformative justice actors, the BCOCTIP redirected attention towards domestic trafficking and migrant workers, further advancing sites of racialized and gendered policing. In turn, such government–nongovernment models of collaboration serve to reproduce the priorities of the nation-state by providing rights-based partnerships that soften the implementation of crime control measures. In doing so, these efforts also reproduce and necessitate such state-based strategies of intervention, often at the expense of the safety and security of individuals criminalized in or through the mechanism of intervention. Even though coordinating bodies like ACT and BCOCTIP work effectively to advocate for supports such as TRPs, this work continues in a context of widespread precarity that reproduces and legitimizes state controls. As seen in cases of low-skilled temporary migrant workers, connecting service provisions with enforcement approaches has significant implications for the criminalization of racialized migrant workers.

In the meantime, there remains a need to address the harms occurring from and within the nation-state. Abandoning the practices of the state altogether is also to abandon the lives of colonized persons and colonial resistance within state systems. As Arvin, Tuck, and Morrill (2013: 14) write, "This is not to deny that the pursuit of civil rights within the nation-states that claim authority over Indigenous peoples is important and often vitally necessary, but simply to encourage ideas of social change and social justice that do not *only* look to the models of governance and community that settler nation-states are founded on." Thus, there is work to be done to address the inequalities within the criminal justice system, the social intervention system, and the system of national boundary maintenance. In this, resistance requires mobilized change from within these systems without erasing the conditions in which such systems operate.

Anti-trafficking in Canada has maintained a focus on symptomatic violence: violence rooted in the foundational narrative of the country and that facilitated the production of nationalist settler identities of civility and humanitarianism. In doing so it sanitizes the messy realities of settler colonialism and its relationship to human trafficking and humanitarian impulses. Anti-trafficking discourses have become a powerful means to shape policies in broad and highly contentious areas, including anti–sex work policies and restrictive policies affecting asylum, temporary migrant labour, and economic immigration. In this way, human trafficking has become a key player in the "global agenda of high politics" and has led to the uncritical acceptance of policies justified by "moral panic" and "potential risk." Rooted in the broader project of development and the ongoing operation of settler colonialism that restricts certain forms of knowledge and power, both human rights abuses and humanitarian responses emerge in a context of structural inequality and inherit the problem of colonial logics and the corresponding misappropriations of social justice that stifle human dignity and limit the realization of social transformation. Yet just as dominant constructions limit consideration of alternate ways of organizing and achieving social change, sustained critical reflection provides a conceptual space to locate resistance and subvert cycles of exclusion. In these spaces the possibilities for social transformation reside.

And so, it is here that I hear my student's voices and other socially minded people asking, "what can we do?" It is perhaps not surprising that other critical approaches to the subject, like that of Julietta Hua, have raised the same question and their responses are similar to my own: there are no straightforward answers. While I use to feel anxious at not having an adequate response to this question, I have come to respect the inherent discomfort of decolonial processes. As Amber Dean (2015: 32) clearly demonstrates, definitive conclusions – "as though such finality were possible" – are not compatible with the aim of transformative change. Rather, this work, like Dean's, seeks to "contribute to the formation of an 'us' committed to transforming the present, now, into a present entirely otherwise than the one in which we find ourselves" – a present in which settler colonial gendered violence remains an ongoing, daily crisis. It is only through such discomfort that we find space to ask: "how am I implicated in the unjust social conditions and arrangements of ongoing settler colonialism" (Dean 2015: xxvii). As we individually and collectively wrestle with "how we are implicated," a useful starting point is to decentre the settler imperative of needing to *do something* by foregrounding the role of what the settler colonial state *has done* in forced movement, displacement, dislocation, and dispossession – in "trafficking" people – and what it continues *to do* in subjecting gendered and racialized bodies to ongoing colonial gender violence. From this space, the centering of ongoing resistances from Indigenous feminist, migrant, and anti-colonial organizing can occur and social transformations that change the material and structural conditions of precarity and violence might be altered.

From this perspective, anti-trafficking is recast as "anticolonial state violence," and contradictory notions of the "state as saviour" and "state as oppressor," both of which reinforce state restrictions and interventions, are abandoned to create space for the possibility of reciprocity. In turn, such a reflexive accounting of privileges and penalties negotiated within settler colonial contexts necessitates decentring the settler colonial state (and settler colonial state actors) and corresponding interventions. Decentring is about making space for the work already being done: the rebuilding of Indigenous sovereignties and self-determination alongside the dismantling of violent colonial structures. By grappling with our own position in settler colonial relations and foregrounding reciprocity and interrelatedness, we enact responsibility for land that is not terra nullius and responsibility in *relationships* of care with persons who are not humanitas nullius. In this space, where Indigenous, migrant, and sex worker communities are centred – rather than disciplined and erased – lies the potential for decolonial anti-trafficking and anti-violence measures and organized resistance to the ongoing imposition of settler colonial dominion in Canada.

List of Selected Government and Nongovernment Organizations Represented by Participants in One-on-One Interviews

National and International

Canadian Council of Refugees (CCR)
Citizenship and Immigration Canada (CIC)
Global Alliance Against Trafficking in Women (GAATW) Canada
United Nations High Commission for Refugees (UNHCR)

Alberta

Action Coalition on Human Trafficking (ACT) Alberta
Alberta Justice
Calgary Catholic Immigration Services
Calgary Communities Against Sexual Assault (CCASA)
Calgary Immigrant Women's Association (CIWA)
Calgary Police Services
Chrysalis Network
SHIFT Calgary
Street Level Consulting and Counseling
Distress Centre

British Columbia

Aboriginal Women's Action Network (AWAN)
British Colombia Coalition of Experiential Communities (BCCEC)
British Columbia Office to Combat Trafficking in Persons (BCOCTIP)
Covenant House
FIRST Decriminalize Sex Work Now!

MOSAIC
No One is Illegal
Providing Alternatives, Counseling and Education (PACE) Society
Resist Exploitation, Embrace Dignity (REED)
Salvation Army
Supporting Women's Alternatives Network (SWAN)
The Future Group
Vancouver Rape Relief
Vancouver Police Department

Manitoba

Assembly of Manitoba Chiefs
Child and Family Services
Ka Ni Kanichihk
Ma Mawi Wi Chi Itata Centre
Mount Carmel Clinic
9 Circles
Sage House
Sexual Exploitation Unit, Province of Manitoba
Street Connections
Transition, Education and Resources for Females (TERF)
Welcome Place
Winnipeg Police Service

Open-Ended Guide for One-on-One Interviews

Nongovernment Organization Employees

1 From your perspective, what are the experiences of trafficked persons?
2 How does your organization define human trafficking?
3 From your perspective, how does the general public understand the issue of human trafficking?
4 How does your organization address the experiences of trafficked persons?
5 From your perspective, what are the service provision needs of trafficked persons?
6 Are these needs being addressed by current anti-trafficking responses and policies?
7 What challenges have you faced in responding to the experiences of trafficked persons?
8 What successes have you had in addressing the issue of human trafficking?
9 Were trafficked persons consulted in designing your anti-trafficking programs?
10 How do you think Canadian anti-trafficking policies can better address the rights and experiences faced by trafficked persons?

Policymakers and Immigration and Law Enforcement Officials

1 How has the adoption of legal instruments, such as Section 279 of the Criminal Code and Section 118 of the Immigration and Refugee Protection Act, addressed or failed to address the issue of human trafficking in Canada?

2 How effective has the temporary resident permit (TRP) program been in addressing the experiences of trafficked women?

3 What are the strengths and limitations of the TRP program?

4 Have TRPs improved access to health care and basic social services for trafficked persons?

5 Do you think there is adequate cooperation at provincial and federal levels to address the issue of human trafficking in Canada?

6 From your perspective, what are the experiences of trafficked persons?

7 What service provision needs do trafficked individuals have?

8 Are Canadian policies effective in addressing the rights and experiences of trafficked persons?

9 Were you consulted in the development of a national strategy to address human trafficking?

10 What issues would you like to see included in a national strategy to address the issue of human trafficking in Canada?

Notes

Preface and Acknowledgments

1 Two of my great-grandparents originate from England (Yorkshire and Basingstoke) and two from Scotland (Crawfordjohn and Edinburgh).

Introduction

1 The Public Safety Canada (2012a) National Action Plan to Combat Human Trafficking includes just over $2 million for a dedicated enforcement team (RCMP and Canada Border Services Agency [CBSA]), $1.3 million for a human trafficking national coordination centre (RCMP), $1.6 million for regional coordination and awareness (RCMP), $445,000 for border service officer training and awareness (CBSA), $96,000 for an anti-crime capacity building program (Department of Foreign Affairs and International Trade). This can be compared with the $500,000 allocated to support victim services.

2 In addition to the listed means of trafficking, Hunt (2008: 2) further highlights that Indigenous people and their "sacred ceremonial regalia have been taken abroad to be put on display in museums and private collections."

3 For the purpose of this book, I do not distinguish between First Nations, Inuit, and Métis. Although I recognize there is no pan-Indigenous identity in Canada, the focus on representations in anti-trafficking discourses requires the use of broader terminology. Therefore, I use the term "Indigenous," which is typically used in international human rights law. However, when discussing state discourses, the term "Aboriginal" is also employed because this is the term documented in the 1982 constitutional amendments to include Inuit, Métis, and First Nations. Language is

selected for pragmatic reasons, but it should be noted that none of these labels are in Indigenous languages or reflect the identity of diverse Indigenous nations and communities. Rather, all of these terms are labels imposed in relation to settler colonial societies.

4 These remarks were made at the 2014 Annual Critical Race and Anticolonial Studies Conference at the University of Alberta in Edmonton.

5 Audra Simpson (2014b) similarly articulated an important discussion of the representations of Indigenous women through an analysis of Canadian discourses about Chief Theresa's Spence's hunger strike in and the inquiry into the gender of settler society. The talk was based on her current book project, *Savage States: Settler Governance in an Age of Sorrow.*

6 As anti-trafficking discourses are the subject of this critical analysis and such discourses are dominated by conversations about violence against women, the book prioritizes women in its analysis. However, this emphasis should be read within the broader structural context of heteropatriarchy that conceals multidimensional conceptions of gender and troubles gender binaries. In particular, erased almost entirely from anti-trafficking discourses are the experiences of Two-Spirit and other individuals who disrupt imposed colonial gender binaries. Despite discursive erasure, individuals facing gendered and racialized forms of oppression are directly affected by the implications of anti-trafficking.

7 The research assumes individuals involved in some form of anti-trafficking work are well-suited to reflect, consider, and evaluate current anti-trafficking initiatives. At the same time, the researcher adopts a critical lens to question how dominant – and oftentimes politicized – discourses are shaping anti-trafficking agendas. As will be discussed, individuals victimized by human trafficking were not specifically recruited for this project; however, some frontline workers involved in anti-trafficking work were previously victimized by trafficking and were invited to share their experiential knowledge. Other formerly trafficked persons were provided information about the research by a frontline worker and initiated contact to participate in the study. Given the limited number of trafficked persons represented in this study, these voices should not be interpreted as representative of trafficking experiences as a whole. Rather, they add richness to the data on anti-trafficking discourses and offer representations of trafficked persons in these discourses.

8 See Dean (2015) who provides an excellent example of upholding the aim of social transformation alongside sustained critique.

9 Adichie uses this quote to discuss the way her roommate imagines the continent of Africa through the lens of a single story. Africans, in this

imagining, are perceived as people "unable to speak for themselves and waiting to be saved by a kind white foreigner." The whiteness of anti-trafficking and its relationship with racialized (i.e., trafficked) persons is similarly important in anti-trafficking imaginings and in the analysis presented in this book.

10 Razack (2004) has also discussed the relevance of this quote in relation to nation-building in Canada, particularly in light of national perceptions of Canada being a peacekeeping country. Such perceptions are discussed in light of racism evident in the violence committed by peacekeepers in Somalia. Tucker and Walton (2012) similarly discuss the limits spectacle places on the story that can be told through their examination of nationalist arguments in relation to Abu Ghraib.

11 See Smith (2014).

12 This narrative was shared by Maria Campbell in response to Sara Ahmed's keynote lecture at the 14th Annual Critical Race and Anticolonial Studies Conference on October 18, 2014, University of Alberta and Athabasca University, Edmonton, Alberta.

13 See RCMP (2004, 2010).

14 Jeffrey (2005) provides an important exception.

15 Kaye, Winterdyk, and Quarterman (2014) provide a critique of anti-trafficking, yet their discussion is not rooted in structural forms of inequality and thereby reproduces recommendations for strengthening coordinated anti-trafficking interventions, albeit while arguing such interventions move beyond a criminal justice framework and take note of power relations involved in such coordinated models of response.

16 According to Mason (2002: 24), qualitative research is "characteristically exploratory, fluid and flexible, data-driven and context sensitive." By responding to the data throughout my analysis, I was able to react to key issues, findings, and puzzles that were raised during the data collection process. In doing so, I remained sensitive to my position as an academic researcher seeking to understand the complex experiences of trafficked persons and the complicated networks of power that underpin human trafficking and anti-trafficking responses.

17 From September 2010 until January 2014, news media was collected using Google Alerts for the search term "human trafficking Canada" and "trafficking in persons Canada."

18 Throughout this book, the term "frontline worker" is understood to mean individuals working in anti-trafficking related employment who have had, or potentially could have, direct contact with trafficked persons. This includes agencies that focus on issues of poverty, the needs of immigrants

and refugees, advocacy and social rights, women's rights, Indigenous rights, and services for individuals victimized by various types of abuse and violence.

19 The participants in this study represent a variety of perspectives from the counter-trafficking field, such as harm reduction and intervention strategies as well as criminal justice response (e.g., border security, immigration and passport sectors, labour standards, city police involved in trafficking cases, legal representatives). Because their participation was based on their positions in institutions of employment, participants from a variety of agencies were contacted directly, provided information about the study, and requested to contact the researcher if they would like to participate. They were asked questions based on their occupational knowledge. All participants were 18 years of age or older and there was no remuneration or compensation offered to those who participated in the study. Consequently, potential participants did not feel coerced or obligated to participate. In order to maintain the confidentiality of participants in a highly contested and politicized area, the particular occupational positions held by participants have been omitted as well as identifying demographic characteristics; however, with the consent of participants, the names of the organizations represented have been included in certain instances and the general type of organizations represented are discussed to provide context to the interview responses.

20 All the interviews were conducted in English and ranged from thirty minutes to two hours in duration, but the majority of the interviews were approximately an hour in length. In all but a couple instances, the interviews were audio recorded, transcribed verbatim, then analysed. A couple participants did not consent to having the interview audio-recorded. In these instances, detailed notes were taken and analysed.

21 Given the potentially traumatic nature of their experiences and related ethical concerns of protecting the anonymity of a limited population, trafficked persons were not directly contacted to participate in this project. Rather, I provided information about the study to frontline workers to pass on to individuals formerly victimized by human trafficking. Trafficked individuals were invited to participate provided they contacted the researcher.

22 As frontline workers assisted in my contact with trafficked persons, those represented have all had some form of engagement with anti-trafficking services.

23 Document analysis also provided useful information for contextualizing the responses of focus group and interview respondents, such as the

mandates of the organizations that the participants represent, their target populations, and mission statements.

24 Two group interviews were held in Vancouver; each engaged with two participants. One focus group was held in Calgary and engaged with five participants. One focus group, engaging four participants, and one group interview with two participants were held in Winnipeg.

25 The discussion groups focused on four key considerations: 1) introducing the project to the group participants and requesting their opinion on the study's main questions and design; 2) uncovering and exploring participants' perceptions of the limitations of existing anti-trafficking policies; 3) observing collective forms of meaning-making; and 4) generating a significant body of information that informed the questions asked during the face-to-face interviews.

26 The primary data informing this book were collected from Winnipeg, Calgary, and Vancouver. In light of this, the empirical findings focus on Western Canada; however, the document and policy analysis examined Canadian discourses as a whole and thereby inform a broader national discussion. The research also includes representatives involved in national and international agencies, such as the RCMP, Citizenship and Immigration Canada, the United Nations, etc.

27 Content-analysis approaches are not homogenous. Used by both qualitative and quantitative researchers, content analysis can assess the repetition of particular words or actions, known as manifest content (e.g., assessing the frequency of specific recurring words, such as consent, victims, etc.) (Babbie and Benaquisto 2002). Another form of content analysis examines the underlying meaning of communications, known as latent content (e.g. assessing the overarching occurrence of themes, such as trafficked persons being portrayed in terms of their victimization, innocence, or resilience). An examination of recurrent and/or significant themes remains sensitive to both manifest and latent content. However, rather than presupposing specific concepts or categories, this research approaches the data with an open, qualitative lens to uncover the thoughts, ideas, and meanings of the research participants (Strauss and Corbin 1998). Because this project is concerned with depth and nuance, which are necessary to understand a diverse range of experiences, such an approach uncovers how participants represent human trafficking and anti-trafficking initiatives and policies.

28 See Strauss and Corbin (1998).

29 Stenvoll's (2002) critical discourse analysis of national newspaper reports on cross-border prostitution in northern Norway provides a useful

example of how to apply the ideas of critical discourse analysis in a related field of inquiry.

1 The Production of International and Domestic Anti-trafficking in Settler-Colonial Canada

1 As will be discussed in more depth, the concept of human trafficking entered international discourse in the early twentieth century alongside concerns over white slavery. Although such discussions waned in the post–Second World War era, they resurfaced following the Vietnam War. As Jeffrey (2005) points out, the Canadian government entered this later iteration of trafficking discussions in the mid-1990s, nearly a decade after such debates had resurfaced in a prominent way in international policy debates. Similarly, anti-trafficking responses, including responses aimed at mitigating the effects of anti-trafficking on migration emerged at this time. Global Alliance Against Traffic in Women (GAATW)–Canada, for instance, was formed in 1996; "its aim is not to stop the migration of women, but to safeguard and promote the human rights of women who migrate and who are trafficked" (GAATW n.d.).

2 For other critical examinations of stereotypical portrayals of human trafficking, see Jeffrey (2005), Agustín (2007), and Kempadoo, Sanghera, and Pattanaik (2012).

3 See Barry (1995); Leidholdt (2003); Farley (2004); Raymond (2005); and Jeffreys (2008).

4 *Exploitation* remains a contested term, and language in general remains problematic in trafficking studies. The terms sexual exploitation and sex trafficking have been conflated with sex work and prostitution in anti-trafficking literature (see, for example, Barry 1984, 1995; Raymond 2005). This study uses the phrase "sex trafficking" in recognition that sex industries represent one site where human trafficking can occur (Sanghera 2005). This aligns with the definition outlined in the UN Trafficking Protocol (to be discussed in Chapter 2), wherein exploitation includes the "exploitation of the prostitution of others or other forms of sexual exploitation." However, the term remains problematic and the use of the phrase "sexual exploitation" was criticized in the discussion leading to the protocol for being "a catch-all phrase with an abolitionist genealogy" (Doezema 2010: 162). In particular, the emphasis on sexual exploitation has been used to silence sex worker–rights movements and the space of agency carved out by sex workers to fully legitimize sexual labour. Although the issue of language clearly remains problematic, this research

recognizes that not all forms of sexual labour are exploitive; however, human trafficking, by nature, requires exploitation to occur. At the same time, the research problematizes the power dynamics underlying who has the right and power to define another as exploited.

5 As Weitzer (2007: 455) identifies, "there are no reliable statistics on the magnitude of trafficking."

6 For critical discussions of human trafficking centred on criminal justice responses, see Lepp (2002, 2003); Jeffrey (2005); Langevin (2007); Bernstein (2007); and Lee (2010).

7 See Pearson (2002); Chapkis (2003); Agustín (2007); Kempadoo (2005); Andrijasevic (2007); Weitzer (2007); and Merry (2011).

8 For Canadian discussions, see Lepp (2002, 2003); Jeffrey 2005; Generally, see Pearson 2002; Sharma 2003; Dottridge 2007; Dewey 2008; and Lee 2010

9 For example, Lepp (2002, 2003); Sharma (2003); Jeffrey (2005); Lee (2011)

10 For similar discussions, see Kapur (2003); Parrenas (2001); Sharma (2003); and Andrijasevic (2007).

11 See Kapur (2003); Lepp (2002, 2003); Agustín (2007); and Jeffrey (2005).

12 A significant body of Canadian research examines the labour conditions and labour rights movements of sex workers, for example, Van der Meulen, Durisin, and Love (2013); Parent et al. (2013); McCarthy, Benoit, and Jansson (2014); Benoit et al. (2014); Brock (2009); Jeffrey and MacDonald (2006); and Jeffrey and MacDonald (2007).

13 See Sharma (2003), Andrijasevic (2007), Doezema (2002), and Kempadoo (2005).

14 See also Sharma (2003); Kapur (2003); and Agustín (2007).

15 Farley et al. (1998: 419), for instance, concluded that prostitution is "inherently traumatizing." Such conclusions have undergone sustained critique. See Vanwesenbeeck (2001) and Weitzer (2005).

16 This is what anti-trafficking advocates disparagingly refer to as the "pro-prostitution lobby"; however, anti-trafficking discourses frequently conflate all perspectives that contest the inherent oppression of prostitution under this banner, including advocates of decriminalization.

17 See Vanwesenbeeck (1994, 2001); Weinberg, Shaver, and Williams (1999); Benoit and Shaver (2006); Brock (2009); McCarthy et al. (2012); Weitzer (2009, 2010, 2012); Benoit et al. (2014); and McCarthy, Benoit, and Jansson (2014).

18 Further critiques that contextualize sex work within the social, political, and economic framework in which it occurs include Jeffrey and MacDonald (2006) and McCarthy, Benoit, and Jansson (2014).

19 In the second half of the twentieth century, radical feminists and neo-abolitionists positioned "prostitution" as one of many forms of male

violence and oppression against women (e.g., Barry 1984, 1995; Leidholdt 2003).

20 For detailed reviews of the literature, see Vanwesenbeeck (2001); Weitzer (2012). For Canadian reviews from the standpoint of sex workers, community-based researchers, and sex work rights activists see Van der Meulen, Durisin, and Love (2013) and Parent et al. (2013).

21 See Bernstein (2007).

22 See Vosko (2010); Andrijasevic (2010); Kempadoo (2012); and LeBaron (2013).

23 The profits derived from trafficking in persons have been used to justify the immediacy of response. In particular, human trafficking was initially declared the "third most profitable business for organized crime" (United Nations Office on Drugs and Crime 2000), but has since been elevated to the second most profitable form of organized criminal activity in the world, alongside drug trafficking and arms dealing. Numerous sources attribute this latter claim to the US Department of Health and Human Services (Jordan and Burke 2011; United Nations High Commissioner for Refugees 2010); however, the claim is no longer available on the department's website. In spite of the uncertain validity of the estimate, the claim proliferates awareness-raising materials and associated "fact" sheets on human trafficking with no reference to its original source. For examples, see Global Ministries (2008); International Justice Mission (2010); and Office of Refugee Resettlement (2012).

24 For discussion of carceral feminism in relation to human trafficking, see Bernstein (2010).

25 See Aradau (2004) on the disciplining of women migrating into sex industries for their "risky" (i.e., at risk) behaviour and the marriage of discursive regimes of trafficked women as simultaneously a threat to the state and a victim invoking sympathy.

26 The Protocol to Prevent, Suppress and Punish Trafficking in Persons, especially Women and Children is one of two Palermo Protocols adopted under the Convention against Transnational Organized Crime. The other protocol is the Protocol against the Smuggling of Migrants by Land, Sea and Air. In 2000, both were adopted by the United Nations in Palermo, Italy.

27 Deer (2011) similarly identifies the role of the state as "trafficker" within the context of anti-trafficking definitions in the United States. On the politics of recognition and settler colonialism in Canada, see Coulthard (2014).

28 For examples of works from a variety of perspectives on trafficking in relation to Indigenous women and girls in Canada, see Oxman-Martinez,

Lacroix, and Hanley (2005); Farley, Lynne, and Cotton (2005); Sethi (2007); Standing Committee on the Status of Women (2007); Sikka (2009); Totten (2009); Hunt (2008), West Coast Legal Education and Action Fund (2009); Perrin (2010a); Tocher (2012); Totten (2010); and Boyer and Kampouris (2014).

29 See Sethi 2007; Sikka 2009; and Perrin 2010. For a discussion from an American context, see Deer (2011).

30 In 2010, Aboriginal women comprised one out of every three women in federal incarceration (Public Safety Canada 2012c). See also Perreault (2011).

31 See Sethi 2007 and Sikka 2009. Also note, the term *victim* remains contested in anti-trafficking studies and language in general is problematic in the trafficking literature. Because "victim" is the label adopted by the criminal justice system, I use the term when situating the discourse as part of the dominant criminal justice approach to trafficking in Canada. However, I recognize that the victim label has been used in anti-trafficking discourses to undermine the agency of individuals in a variety of areas, particularly sex trade industries where "victim status" is frequently rejected (Downe, 2006: 66; Soderlund, 2005).

32 As discussed in the preface, my experience working in anti-trafficking initiatives and social serving agencies means I am not a dispassionate observer of these responses. Thus, I also do not consider myself disconnected from the critiques depicted in this book.

33 See Arvin, Tuck, and Morrill (2013) on the ongoing social structure of settler colonialism.

34 In her discussion of First Nations' independence, the late Patricia Monture suggests the following: "The question ought to be: How do we achieve justice for Aboriginal Peoples domiciled in Canada? ... How can a process that capitalizes on our oppression be seen as a viable solution?" (Monture 1999: 17). In this way, Monture reminds us that self-determination remains irrelevant if it fails to account for state systems, where many Indigenous women currently reside in overrepresented and disproportionate numbers.

35 As Heron (2007: 92) suggests, "bourgeois" signifies race, class, gender, and space: Northern, white, middle-class, heteronormative male. White middle-class women, who are "simultaneously insiders and outsiders," are "discursively produced to aspire to the mythological bourgeois ideal/ norm" while "fitted to accept and perform a subordinate, feminized variation thereof."

36 It should be noted, this book focuses on analysing how trafficked persons are represented and the implications of discursively situating trafficked individuals as "international" versus "internal." Subaltern studies, however,

advance the work of Spivak to focus on the agency of subaltern voices and whether the subaltern, or Other, can self-represent given structural forms of domination. In other words, Spivak raised the question of representation and the right and ability of investigators to represent the experiences of an oppressed "other." This book does not provide a corrective to self-representation; rather, it traces discursive practices that foreground colonial legacies while hiding ongoing colonial occupations and colonial continuities.

37 The rise of the so-called Asian Tigers or newly industrializing countries (NICs) are frequently cited as an exception and, although these countries reveal that the global economic system is anything but static, they have not substantially altered global economic inequalities. The expansion of NICs undermined Third World resistance to the liberalization of international financial markets and structural adjustment programs (McMichael 2012). In the end, the debt crisis concentrated the power of international financial institutions (i.e., the World Bank and International Monetary Fund) to disproportionately influence development strategies in the Global South. The NICs were also affected by the debt crisis in 1997, a decade later than most of the Global South. It is also worth noting, the rise of NICs was not primarily driven by a neoliberal capitalist strategy; rather, NICs adopted a mixed economy that included forms of state management.

38 See McGrew (2000); Sassen (2002); McMichael (2012); Battacharyya (2005); Brysk and Shafir (2004); and Fortin et al. (2012).

39 Kothari (2005) problematizes conventional discussions of development history that identify 1945 as the "start date" of development. Instead she traces the relationship between colonialism and contemporary development studies. See also George (2003).

40 Jeffrey (2005), for example, provides a postcolonial examination of trafficking in relation migrant sex work and Canadian foreign policy. More broadly, Agustín (2007) provides a postcolonial critique of the "rescue industry" for disempowering and controlling cross-border migration, particularly by casting migrants who sell sex as "trafficked." See also Kempadoo (2007).

41 As Kothari (2001) argues, power may not be expressed solely (or even predominately) in terms of material inequality.

42 Although the concept of power, specifically political power, has been highly contested in the literature (e.g., Boulding 1989; Foucault 1980, 1982; Scott 2001; Lukes 2005; Morriss 2006), Béland (2010: 147) emphasizes the unequal distribution of "power resources" to conceptualize political power in liberal democracies as "the unequally distributed capacity to act together and affect the behaviour of others in order to shape political outcomes." In this way, political power is distinct from domination. For

Béland (2010: 147), domination refers to "the structural maintenance of unequal social and political relations that mainly serve the perceived interests of the rulers." Thus, while political power can lead to domination, the concepts are analytically distinct.

43 Anderson (2006) underscores that national identities delineate a social arrangement that demarcates boundaries between "us" and "them." See also Lamont and Molnár (2002).

44 See Anderson (2006) on the socially constructed or "imagined" nature of nations.

45 See Mies (1998) and Wade (2004).

46 See Lee (2011) and LeBaron (2013).

47 LGBTTQQIA refers to lesbian, gay, bisexual, transgender, transsexual, queer, questioning, intersex, and asexual.

48 See Razack (2002); Sharma (2006); and Thobani (2012).

49 Given the dominance of representations of women in anti-trafficking discourses, this book primarily focuses on representations of women; however, examinations of anti-trafficking as a particular site to reproduce settler colonial relations through binary gender constructions provides an important area for further critical research.

50 For example, Lepp (2002, 2003); Sharma (2003); Jeffrey (2005); Global Alliance Against Traffic in Women (2007); and Lee (2011).

51 For broader theoretical discussion of the construction of risk and "potential threats" see Beck (1992) and Adam, Beck, and van Loon (2000). For an alternate critical discussion see Béland (2008).

2 Settler Colonialism and the Construction of Anti-trafficking

1 See Kempadoo (2005); Gallagher (2010); Doezema (2010).

2 Sex workers–rights advocates argue against the use of the stigmatizing term *prostitution* in favour of *sex work*. In this book, both are used to maintain consistency with the opinions and/or standpoints being represented. Prostitution is used when discussing early twentieth-century portrayals, legislative frameworks that maintain the terminology, and abolitionist depictions, whereas sex work is used when discussing sex worker rights and sex industries in general. Throughout, I maintain the terminology used in original quotations.

3 See, for example, Connelly (1980); Guy (1991); and Corbin (1996).

4 For a related discussion see Doezema (2000); Bruckert and Parent (2002).

5 According to Kempadoo (2005: x), "these migrations were lodged in the large-scale international relocations and massive displacements of people

that followed the abolition of slavery in the nineteenth and twentieth century, and which accompanied the internationalization of waged labour embedded in the period of globalization of capitalism between 1850 and 1914. See Stalker (2000) on the relationship between migration and the social and economic changes associated with globalization.

6 See Doezema (2000) and Kempadoo (2005).

7 See Roberts (1992).

8 For further discussion, see Doezema (2010).

9 See Ward (2002) for a detailed discussion of the racism and hostility that underpinned the anti-immigration policies defining the Komagata Maru experience.

10 The potlatch, as Mawani (2002: 52) identifies, "brought together Native peoples from various bands who feasted and gave gifts to commemorate major events including births, marriages, and deaths." Yet drawing on assumptions of Indigenous persons as "uncivilized Others," colonial perceptions of the potlatch provide an example of how "Euro-Canadians inferiorized aboriginal peoples and indigenous spaces" while building up "their own identities as racially superior."

11 Barman (2004) provides the example: "Indian Girl Sold for 1000 Blankets."

12 On the construction of sex work as a social problem, see Brock (2009); on the relationship between white slavery and contemporary anti-trafficking campaigns in Canada generally, see Bruckert and Parent (2002); see also Doezema (2010) and Bernstein (2010).

13 For more detailed discussions see Backhouse (1985) and Erickson (2011).

14 For related discussions of the Indian Act, see Monture (1999); Thobani (2007); and Anderson (2000).

15 See Roberts (1992).

16 See Doezema (2002) and Williams and Masika (2002). See also Sanghera (2005) on the problematic conflation of women and girls in anti-trafficking discourses, which further "domesticates" women seen to require the direction and discipline of a patriarch in the household.

17 Also discussed in Doezema (2010) and Lee (2011).

18 Radical feminists equate sexual slavery, trafficking, and prostitution, arguing that prostitution represents an inherent violence against women. As Kempadoo (2005: xi) states, radical feminists view prostitution, which is perceived as trafficking, as "the very worst of patriarchal oppression and the greatest injury to women" (Kempadoo 2005: xi). For a radical feminist perspective of human trafficking see Barry (1984) and Raymond (2005).

19 See Lepp (2003) and Kapur (2003).

20 See Sen and Grown (1987) and Aradau (2004).

21 Members of the Human Rights Caucus (HRC) include International Human Rights Law Group, Foundation Against Trafficking in Women, Global Alliance Against Traffic in Women, Asian Women's Human Rights Council, La Strada, Ban-Ying, Fundación Esperanza, Foundation for Women, KOK-NGO Network Against Trafficking in Women, Women's Consortium of Nigeria, Women, and Law and Development in Africa (Nigeria) (Jordan 2002). The Network of Sex Work Projects (NSWP) also supported the position of the HRC. The Coalition Against Trafficking in Women (CATW), on the other hand, worked with a coalition of NGOs called the International Human Rights Network (IHRN) (CATW n. d.). Of note, both of the polarized groups comprise human rights and feminist advocates from countries of the Global North and Global South (Doezema 2010).

22 See Nagle (1997); Kempadoo (1998); and Doezema (1998).

23 See Leidholdt (2003) and Raymond (2005).

24 Dominant discourses of human trafficking, particularly in the fields of research, enforcement, service provision, and prevention, emphasize that human trafficking is primarily a woman's issue by pointing to the overrepresentation of women and girls among trafficked persons and the gender-based violence and discrimination of women underlying human trafficking syndicates (see Williams and Masika 2002; Popli 2008; Lee 2007, 2011). While estimates of human trafficking remain highly unreliable, most estimates indicate that women and girls are overrepresented in international and internal types of trafficking (see Williams and Masika 2002; Laczko and Gozdziak 2005; US State Department 2008; International Labour Organization [ILO] 2012; International Organization for Migration 2010; and Ogrodnik 2010). While it is problematic to place women and girls – or women and children for that matter – in the same category given differing capacities of agency and ability to consent, many estimates of human trafficking rely on such groupings. Feingold (2005) further problematizes representations focusing predominantly on sex trafficking (see also Feingold 2010), arguing that trafficking for the purpose of labour exploitation is likely more prevalent than trafficking for forced prostitution. Similarly, according to an ILO (2005) report, less than half of all trafficked individuals are involved in sex industries. Despite controversial estimates of the nature of human trafficking, anti-trafficking discourses are nonetheless dominated by discussions of women trafficked for the purpose of sexual exploitation.

25 For example, anti-slavery advocates frequently issue calls to action, such as those declared through reference to Margret Mead's famous quote: "Never doubt that a small group of thoughtful, committed citizens can change the world. Indeed, it's the only thing that ever has," or Edmund

Burke's: "[A]ll that is necessary for the triumph of evil is that good men do nothing" (see Campbell 2010; Perrin 2010a). In Canada, groups that equate prostitution with modern-day slavery further seek to abolish prostitution through legal regulations, admonishing, "Every woman in this country deserves our defense. Prostituted women and those at risk are voiceless and vulnerable" (Defend Dignity 2012). Again, "voiceless" women are portrayed as dependent on the good intentions of a self-appointed group of individuals campaigning to end modern day slavery through the "abolition of prostitution in Canada."

26 See Kaye, Winterdyk, and Quarterman (2014).
27 For a related discussion, see Smith and Kangaspunta (2012).
28 For a similar discussion based on this data, see Kaye and Hastie (2015).
29 See, generally, United Nations Office on Drugs and Crime Research Database; RCMP (2010).
30 As discussed throughout this book, definitional discrepancies and contested definitions influence efforts to shape trafficking-related policies. Such discrepancies make prevention particularly challenging in persons.
31 According to a Canadian policymaker (personal communication [2012]), this approach was adopted because Canada already has provisions in the Criminal Code for addressing the offences covered under the "means" section: threat, force, coercion, abduction, fraud, deception, abuse of power, or bribes.
32 From an "agency" perspective, the UN Trafficking Protocol successfully diverges from the abolitionist roots of the 1949 Convention by connecting trafficking to multiple labour sites and the use of threat, force, or coercion (Doezema 2002). At the same time, the UN Trafficking Protocol includes stipulations about the abuse of "a position of vulnerability," which refers to "any situation in which the person involved has no real and acceptable alternative but to submit to the abuse involved" (UN Interpretive Footnote in Jordan 2002: 4). This stipulation draws on "victim" discourses that suggest trafficking can occur in the absence of coercion to include persons who have "no culturally acceptable or legal means to refuse and so they 'submit' to the situation" (Jordan 2002: 8). In doing so, advocates of women's agency argue the stipulation can be used to silence the voices of women from economically marginalized situations by declaring them passive victims of their circumstances. Yet victim advocates insist the stipulation considers the hidden forms of manipulation that traffickers use to lure women into trafficking for sexual exploitation (see Perrin 2010a).
33 See Perrin (2010a).
34 See Jordan (2002); Williams and Masika (2002); and Kempadoo (2005).

35 See Vanwesenbeeck (2001); Lee (2011); and Weitzer (2012)
36 See Pearson (2002) and Dottridge (2007)
37 The discussions leading to the adoption of the protocol were preoccupied
    with debates over the "victim" or "agent" status of trafficked women.
    As no consensus was achieved and interpretations of human rights were
    at the center of these debates, the UN Protocol was unable to advance a
    strong stance on the rights of trafficked persons. See Gallagher (2001);
    Jordan (2002); Kempadoo (2005); O' Connell Davidson (2006, 2015)
38 Jordan (2002); GAATW (2000).
39 Sanghera (2005); Lee (2011); O'Connell Davidson (2013).
40 Canada Immigration and Job Consultants (2009) and Future Group (2006)
    critique the working group for not developing a national action plan.
41 See Bales (2007); Kara (2009); United Nations Office on Drugs and Crime
    (2009); and European Commission (2012). As discussed, scholars and
    journalists have also drawn on sensationalized discourses. Some recent
    titles of books on the issue include: *Slave Hunter: One Man's Global Quest to
    Free Victims of Human Trafficking* (Cohen and Buckley 2009); *The Slave Next
    Door: Human Trafficking and Slavery in America Today* (Bales and Soodalter
    2009); *More Than Rice: A Journey through the Underworld of Human Trafficking*
    (Chestnut 2010).
42 Bales (1999, 2005), for instance, argues that proportionally more people are
    held in situations of bondage today than at any other point in history.
43 For instance, in 2002, the US. State Department offered the highly imprecise
    estimate that "at least 700,000, and possibly as many as four million men,
    women and children worldwide were bought, sold, transported and held
    against their will in slave-like conditions" (US State Department 2002). Two
    years later, the annual *Trafficking in Persons (TIP) Report* revised this claim
    to the widely cited estimate that 600,000 to 800,000 people are "victims"
    of human trafficking annually (US State Department 2004). However, in
    2006, the US Government Accountability Office declared many of the US
    government estimates of human trafficking as "questionable" given a lack
    of methodological rigor, reliability measures, and comparability of country-
    specific data. As a result, in the same year, the US State Department's *TIP
    Report* sought to overcome these challenges by relying on data from the
    International Labour Organization (ILO) (e.g. Shelley 2010), making the ILO
    estimates the most popularly cited human trafficking figures. Based on data
    from 1995–2004, the ILO (2005) estimates a minimum of 12.3 million people
    are victimized by human trafficking at any point in time and approximately
    two-thirds of these individuals are women and children trafficked for the
    purpose of sexual exploitation. In 2012, the ILO revised their capture–

recapture methodology and estimated 20.9 million people are victimized
by forced labour at any given time. This estimate is based on data from
2002–2011 (ILO 2012). According to the ILO (2012: 13), "human trafficking
can also be regarded as forced labour, and so this estimate captures the
full realm of human trafficking for labour and sexual exploitation, or what
some call 'modern day slavery.'" The figures do not include trafficking
for the removal and sale of human organs or forced marriages/adoptions.
According to this report, women and girls represent 11.4 million victims
(55 per cent), while men and boys represent 9.5 million (45 per cent)
(ILO 2012). This varies substantially from the above-mentioned "two-thirds"
estimate and the *TIP Report* that estimated 80 per cent of internationally
trafficked persons are women and 70 per cent are women trafficked for
the purpose of sexual exploitation (US State Department 2008). For related
discussions, see Feingold (2010) and Goodey (2012).

44 See Clancey, Khushrushahi, and Ham (2014).

45 Compare this with the $500,000 allocated for victim services.

46 Section 279.011 further criminalizes the trafficking of a person under
    the age of 18 years. Although this manuscript focuses predominantly on
    trafficking discourses in relation to adults, youth feature prominently in
    Canadian anti-trafficking discourses. For the purposes of this book, youth
    are considered when such discourses are conflated with those of adults,
    most notably women.

47 For the purposes of Sections 279.01 to 279.03, a person exploits another
    person if they 1) cause them to provide, or offer to provide, labour or a
    service by engaging in conduct that, in all circumstances, could reasonably
    be expected to cause the other person to believe that their safety or the
    safety of a person known to them would be threatened if they failed to
    provide, or offer to provide, the labour or service; or 2) cause them, by
    means of deception or the use or threat of force or of any other form of
    coercion, or to have an organ or tissue removed.

48 See Global Alliance Against Traffic in Women (2007).

49 See Hastie (2012, 2013); Dowling, Moreton, and Wright (2007).

50 The revised Section 279.04 includes the following provision: "In
    determining whether the accused exploits another person under
    subsection 1) the Court may consider, among other factors, whether the
    accused a) used or threatened to use force or another form of coercion;
    b) used deception; c) abused a position of trust, power or authority"
    (Statutes of Canada 2012).

51 While public solicitation of customers on the street remained illegal, the
    decision enabled sex workers to work indoors in organized bawdy houses

and to hire drivers, bodyguards, and other support staff to help facilitate safer practices.

52 The court withheld implementation of the law for a period of one year to enable the sitting federal government to amend the Criminal Code.

53 Meanwhile, Vancouver advocates, particularly Sheryl Kiselbach, a former sex worker, and the Downtown Eastside Sex Workers United Against Violence Society, were granted the right to challenge Canada's prostitution laws on the basis that the law violates the constitutional rights of sex workers to equality, freedom of expression, and freedom of association (*Globe and Mail* 2012, September 21). This right was granted following a unanimous ruling that dismissed the then federal government's appeal to prevent the case from proceeding to the British Columbia Supreme Court. However, the applicants opted to stay the case pending the ruling of the Supreme Court of Canada (Canada v. Bedford, 2013 SCC 72).

54 This approach relies substantially on the contested research of Farley et al. (1998).

55 See Global Alliance Against Traffic in Women (2007).

56 See Chapkis (2003). See also Pratt and Valverde (2002) for related discursive shifts affecting refugees in Canada.

57 Although Citizenship and Immigration Canada considers whether the person can assist law enforcement in criminal proceedings, the policy clearly states, "In Canada, you do not have to testify against your trafficker to get temporary or permanent resident status" (CIC 2016).

3 Anti-trafficking in Canada: Negotiating "Domestic" versus "International"

1 From 2007 until the end of the 2010 fiscal year, the annual budget remained at $650,000 and was reduced to $300,000 in 2011.

2 From 2007–2012, the BC Office to Combat Trafficking in Persons (BCOCTIP) offered assistance to trafficked persons by referring potential cases to the RCMP's Human Trafficking Coordinator for BC/Yukon (a position that no longer exists) or municipal law enforcement (British Columbia Ministry of Justice 2013). BCOCTIP also monitors the investigation and prosecution when trafficking charges are pursued in that province.

3 For example, Amnesty International (2004)

4 My own research has similarly constructed power imbalances problematically in this fashion (see Kaye, Winterdyk, and Quarterman 2014).

5 This finding is consistent with preliminary research findings exploring the link between the EUFA European Championships in 2012 and human trafficking. Based on the preliminary findings, the International Organization for Migration (IOM) Ukraine (2012) indicates the event did not result in heightened levels of human trafficking for the purpose of sexual or other forms of exploitation. These results are also consistent with the IOM's previous statements after monitoring the World Cup games in Germany in 2006 and South Africa in 2010. In a statement on the EUFA 2012 findings, Ruth Krcmar, Coordinator of IOM Ukraine's Counter Trafficking Programme, indicates, "The scare of increased human trafficking for sexual exploitation comes up every time there is a large sporting event on the horizon, although our experience only reinforces earlier findings in other countries. We hope studies like ours will eventually put an end to the myth, which results in scarce counter-trafficking resources being spent on one-off campaigns rather than long-term solutions and victim assistance" (IOM Ukraine 2012).

6 It is worth noting that although no charges of human trafficking were laid, one abolitionist agency claims to have offered services to "five victims of human trafficking" during the Olympic events (frontline worker, Vancouver). Other organizations highlight cases of trafficking in the preparation of the infrastructure for the Vancouver Olympic games.

7 As of February 2011, the time of conducting field research in Winnipeg for this study, the team had not yet identified any cases of human trafficking.

8 Although no source is provided in support of this claim, the Government of Manitoba presents it as a clear statement of fact. The statement is consistent with the findings of Farley et al. (1998), who compare five countries from the standpoint that prostitution is a form of violence against women and a human rights violation. According to them, the average age of entry is 13 years old. At this point, it is important to reiterate, the goal of this research is not to demonstrate or contest the legitimacy of these specific claims; rather, this research examines how anti-trafficking discourses have informed the strategy adopted by the province and, in turn, how the strategy effects the complex experiences of trafficked individuals.

9 See Agustín (2007), Doezema (2010), and others.

10 See, for example, Swift (1995). See also Satzewich and Wotherspoon (2000) and Rutman and Armitage (1993) on the role of child welfare and the reproduction of colonial domination.

11 See McManus (2001).

12 See "The Numbered Treaties (1871–1921)" (Indigenous and Northern Affairs Canada 2013).

13 See Bourgeois (2015); Isaacs (2014); Mancuso (2011); Jeffery (2010).
14 See Carroll (2007).
15 The Alberta Victims of Crime Fund emerged from the Victims of Crime Act. The fund is supported by surcharges on provincial fines and surcharges imposed by the courts under the Criminal Code of Canada (Ministry of Justice and Solicitor General. 1995–2013).
16 From October 2011 until June 2012, I was hired on a contract basis with ACT Alberta to coordinate the Calgary chapter during a time of transition within the organization. My role included managing the network of stakeholders and coordinating services when cases of trafficking emerged in the city. From June 2012 until the time of writing, I served as the Research Advisor for ACT Alberta and have participated in the development of the provincial response to human trafficking in Alberta. This work certainly informs my perspective; however, for the purposes of this book, I adopt a broader sociological lens that critically considers the structural factors shaping existing discussions and responses in the country. I have not hesitated to place my own labours under scrutiny in the context of settler colonialism and this exploration of how settler colonial domination reproduces national, racial, and sexual priorities.
17 This data were first released in Kaye (2015).
18 In terms of gender, there was only information available for 80 per cent of cases.

4 Settler Colonialism, Sex Work, Criminalization, and Human Trafficking

1 See, for example, Erickson's (2011: 63) discussion of early Criminal Code legislation, which "categorized Aboriginal prostitution as an indictable offence against morality" whereas other forms of prostitution fell under notions of vagrancy and nuisance.
2 In light of this highly politicized environment, research emerging from the context of Vancouver must be critically assessed. Multiple interview respondents referenced intentional biasing of research findings in support of predetermined ideological viewpoints. Given the researcher's position as an outsider of the city, this study engaged in interviews with individuals from multiple perspectives.
3 Mensah (2006) documents similar exchanges between abolitionist and sex worker–rights advocates in Quebec and similarly argues that both sides engage in silencing of the "other" (see Benoit and Shaver 2006). Further,

see Brock (2009) for a discussion of political organization among sex workers in resistance to victim labeling.

4 Although some individual police officers worked hard to address the violence, such officers worked in the context of "systemic inadequacies and repeated patterns of error" (British Columbia Missing Women Commission of Inquiry 2012, Volume IIA: 3).

5 Ferris (2015: 142) similarly notes that before the Native Women's Assocation of Canada's participation in the Women's Coalition for the Absolution of Prostitution there was "no clear anti-prostitution position" documented in their materials.

6 See Amnesty International (2004).

7 An informal discussion with a past participant of an abolition-based program in Calgary revealed that she was not permitted to share her story on behalf of this organization because she was unwilling to describe herself as a "victim." While she was grateful to the organization for helping her exit the sex trade, she did not view herself as a victim of the sex trade.

8 Observational note from the researcher: During my time participating in the Calgary Network on Prostitution (CNOP) (October 2011–June 2012), it became clear that although representatives from abolitionist and sex worker–rights approaches engaged in open dialogue, the abolitionist standpoint – that all forms of prostitution constitute sexual exploitation – prevented abolitionists from taking seriously the claims made by supporters of sex worker rights.

5 Anti-trafficking and Border Secularization: Reproducing the Citizen–Subject through Restrictive Measures and Potential Threats

1 According to the UN Convention Against Transnational Organized Crime (the Convention that houses the UN Trafficking Protocol), an organized criminal group refers to a structured group of three or more persons, existing for a period of time and acting in concert with the aim of committing one or more serious crimes or offences established in accordance with this Convention, in order to obtain, directly or indirectly, a financial or other material benefit (United Nations Office on Drugs and Crime 2000: Article 2).

2 See Salt (2000).

3 See Aronowitz (2001) and O'Connell Davidson (2013).

4 This department has since been expanded and renamed Human Resources and Skills Development Canada.

5 Similarly, recent changes to the temporary foreign worker (TF) program in Canada permit certain industries to be "fast tracked" for approval under the Low-Skill Pilot Project (LSPP), renamed the Pilot Project for Occupations Requiring Lower Levels of Formal Training (PPORLLFT).

6 See Macklin (2003) and Library of Parliament (2012).

7 See Ross (2003).

8 See Hughes (2005).

9 Of note, following a review, the federal ethics commissioner, Bernard Shapiro, cleared Judy Sgro of wrongdoing.

10 For example, as will be discussed further in the next chapter, bills C-17, C-57, and C-45 aimed to restrict and/or eliminate the exotic dancer visa program.

11 It is important to note, the prevention strategies outlined in the National Action Plan to Combat Human Trafficking are more broad-based than merely recommending such restrictive measures. With respect to prevention, suggested strategies also include awareness-raising activities, the development of diagnostic tools to enhance identification of trafficked persons in Canada, and targeted support for the Canadian International Development Agency (CIDA) to address the experiences of "women and girls living in poverty" (Public Safety Canada 2012a: 31). However, many of these preventive measures overlap with securitization efforts (e.g. enhanced identification tools) and, on the whole, the plan emphasizes enforcement-based controls.

12 See Jeffrey and MacDonald (2006) for a detailed critical analysis that relies on interviews with sex workers in the Maritimes to contextualize sex work within the social, political, and economic framework in which it occurs.

13 As Bakan and Stasiulis (2012: 204) point out, there is no shortage of Canadian workers; rather, "there is a shortage of 'free' wage labourers in the Canadian labour market who are willing to work for low wages" and substandard working conditions. SeeSatzewich (1991) and Hanley et al. (2012).

14 See Nakache and Kinoshita (2010); Hanley et al. (2006); Hastie (2013); Hennebry (2012); and Sassen (2008).

15 See Faraday (2012) and Citizenship and Immigration Canada (2010).

16 See Sharma (2006); Lenard and Straehle (2012); and Crépeau and Nakache (2006).

17 See Nakache and Kinoshita (2010).

18 Although the focus of this section is on matters of precariousness and insecurities faced by low-skill migrant workers, the role of migrant workers in resisting and organizing against such exploitation should not be underemphasized (see, for example, Hanley et al. 2012). Further, the aim of this section is not to assert that low-skill TFWs are trafficked

persons, but to situate instances of labour trafficking in the broader context of precariousness faced by low-skill migrants and to problematize the application of anti-trafficking discourses that further restrict rather than empower migrant communities. See also Hanley et al. (2006); Hastie (2013); and Hennebry (2012).

19 For detailed discussion, see Bakan and Stasiulis (2012).

20 Human trafficking charges for the purposes of forced labour have been laid in Alberta, Ontario, and British Columbia (Public Safety Canada 2012a).

21 See Bradimore and Bauder (2011) and Krishnamurti (2013).

22 In January 2013, the British Colombia Supreme Court struck down Section 117 of the human smuggling offence in the Immigration and Refugee Protection Act for violating the Canadian Charter of Rights and Freedoms and criminalizing humanitarian actions associate with asylum. The ruling indicated the definition of smuggler was too broad in its declaration that "no person shall knowingly organize, induce, aid or abet the coming into Canada of one or more persons who are not in possession of a visa, passport or other documentation required by this Act" (British Columbia Supreme Court 2013). The Crown appealed the ruling, arguing that Section 117 required a broad scope because its intended aim was to address a broader purpose than human smuggling legislation.

23 In support of the prime minister's claim regarding Canadian perceptions of mass arrival, an Angus Reid (2010) opinion poll conducted on August 17–18, 2010, indicated that close to half (48 per cent) of all Canadians thought the migrants should be deported even if they were determined to be legitimate refugees and more than half (63 per cent) thought the ship should have been turned back before reaching Canadian waters. Additionally, three-quarters (72 per cent) expected more migrant ships to arrive to Canada in the months following the arrival of the Sun Sea. Finally, more than half (64 per cent) of Canadians indicated they were "very closely" or "moderately closely" following the media coverage of the arrival of the ships.

24 Article 31 of the Refugee Convention prohibits state parties from prosecuting asylum claimants for arriving without legal documentation, regardless of how they arrive.

25 At the time, discussions indicated this would set the precedent for the 470 migrants whose refugee cases were still pending at the time of the ruling. However, the ruling has since been overturned by the Federal Court of Canada (*National Post*, 2013 January 21). Nonetheless, at the time of this ruling, twenty-three migrants had been determined inadmissible to Canada and thirty-four had obtained refugee status (CTV BC 2012, September 21).

26 In response to significant pressure from refugee advocates and political interest groups, Bill C-31 withdrew a key controversial element of the proposed Bill C-4 by exempting minors (under the age of 16 years) from detention.

27 Some measures of the legislation came into effect in the fall of 2012, yet most came into effect December 2012.

28 Of note, the connection between the experiences of the Roma community and the human trafficking case should also be understood in the context of significant public discourse whereby the minister of citizenship and immigration repeatedly connects the Roma population to abuses of the system of asylum. For example, quoted in the *National Post*, Jason Kenney declared the following: "Almost none of these European asylum claimants even show up for their hearings – they just overwhelmingly abandon them and withdraw their own claims ... But they all do show up in Ontario's welfare program" (*National Post* 2012, April 22). See Levine-Rasky, Beaudoin, and St Clair (2013) for a discussion of the federal government's response to the arrival of European Roma refugee claimants and a discussion of systematic exclusion as a form of institutional racism. Additionally, it is worth noting the Hamilton human trafficking case was also referenced in support of adding Hungary to the list of "designated countries of origin" (DCO) or so-called safe countries. Based on the assumption that asylum claims from DCOs are likely unfounded, the federal government expedites the claims process and failed claimants do not have access to the Refugee Appeal Division.

29 See Mountz (2010).

30 See, for example, Global Network of Sex Work Projects (2014b); SWAN Vancouver Society (2015); *National Post* (2015, May 13); GAATW (2007)

31 For a discussion of this clause, see Caron and Partners LLP (2012).

32 This waiting period is increased to thirty-six months for failed claimants from "a designated country of origin" (CIC 2012c).

Conclusion

1 See Thobani (2012); Coulthard (2014); and Simpson (2014a). On the "invisibilized dynamics of settler colonialism" see Tuck and Yang (2012).

2 See Arvin, Tuck, and Morrill (2013:12), who similarly argue the state "continues to exploit Indigenous, black, and other peoples deemed 'illegal' (or otherwise threatening and usurping) immigrants."

3 see Aradau (2004).

4 See Jeffrey (2005).

References

Aboriginal Women's Action Network (AWAN). 2007. "Statement Opposing Legalized Prostitution and Total Decriminalization of Prostitution." Vancouver: Aboriginal Women's Action Network. (http://www.awanbc.ca/aboutus.html#Oppose).

Acoose, Janice. 1995. *Iskwewak: Neither Indian Princess nor Easy Squaws*. Toronto: Women's Press.

Action Coalition on Human Trafficking (ACT) Alberta. 2012. "Mission and Philosophy: ACT Alberta Mission." Edmonton: ACT Alberta. http://www.actalberta.org/about-act.php?sid=70.

Action Coalition on Human Trafficking (ACT) Alberta. 2015. "Human Trafficking in Alberta: Myths vs. Realities" Edmonton: Act Alberta. http://www.actalberta.org/uploads/060515_9Zx8yB9VDceE5Wn_100744.pdf.

Adam, Barbara, Ulrich Beck, and Joost van Loon. 2000. *The Risk Society and Beyond: Critical Issues for Social Theory*. London: Sage Publications.

Adichie, Chimimanda. 2009. "The Danger of a Single Story." New York: TED Talks. https://www.ted.com/talks/chimamanda_adichie_the_danger_of_a_single_story?language=en.

Agustín, Laura. 2007. *Sex at the Margins: Migration, Labour Markets and the Rescue Industry*. New York: Zed Books.

Ahmed, Sara. 2014. *Willful Subjects*. Durham: Duke University Press. htWootp://dx.doi.org/10.1215/9780822376101.

Alfred, Taiaiake. 2005. *Wasáse: Indigenous Pathways of Action and Freedom*. Toronto: University of Toronto Press.

Alfred, Taiaiake, and Jeff Corntassel. 2005. "Being Indigenous: Resurgences Against Contemporary Colonialism." Victoria, BC: www.corntassel.net. http://www.corntassel.net/articles.htm.

Amnesty International. 2004. "Stolen Sisters: A Human Rights Response to Discrimination and Violence Against Indigenous Women in Canada." Ottawa: Amnesty International Canada. https://www.amnesty.ca/sites/amnesty/files/amr200032004enstolensisters.pdf.

Anderson, Benedict. 2006. *Imagined Communities: Reflections on the Origin and Spread of Nationalism*. New York: Verso.

Anderson, Kim. 2000. *A Recognition of Being: Reconstructing Native Womanhood*. Toronto: Sumach Press.

Andrijasevic, Rutvica. 2007. "Beautiful, Dead Bodies: Gender, Migration and Representation in Anti-Trafficking Campaigns." *Feminist Review* 86: 24–44.

Andrijasevic, Rutvica. 2010. *Migration, Agency and Citizenship in Sex Trafficking*. New York: Palgrave Macmillan. http://dx.doi.org/10.1057/9780230299139.

Angus Reid. 2010. *Almost Half of Canadians Believe Tamil Migrants Should be Deported*. Vancouver: Angus Reid Institute; http://angusreidglobal.com/wp-content/uploads/2010/08/2010.08.19_Migrants_CAN.pdf.

Aradau, Claudia. 2004. "The Perverse Politics of Four-Letter Words: Risk and Pity in the Securitisation of Human Trafficking." *Millennium* 33 (2): 251–77. http://dx.doi.org/10.1177/03058298040330020101.

Aronowitz, Alexis A. 2001. "Smuggling and Trafficking in Human Beings: The Phenomenon, the Markets that Drive it and the Organizations that Promote it." *European Journal on Criminal Policy and Research* 9 (2): 163–95. http://dx.doi.org/10.1023/A:1011253129328.

Arvin, Maile, Eve Tuck, and Angie Morrill. 2013. "Decolonizing Feminism: Challenging Connection Between Settler Colonialism and Heteropatriarchy." *Feminist Formations* 25 (1): 8–34. http://dx.doi.org/10.1353/ff.2013.0006.

Babbie, Earl, and Lucia Benaquisto. 2002. *Fundamentals of Social Research.*. Scarborough: Nelson.

Backhouse, Constance. 1985. "Nineteenth Century Canadian Prostitution Law Reflection of a Discriminatory Society." *Social History* XVIII (36): 387–423.

Bakan, Abigail, and Daiva K. Stasiulis 2012. " Live-in Caregivers: A Case Study of Unfree Labour." In *Legislated Inequality: Temporary Labour Migration in Canada*, ed. P. Lenard and C. Straehle. Montréal: McGill-Queens University Press.

Bales, Kevin. 1999. *New Slavery in the Global Economy*. Berkeley: University of California Press.

Bales, Kevin. 2005. *Understanding Global Slavery*. Berkley: University of California Press. http://dx.doi.org/10.1525/california/9780520245068.001.0001.

Bales, Kevin. 2007. *Ending Slavery: How We Free Slaves Today*. Berkeley: University of California Press.

Bales, Kevin, and Ron Soodalter. 2009. *The Slave Next Door: Human Trafficking and Slavery in America Today*. Berkley, CA: University of California Press.

Barman, Jean. 2004. "Taming Aboriginal Sexuality: Gender, Power, and Race in British Columbia, 1850-1900." In *In the Days of Our Grandmothers: A Reader in Aboriginal Women's History in Canada*, ed. M.E. Kelm and L. Townshend, 270–300. Toronto: University of Toronto Press.

Barry, Kathleen. 1984. *Female Sexual Slavery*. New York: New York University Press.

Barry, Kathleen. 1995. *The Prostitution of Sexuality*. New York: New York University Press.

Barnett, Laura. 2008. "Trafficking in Persons." In *Parliamentary Information and Research Services*. Ottawa: Library of Parliament; http://www2.parl.gc.ca/Content/LOP/ResearchPublications/prb0624-e.pdf.

Barnett, Laura. 2011. *Prostitution in Canada: International Obligations, Federal Law, and Provincial and Municipal Jurisdiction*. Ottawa: Library of Parliament; http://www.lop.parl.gc.ca/Content/LOP/ResearchPublications/2011-119-e.htm.

Beads, Tina, and Ruana Kuokkanen. 2007. "An Aboriginal Feminist on Violence Against Women." In *Making Space for Indigenous Feminism*, ed. J. Green, 221–232. Nova Scotia: Fernwood.

Beck, Ulrich. 1992. *Risk Society: Towards a New Modernity*. London: Sage Publications.

Bedford v. Canada. 2010. ONSC 4264. Toronto: Ontario Superior Court of Justice.

Béland, Daniel. 2008. *States of Global Insecurity: Policy, Politics, and Society*. Worth Publishers.

Béland, Daniel. 2010. "The Idea of Power and the Role of Ideas." *Political Studies Review* 8 (2): 145–54. http://dx.doi.org/10.1111/j.1478-9302.2009.00199.x.

Benoit, Cecilia, and Frances Shaver. 2006. "Critical Issues and New Directions in Sex Work Research." *Canadian Review of Sociology and Anthropology. La Revue Canadienne de Sociologie et d'Anthropologie* 43 (3): 243–52. http://dx.doi.org/10.1111/j.1755-618X.2006.tb02222.x.

Benoit, Cecilia, Chris Atchison, Lauren Casey, Mikael Jansson, Bill McCarthy, Rachel Phillips, Bill Reimer, Dan Reist, and Frances M. Shaver. 2014. *A 'Working Paper' Prepared as Background to Building on the Evidence: An International Symposium on the Sex Industry in Canada*. Victoria: University of Victoria; http://www.understandingsexwork.com,.

Bernstein, Elizabeth. 2007. *Temporarily Yours: Intimacy, Authenticity, and the Commerce of Sex*. Chicago: University of Chicago Press. http://dx.doi.org/10.7208/chicago/9780226044620.001.0001.

Bernstein, Elizabeth. 2010. *Temporarily Yours: Intimacy, Authenticity, and the Commerce of Sex*. Chicago: University of Chicago Press.

Bhabha, Homi. K. 1990. *Nation and Narration*. London: Routledge.

Bhattacharyya, Gargi. 2005. *Traffick: The Illicit Movement of People and Things*. London: Pluto Press.

Boulding, Kenneth E. 1989. *Three Faces of Power*. London: Sage Publications.

Bourgeois, Robyn. 2015. "Colonial Exploitation: The Canadian State and the Trafficking of Indigenous Women and Girls in Canada." *UCLA Law Review. University of California, Los Angeles. School of Law* 62: 1426–63.

Bowen and Shannon Frontline Consulting. 2009. *Human Trafficking, Sex Work Safety and the 2010 Games: Assessments and Recommendations*. Vancouver: Sex Industry Worker Safety Action Group (SIWSAG). http://www.straight.com/files/pdf/sextraffic2010games.pdf.

Boyer, Yvonne, and Peggy Kampouris. 2014. "Trafficking in Aboriginal Women and Girls." Ottawa: Public Safety Canada. http://publications.gc.ca/collections/collection_2015/sp-ps/PS18-8-2014-eng.pdf.

Bradimore, Ashley, and Harald Bauder. 2011. "Mystery Ships and Risky Boat People: Tamil Refugee Migration in the Newsprint Media." *Canadian Journal of Communication* 36 (4): 637–61.

British Columbia Missing Women Commission of Inquiry. 2012. "Forsaken: The Report of the Missing Women Commission of Inquiry." Volume IIA. Victoria: Government of British Columbia http://www.ag.gov.bc.ca/public_inquiries/docs/Forsaken-Vol_2A.pdf.

British Columbia Ministry of Justice. 2013. *BC's Action Plan to Combat Human Trafficking 2013–2016*. British Columbia.

British Columbia Supreme Court. 2013. "R. v. Appulonapp, 2013: BCSC 31." Vancouver: CanLII. http://www.canlii.org/en/bc/bcsc/doc/2013/2013bcsc31/2013bcsc31.html.

Brock, Deborah. 1989. *The Impact of Bill C-49 on Street Prostitution: A Summary*. Ottawa: National Action Committee on the Status of Women.

Brock, Deborah. 2009. *Making Work, Making Trouble: The Social Regulation of Sexual Labour*. Toronto: University of Toronto Press.

Brown, Wendy. 2005. *Edgework: Critical Essays on Knowledge and Politics*. Princeton, NJ: Princeton University Press.

Brubaker, Rogers. 1992. *Citizenship and Nationhood in France and Germany*. Cambridge: Harvard University Press.

Bruckert, Christine, and Colette Parent. 2002. "Trafficking in Human Beings and Organized Crime: A Literature Review." Research and Evaluation Branch: Community, Contract and Aboriginal Policing Services Directorate. Ottawa: RCMP. http://lastradainternational.org/lsidocs/bruckert_02_crime_0708.pdf.

Brysk, Alison, and Gershon Shafir, eds. 2004. *People out of Place: Globalization, Human Rights, and the Citizenship Gap*. New York: Routledge.

Butterfly (Asian and Migration Sex Workers Support Network). 2015. "Stop Harm from Anti-trafficking Policies and Campaigns: Support Sex Workers' Rights, Justice, and Dignity." Toronto: Migrant Sex Workers Project. http://www.migrantsexworkers.com/press/harper-conservatives-set-to-pour-another-60-million-on-failed-programs-that-target-people-in-the-sex-trade.

Byl, Yessy. 2009. *Entrenching Exploitation*. Edmonton: Alberta Federation of Labour. http://aaisa.ca/wp-content/uploads/2013/02/Entrenching-Exploitation2.pdf.

Byrd, Jodi A. 2011. *The Transit of Empire: Indigenous Critiques of Colonialism*. Minneapolis: University of Minnesota Press. http://dx.doi.org/10.5749/minnesota/9780816676408.001.0001.

Calgary Economic Development. 2011. "Financial Services." Calgary: CED. http://www.calgaryeconomicdevelopment.com/industries/focus-areas/financial-services.

Cameron, Michelle. 2009. "Two Spirited Aboriginal People: Continuing Cultural Appropriation by Non-Aboriginal Society." *Canadian Woman Studies* 24.2–3(2005): 23–27.

Campbell, June. 2010. "Human Trafficking: Modern Day Slavery." *Perspectives* 75: 6–7. Toronto: The Presbyterian Church in Canada. http://www.presbyterian.ca/files/webfm/ourresources/mcv/wim/WP%20Jan2010.pdf.

Canada Immigration and Job Consultants. 2009. "Confronting Human Trafficking in Canada," blog entry by Benjamin Perrin, February 6, 2009. http://www.lawyersweekly.ca/index.php?section=article&articleid=849.

Canadian Women's Foundation. 2013. "End Sex Trafficking." http://canadianwomen.org/m/our-work/end-human-trafficking.

Caron and Partners. 2012. "Pre-removal Risk Assessments." Calgary: Caron and Partners. http://www.caronpartners.com/immigration-blog/2016/1/19/pre-removal-risk-assessments-prra.

Carroll, William K. 2007. "From Canadian Corporate Elite to Transnational Capitalist Class: Transitions in the Organization of Corporate Power." *Canadian Review of Sociology and Anthropology. La Revue Canadienne de Sociologie et d'Anthropologie* 44 (3): 265–88. http://dx.doi.org/10.1111/j.1755-618X.2007.tb01186.x.

CBC News. 2005, June 21. "Judy Sgro Timeline.". Toronto: CBC News. (http://www.cbc.ca/news/background/cdngovernment/sgro-judy.html).

CBC News. 2009, September 22. "Critics Upset With New Caregiver Bill." Toronto: CBC. http://www.cbc.ca/news/canada/toronto/story/2009/09/22/caregiver-bill.html.

CBC News. 2010, September 7. "Tories Target Human Trafficking in Campaign." *Power & Politics*. Toronto: CBC. http://www.cbc.ca/news/canada/story/2010/09/07/toews-human-smuggling-tamil-ship.html.

CBC News. 2010, October 21. "Tories Fortify Human Smuggling Laws" Toronto: http://www.cbc.ca/news/canada/story/2010/10/21/human -smuggling-refugee-kenney-toews.html.

CBC News. 2012, March 29. "Smuggling And Trafficking Big Business In Canada." Toronto: CBC. http://www.cbc.ca/news/canada/ story/2012/03/28/f-human-smuggling-overview.html).

CBC News. 2012, December 5. "Romanian Human Smuggling Ring Busted In Ontario: Foreign Nationals Crossed Canadian Border From U.S. At Stanstead, Que." Toronto: CBC. http://www.cbc.ca/news/politics/ romanian-human-smuggling-ring-busted-in-ontario-1.1292783.

CBC News. 2013, January 23. "Full Text Of Declaration That Will End Attawapiskat Chief's Six-Week Protest." Toronto: CBC. http://www.cbc.ca/ newsblogs/politics/inside-politics-blog/2013/01/full-text-of-declaration -that-will-end-attawapiskat-chiefs-six-week-protest.html.

CBC News. 2015, November 3. "Increasing Community Awareness Top Priority of Strategic Initiative." Toronto: CBC. http://www.cbc.ca/m/ touch/aboriginal/story/1.3301726.

Chant, Sylvia. 2006. "Re-thinking the Feminization of Poverty in Relation to Aggregate Gender Indices." *Journal of Human Development* 7 (2): 201–20. http://dx.doi.org/10.1080/14649880600768538.

Chapkis, Wendy. 2003. "Trafficking, Migration, and the Law: Protecting Innocents, Punishing Immigrants." *Gender & Society* 17 (6): 923–37. http:// dx.doi.org/10.1177/0891243203257477.

Chestnut, Pamala. 2010. *More Than Rice: A Journey through the Underworld of Human Trafficking*. Yorkshire.

Christianity Today. 2008. "Catherine Booth: Compelling Preacher an Co-Founder of the Salvation Army." Carol Stream: ChristianityToday.org. http://www .christianitytoday.com/history/people/activists/catherine-booth.html.

Chrysalis Anti-Human Trafficking Network. 2013. *Now Recruiting Child Sex Workers*. Advertisement [Poster]. Edmonton: ChrysalisNetwork.org.

Chuang, Janie. 2006. "Beyond a Snapshot: Preventing Human Trafficking in the Global Economy." *Indiana Journal of Global Legal Studies* 13 (1): 137–63. http://dx.doi.org/10.2979/GLS.2006.13.1.137.

Citizenship and Immigration Canada (CIC). 2009. "Protection and Assistance for Victims of Human Trafficking." Ottawa: Citizenship and Immigration Canada. http://www.cic.gc.ca/english/information/applications/trp.asp.

Citizenship and Immigration Canada (CIC). 2010. "Facts and Figures 2009 – Immigration Overview: Permanent and Temporary Residents." Ottawa: Citizenship and Immigration Canada. http://www.cic.gc.ca/english/ resources/statistics/facts2009/.

Citizenship and Immigration Canada (CIC). 2012a. "Limits on Pre-Approval Risk-Assessments and Applications for Humanitarian and Compassionate Consideration." Ottawa: Citizenship and Immigration Canada. http://www.cic.gc.ca/english/refugees/reform-ppra.asp.

Citizenship and Immigration Canada (CIC). 2012b. "Speaking Notes for the Honourable Jason Kenney, P.C., M.P. Minister of Citizenship and Immigration and Multiculturalism." Ottawa: Citizenship and Immigration Canada. http://www.cic.gc.ca/english/department/media/speeches/2012/2012-07-04.asp.

Citizenship and Immigration Canada (CIC). 2012c. "Notice on Proposed Regulatory Amendments – Processing Time Lines for Asylum Claims in Canada." Ottawa: Citizenship and Immigration Canada. http://www.cic.gc.ca/english/department/media/notices/notice-asylum.asp.

Citizenship and Immigration Canada (CIC). 2016. "Protection and Assistance for Victims of Human Trafficking." Ottawa: Citizenship and Immigration Canada. http://www.cic.gc.ca/english/information/applications/trp.asp.

City of Vancouver. 2015. "About Vancouver." Vancouver: City of Vancouver. http://vancouver.ca/about-vancouver.aspx

Clancey, Alison, Noushin Khushrushahi, and Julie Ham. 2014. "Do Evidence-Based Approaches Alienate Canadian Anti-Trafficking Funders?" Anti-Trafficking Review 3: 87–108. http://www.antitraffickingreview.org/index.php/atrjournal/article/view/66/85). http://dx.doi.org/10.14197/atr.20121435.

Coalition Against Trafficking in Women. n.d. "An Introduction to CATW." New York: Coalition Against Trafficking Women. http://www.catwinternational.org/.

Cohen, Aaron, and Christine Buckley. 2009. Slave Hunter: One Man's Global Quest to Free Victims of Human Trafficking. New York: Simon & Schuster.

Cohen, Edward. 2001. "Globalization and the Boundaries of the State: A Framework for Analyzing the Changing Practice of Sovereignty." Governance: An International Journal of Policy, Administration and Institutions 14 (1): 75–97. http://dx.doi.org/10.1111/0952-1895.00152.

Collins, Patricia H. 2000. Black Feminist Thought: Knowledge, Consciousness, and the Politics of Empowerment, 2nd ed. New York: Routledge.

Connelly, Mark Thomas. 1980. The Response to Prostitution in the Progressive Era. North Carolina: University Press.

Corbin, Alain. 1996. Women for Hire: Prostitution and Sexuality in France after 1850, trans. Alan Sheridan. Harvard University Press.

Corriveau, Patrice. 2013. "Regulating Sex Work." In Sex Work: Rethinking the Job, Respecting the Workers, ed. C. Parent, C. Bruckert, P. Corriveau, M.N. Mensah, and L. Toupin, trans. Käthe Roth, 31–56. Vancouver: UBC Press.

Coulthard, Sean G. 2014. *Red Skin, White Masks: Rejecting the Colonial Politics of Recognition*. Minneapolis: University of Minnesota Press. http://dx.doi.org/10.5749/minnesota/9780816679645.001.0001.

Court of Appeal for Ontario. 2012. "Canada (Attorney General) v. Bedford (2010 ONCA 186)." Ottawa: The Canadian Legal Information Institute. http://www.canlii.org/en/on/onca/doc/2012/2012onca186/2012onca186.pdf.

Crépeau, François, and Delphine Nakache. 2006. "Controlling Irregular Migration in Canada: Reconciling Security Concerns with Human Rights Protection." *Immigration and Refugee Policy Choices* 12 (1): 1–42.

Criminal Code, R.S.C. 1985, c. C-49, s. 294.04. Ottawa: Justice Laws Website. http://laws-lois.justice.gc.ca/eng/acts/C-46.

CTV BC. 2012, September 21. "Canada's Tough Talk On Tamil Migrants Backfires." Vancouver: Bell Media. http://bc.ctvnews.ca/canada-s-tough-talk-on-tamil-migrants-backfires-1.967043.

CTV News. 2013, November 22. "Woman Found Not Guilty of Human Trafficking of Young African Woman." Vancouver: Bell Media. http://www.ctvnews.ca/canada/woman-found-not-guilty-of-human-trafficking-of-young-african-woman-1.1555983.

Danforth, Jessica. 2013. "Activism in and beyond the Academy." Paper presented at the Critical Ethnic Studies Association conference Decolonizing Future Intellectual Legacies and Activist Practices. Chicago: University of Illinois, September 19–21.

Dean, Amber. 2015. *Remembering Vancouver's Disappeared Women: Settler Colonialism and the Difficult of Inheritance*. Toronto: University of Toronto Press.

Deer, Sarah. 2011. "Relocation Revisited: Sex Trafficking and Native Women in the United States." *William Mitchell Law Review* 36 (2): 621–83.

Defend Dignity. 2012. "Welcome to Defend Dignity 2.0!" Regina: Defend Dignity. http://defenddignity.ca/.

Department of Justice. 2016. "Human Trafficking." Ottawa: Department of Justice. http://www.justice.gc.ca/eng/cj-jp/tp/index.html.

De Vries, Maggie. 2003. *Missing Sarah*. Toronto: Penguin Group.

Dewey, Susan. 2008. *Hollow Bodies: Institutional Responses to Sex Trafficking in Armenia, Bosnia, and India*. Sterling: Kumarian Press.

Dhamoon, Rita K. 2015. "A Feminist Approach to Decolonizing Anti-Racism: Rethinking Transnationalism, Intersectionality, and Settler Colonialism." *feral feminisms* 4: 20–37. http://feralfeminisms.com/rita-dhamoon/.

Doezema, Jo. 1998. "Forced to Choose: Beyond the Voluntary v. Forced Prostitution Dichotomy." In *Global Sex Workers: Rights, Resistance, and Redefinition*, ed. K. Kempadoo and J. Doezema, 34–50. New York: Routledge.

Doezema, Jo. 2000. "Loose Women or Lost Women: The Re-emergence of the Myth of White Slavery in Contemporary Discourses of Trafficking in Women." *Gender Issues* 1 (1): 23–50.

Doezema, Jo. 2002. "Who Gets to Choose? Coercion, Consent, and the UN Trafficking Protocol." *Gender and Development* 10 (1): 20–7. http://dx.doi.org/10.1080/13552070215897.

Doezema, Jo. 2010. *Sex Slaves and Discourse Masters: The Construction of Trafficking*. London: Zed Books.

Dottridge, Mike. 2007. "Introduction." In *"Collateral Damage: The Impact of Anti-Trafficking Measures on the Human Rights around the World*, 1–27. Bangkok: GAATW. http://www.gaatw.org/Collateral%20Damage_Final/singlefile_CollateralDamagefinal.pdf.

Dowling, Samantha, Karen Moreton, and Leila Wright. 2007. "Trafficking for the Purposes of Labour Exploitation: A Literature Review." London: GOV. UK. www.homeoffice.gov.uk.

Downe, Pamela. 2006. "Two Stories of Migrant Sex Work, Cross-Border Movement and Violence." *Canadian Women's Studies* 25 (1–2): 61–6.

Eberts, Mary. 2014. "Victoria's Secret: How to Make a Population of Prey." In *Indivisible: Indigenous Human Rights*, ed. J. Green, 144–165. Halifax, Nova Scotia: Fernwood Publishing.

Elabor-Idemudia, Patience. 2002. "Participatory Research: A Tool in the Production of Knowledge in Development Discourse." In *Feminist Post-Development Thought: Re-Thinking Modernity, Post-Colonialism, and Representation*, ed. K. Saunders, 227–254. London, UK: Zed Books.

Employment and Social Development Canada. 2012. "Government of Canada Takes Action to Protect Temporary Foreign Workers." Ottawa: ESD Canada. http://news.gc.ca/web/article-en.do?nid=684419.

Erickson, Lesley. 2011. *Westward Bound: Sex, Violence, the Law, and the Making of a Settler Society*. Vancouver: UBC Press.

Escobar, Arturo. 1995. *Encountering Development: The Making and Unmaking of the Third World*. Princeton, NJ: Princeton University Press.

European Commission. 2012. "The EU Strategy Towards the Eradication of Trafficking in Human Beings 2012-2016." Viena: UNODC. http://www.ungift.org/doc/knowledgehub/resource-centre/The_EU_Strategy_towards_the_Eradication_of_Trafficking_in_Human_Beings_2012-2016.pdf.

Fairclough, Norman, and Ruth Wodak. 1997. "Critical Discourse Analysis." *Discourse Studies: A Multidisciplinary Introduction* 2: 258–84.

Faraday, Fay. 2012. "Made in Canada: How the Law Constructs Migrant Workers' Insecurity." Toronto: Metcalf Foundation. http://metcalffoundation.com/publications-resources/view/made-in-canada/.

Farley, Melissa. 2004. "'Bad for the Body, Bad for the Heart': Prostitution Harms Women Even if Legalized or Decriminalized." *Violence Against Women* 10 (10): 1087–125. http://dx.doi.org/10.1177/1077801204268607.

Farley, Melissa, Isin Baral, Merab Kiremire, and Ufuk Sezgin. 1998. "Prostitution in Five Countries: Violence and Post-Traumatic Stress Disorder." *Feminism & Psychology* 8 (4): 405–26. http://dx.doi.org/10.1177/0959353598084002.

Farley, Melissa, Jacqueline Lynne, and Ann Cotton. 2005. "Prostitution in Vancouver: Violence and the Colonization of First Nations Women." *Transcultural Psychiatry* 42 (2): 242–71.

Feingold, David. 2005. "Think Again: Human Trafficking." Sacramento: World Wide Open. http://www.worldwideopen.org/en/resources/detail/627#.USfB_476YXc.

Feingold, David. 2010. "Trafficking in Numbers: The Social Construction of Human Trafficking Data." In *Sex, Drugs and Body Counts: The Politics of Numbers in Global Crime and Conflict*, ed. P. Andreas, 46–74. New York: Cornell University.

Ferris, Shawna. 2015. *Street Sex Work and Canadian Cities: Resisting a Dangerous Order*. Edmonton: University of Alberta Press.

Festa, Lynn. 2010. "Humanity without Feathers." *Humanity: An International Journal of Human Rights* 1 (1): 3–27. https://muse.jhu.edu/article/394859/pdf.

FIRST. 2009. "Open Letter to the Salvation Army of Canada: Rights Not Rescue." Vancouver: firstadvocates.org. http://rabble.ca/babble/feminism/rights-not-rescue-open-letter-salvation-army.

Fischer-Tiné, Harald. 2011. "Reclaiming Savages in 'Darkest England' and 'Darkest India': The Salvation Army as a Transnational Agent of the Civilizing Mission." In *Civilizing Missions in Colonial and Postcolonial South Asia*, ed. C. Watt and M. Mann, 125–64. London: Anthem Press.

Flowers, Rachel. 2015. "Refused to Forgive: Indigenous Women's Love and Rage." *Decolonization: Indigeneity, Education and Society* 4 (2): 32–49.

Fortin, Nicole, David A. Green, Thomas Lemieux, Kevin Milligan, and W. Craig Riddell. 2012. "Canadian Inequality: Recent Developments and Policy Options." *Canadian Public Policy* 38 (2): 121–45. http://www.sfu.ca/~pendakur/teaching/econ104/fortin%20et%20al%20CPP%202012.pdf.

Foucault, Michel. 1975. *Discipline and Punish: The Birth of the Prison*. London: Penguin.

Foucault, Michel. 1980. "Power and Strategies." In *Power/Knowledge: Selected Interviews and other Writings, 1972–1977*, ed. C. Gordon, 134–46. New York: Pantheon Books.

Foucault, Michel. 1982. "The Subject and Power." *Critical Inquiry* 8 (4): 777–95. http://dx.doi.org/10.1086/448181.

Future Group. 2006. "Falling Short of the Mark: An International
Study on the Treatment of Human Trafficking Victims." Calgary: The
Future Group. http://www.oas.org/atip/canada/fallingshortofthemark
.pdf.

Gallagher, Anne T. 2001. "Human Rights and the New UN Protocols
on Trafficking and Migrant Smuggling: A Preliminary Analysis."
Human Rights Quarterly 23 (4): 975–1004. http://dx.doi.org/10.1353/
hrq.2001.0049.

Gallagher, Anne T. 2010. *The International Law of Human Trafficking*. Cambridge
University Press. http://dx.doi.org/10.1017/CBO9780511761065.

George, Susan. 2003. "Globalizing Rights?" In *Globalizing Rights*, ed. M. Gibney,
15–33. New York: Oxford University Press.

Gill, Sheila D. 2002. "The Unspeakability of Racism: Mapping Law's
Complicity in Manitoba's Racialized Spaces." In *Race, Space, and the Law:
Unmapping a White Settler Society*, ed. S. Razack, 157–84. Toronto: Between
the Lines.

Global Alliance Against Traffic in Women (GAATW). 2000. "Human Rights
and Trafficking in Persons: A Handbook." Bangkok: GAATW. http://gaatw
.org/books_pdf/Human%20Rights%20and%20Trafficking%20in%20Person
.pdf.

Global Alliance Against Traffic in Women (GAATW). 2007. "Collateral Damage:
The Impact of Anti-Trafficking Measures on Human Rights around the
World." Bangkok: GAATW. http://www.gaatw.org/Collateral%20Damage
_Final/singlefile_CollateralDamagefinal.pdf.

Global Alliance Against Traffic in Women (GAATW). 2011. "What's the Cost of
a Rumour? A Guide to Sorting out the Myths and the Facts about Sporting
Events and Trafficking." Bangkok: GAATW. http://www.gaatw.org/
publications/WhatstheCostofaRumour.11.15.2011.pdf.

Global Alliance Against Traffic in Women (GAATW). n.d. "GAATW
Members." Bangkok: GAATW. http://gaatw.org/members/theamericas.

Global Alliance Against Traffic in Women (GAATW). 2013. "2010 Winter Games
Analysis on Human Trafficking" Prepared for Law Enforcement and Policing
Branch, Public Safety Canada. https://www.publicsafety.gc.ca/cnt/rsrcs/
pblctns/wntr-gms-2010/wntr-gms-2010-eng.pdf

Global Ministries. 2008. "Human Trafficking Advocacy [PowerPoint
Presentation]." Cleveland: Global Ministries. www.globalministries.org/
get-involved/justice-and-advocacy/human-trafficking.

Global Network of Sex Work Projects. 2014a. "Butterfly – Asian and Migrant
Sex Workers Network." Edinburgh: NWSP. http://www.nswp.org/
members/butterfly-asian-and-migrant-sex-workers-network.

Global Network of Sex Work Projects. 2014b. "Resources: Migration and Trafficking." Edinburgh: NWSP. http://www.nswp.org/resources/theme/ migration-trafficking/types/research-sex-work.

Globe and Mail. 2004, December 2. "Editorial." Toronto: Globe and Mail, Inc. http://www.theglobeandmail.com/servlet/ArticleNews/TPStory/ LAC/20041202/DANCER02/TPNational/.

Globe and Mail. 2010, August 17. "PM Takes a Hard Line on Tamil Migrants." Toronto: Globe and Mail, Inc. http://www.theglobeandmail.com/news/ politics/ottawa-notebook/pm-takes-hard-line-on-tamil-migrants/ article1368937/.

Globe and Mail. 2012, April 2. "How Hungarian Criminals Built a Slave Trade in Ontario." Toronto: Globe and Mail, Inc. http://www.theglobeandmail. com/news/national/how-hungarian-criminals-built-a-slave-trade-in-ontario/article4097573/,

Globe and Mail. 2012, September 21. "Vancouver Sex Workers Can Proceed with Prostitution Law Challenge: Top Court." Toronto: Globe and Mail, Inc. http:// www.theglobeandmail.com/news/british-columbia/vancouver-sex-workers -can-proceed-with-prostitution-law-challenge-top-court/article4558721/.

Goodey, Jo. 2012. "Data on Human Trafficking: Challenges and Policy Context." In *Human Trafficking: Exploring the International Concerns, Nature, and Complexities*, ed. J. Winterdyk, B. Perrin, and P. Reichel, 39–56. CRC Press.

Goodyear, Michael, and Cheryl Auger. 2013. "Regulating Women's Sexuality: Social Movements and Internal Exclusion." In *Selling Sex: Experience, Advocacy, and Research on Sex Work in Canada*, ed. E. van der Meulen, E. Durisin, and V. Love, 211–29. Vancouver: UBC Press.

Government of Manitoba. 2012. "Tracia's Trust: Manitoba's Sexual Exploitation Strategy." Winnipeg: Government of Manitoba. http://www.gov.mb.ca/fs/ traciastrust/index.html.

Green, Joyce. 2007. "Taking Account of Aboriginal Feminism." In *Making Space for Indigenous Feminism*, ed. J. Green, 20–32. Black Point, NS: Fernwood.

Grimm, Jacob, and Wilhelm Grimm. 1884. *Household Tales*. Vol. 2. Trans. Margaret Hunt. London: George Bell.

Guy, Donna. 1991. *Sex and Danger in Buenos Aires: Prostitution, Family, and Nation in Argentina*. Lincoln: University of Nebraska Press.

Hallgrimsdottir, Helga Kristin, Rachel Phillips, and Cecilia Benoit. 2006. "Fallen Women and Rescued Girls: Social Stigma and Media Narratives of the Sex Industry in Victoria, B.C., from 1980 to 2005." *Canadian Review of Sociology and Anthropology. La Revue Canadienne de Sociologie et d'Anthropologie* 43 (3): 265–80. http://dx.doi.org/10.1111/j.1755-618X.2006. tb02224.x.

Hamilton Spectator. 2012, January 12. "Human Trafficking Case Puts Spotlight on Refugee System." Hamilton: Metroland Media Group, Ltd. http://www.thespec.com/news/crime/article/653197--human-trafficking-case-puts-spotlight-on-refugee-system.

Hanley, Jill, Jacqueline Oxman-Martinez, Marie Lacroix, and Gal Sigalit. 2006. "The 'Deserving' Undocumented? Government and Community Responses to Human Trafficking as a Labour Phenomenon." *Labour Capital and Society. Travail Capital et Société* 39 (2): 78-103.

Hanley, Jill, Eric Shragge, Andre Rivard, and Jahhon Koo. 2012 "'Good Enough to Work? Good Enough to Stay!' Organizing Among Temporary Foreign Workers." In *Legislated Inequality: Temporary Labour Migration in Canada*, 245–71 Montreal: McGill-Queen's University Press.

Hastie, Bethany. 2012. "Doing Canada's Dirty Work: A Critical Analysis of Law and Policy to Address Labour Exploitation and Trafficking." In *Labour Migration, Human Trafficking and Multinational Corporations: The Commodification of Illicit Flows*, ed. A. Quayson and A. Arhin, 121–137. New York: Routledge.

Hastie, Bethany. 2013. "To Do the Dirty Work in Canada: A Critical Analysis of Laws and Policies Related to Forced Labor and Human Trafficking." Paper presented at the Responding to Human Trafficking: Towards Integrated Action SYMPOSIUM. Montreal: CATHII and McGill University, April 11.

Hennebry, Jenna. 2012. *Permanently Temporary? Agricultural Migrant Workers and Their Integration in Canada*. Montreal: Institute for Research on Public Policy. http://www.irpp.org/pubs/IRPPstudy/IRPP_Study_no26.pdf.

Heron, Barbara. 2007. *Desire for Development: Whiteness, Gender, and the Helping Imperative*. Waterloo: Wilfrid Laurier University Press.

Hoogvelt, Ankie. 1997. *Globalization and the Post-colonial World: The New Political Economy of Development*. London: Macmillan Press. http://dx.doi.org/10.1007/978-1-349-25671-6.

Hua, Julietta. 2011. *Trafficking Women's Human Rights*. Minnesota: University of Minnesota Press. http://dx.doi.org/10.5749/minnesota/9780816675609.001.0001.

Hughes, Donna M. 2005. "The Demand for Victims of Sex Trafficking." Kingston: University of Rhode Island. http://www.uri.edu/artsci/wms/hughes/demand_for_victims.pdf.

Hunt, Sarah. 2008. "Trafficking of Aboriginal Girls and Youth: Risk Factors and Historical Context." Vancouver: Safe Online Research. http://www.safeonlineoutreach.com/pdf/sara_hunt-human_trafficking_speech%20copy.pdf.

Hunt, Sarah. 2013. "Sex Work and Self-Determination: In Solidarity with the Bedford Case." Sarah Hunt: Becoming Collective. https://becomingcollective.wordpress.com/2013/06/12/sex-work-and-self-determination-in-solidarity-with-the-bedford-case/.

Hunt, Sarah. 2014. *Panel Discussion.* "*Red Skin, White Masks: Rejecting the Colonial Politics of Recognition.* Vancouver: Simon Fraser University; http://www.sfu.ca/sfuwoodwards/events/events1/2014-2015-fall/GlenCoulthardRedSkinWhiteMask.html.

Ikebuchi, Shelly D. 2015. *From Slave Girls to Salvation: Gender, Race, and Victoria's Chinese Rescue Home, 1886–1923.* Vancouver: UBC Press.

Immigration Watch Canada. 2007. "UBC Law Professor says Human Traffickers Will View the 2010 Olympics as the Biggest Business Opportunity for Them in Decades." Vancouver: Immigration Watch Canada. (http://www.immigrationwatchcanada.org/index.php?module=pagemaster&PAGE_user_op=view_page&PAGE_id=2220&MMN_position=92:90).

Indigenous and Northern Affairs Canada. 2013. "The Numbered Treaties (1871–1921)." Ottawa: Indigenous and Northern Affairs Canada. https://www.aadnc-aandc.gc.ca/eng/1360948213124/1360948312708.

Indigenous Sex Sovereignty Collective. 2016. "Statement from Indigenous Sex Sovereignty Collective." Indigenous Sex Sovereignty Collective. http://indigenoussexsovereignty.tumblr.com.

International Justice Mission. 2010. "Fact Sheet: Sex Trafficking." Washington: International Justice Mission. https://www.ijm.org/sites/default/files/download/resources/Factsheet-Sex-Trafficking.pdf.

International Labour Organization. 2005. *A Global Alliance Against Forced Labor. Global Report on the follow-up to the ILO Declaration on Fundamental Principles and Rights at Work.* Geneva: ILO.

International Labour Organization. 2012. "ILO Global Estimate of Forced Labour 2012: Results and Methodology." Washington, DC: International Labour Organization. http://www.ilo.org/sapfl/Informationresources/ILOPublications/WCMS_182004/lang--en/index.htm.

International Organization for Migration. 2010. "Global Human Trafficking Database Counter Trafficking Division." Geneva: International Organization for Migration. http://www.iom.int/jahia/webdav/shared/shared/mainsite/activities/ct/iom_ctm_database.pdf.

International Organization for Migration (IOM) Ukraine. 2012. "Human Trafficking in Ukraine Did Not Spike During EURO 2012." Geneva: International Organization for Migration. http://iom.org.ua/en/home-page/news/human-trafficking-in-ukraine-did-not-spike-during-euro-2012.html).

Isaacs, Tracy. 2014. "Collective Responsibility and Collective Obligation." *Midwest Studies in Philosophy* 38 (1): 40–57. http://dx.doi.org/10.1111/misp.12015.

Jeffery, Taylor. 2010. "Capitalist Development, Forms of Labour, and Class Formation in Prairie Canada." In *The West and Beyond: New Perspectives on an Imagined Region*, ed. S. Carter, A. Finkel, and P. Fortna, 159–180. Edmonton: Athabasca University Press.

Jeffrey, Leslie Ann. 2005. "Canada and Migrant Sex Work: Challenging the 'Foreign' in Foreign Policy." *Canadian Foreign Policy* 12 (1): 33–48. http://dx.doi.org/10.1080/11926422.2005.9673387.

Jeffrey, Leslie Ann, and Gayle MacDonald. 2006. "'It's in the Money, Honey': The Economy of Sex Work in the Maritimes." *Canadian Review of Sociology and Anthropology. La Revue Canadienne de Sociologie et d'Anthropologie* 43 (3): 313–27. http://dx.doi.org/10.1111/j.1755-618X.2006.tb02227.x.

Jeffrey, Leslie Ann, and Gayle MacDonald. 2007. *Sex Workers in the Maritimes Talk Back*. Vancouver: UBC Press.

Jeffreys, Sheila. 2008. *The Industrial Vagina: The Political Economy of the Global Sex Trade*. New York: Routledge.

Jordan, Ann. 2002. "The Annotated Guide to the Complete UN Trafficking Protocol." Edinburgh: Global Network of Sex Workers Projects. http://www.nswp.org/.

Jordan, Ann, and Burke Jordan. 2011. "Is Human Trafficking Really the Most Third Most Profitable Business for Organized Crime." Rights Work. http://rightswork.org/2011/03/is-human-trafficking-really-the-third-most-profitable-business-for-organized-crime-3/.

Jordan, Michael. 2005. *The Great Abolition Sham: The True Story of the End of the British Slave Trade*. Stroud, UK: The History Press Ltd.

Kapoor, Ilan. 2013. *Celebrity Humanitarianism: The Ideology of Global Charity*. Abingdon: Routledge.

Kapur, Ratna. 2003. "The 'Other' Side of Globalization: The Legal Regulation of Cross-Border Movements." *Canadian Woman Studies* 22: 6–15.

Kara, Siddharth. 2009. *Sex Trafficking: Inside the Business of Modern Slavery*. New York: Columbia University Press.

Kaye, Julie, and Bethany Hastie. 2015. "The Canadian *Criminal Code* Offence of Trafficking in Persons: Challenges from the Field and within the Law." *Social Inclusion* 3 (1): 88–102. http://dx.doi.org/10.17645/si.v3i1.178.

Kaye, Julie, John Winterdyk, and Lara Quarterman. 2014. "Beyond Criminal Justice: A Case Study of Responding to Human Trafficking in Canada." *Canadian Journal of Criminology and Criminal Justice* 56 (1): 23–48.

Kaye, Julie. 2015. *Intersections of Race, Class, and Gender in Human Trafficking in Alberta: An Environmental Scan*. Edmonton: Government of Alberta Ministry of Human Services.

Kaye, Julie, and John Winterdyk. 2011. "Explaining Human Trafficking." In *Human Trafficking: Exploring the International Nature, Concerns, and*

Complexities, ed. J. Winterdyk, B. Perrin, and P. Reichel, 57–78. Boca Raton, FL: Taylor and Francis.

Kempadoo, Kamala. 1998. "Introduction: Globalizing Sex Workers' Rights." In *Global Sex Workers: Rights, Resistance, and Redefinition*, ed. K. Kempadoo and J. Doezema, 1–28. New York: Routledge.

Kempadoo, Kamala. 2005. "Introduction: From Moral Panic to Global Justice: Changing Perspectives on Trafficking." In *Trafficking and Prostitution Reconsidered: New Perspectives on Migration, Sex Work, and Human Rights*, ed. K. Kempadoo, J. Sanghera, and B. Pattanaik, vii–xxxiv. Boulder, CO: Paradigm Publishers.

Kempadoo, Kamala. 2007. "The War on Human Trafficking in the Caribbean." *Race & Class* 49 (2): 79–85. http://dx.doi.org/10.1177/03063968070490020602.

Kempadoo, Kamala. 2012. "Introduction: Abolitionism, Criminal Justice, and Transnational Feminism: Twenty-First-Century Perspectives on Human Trafficking." In *Trafficking and Prostitution Reconsidered: New Perspectives on Migration, Sex Work, and Human Rights,* 2nd ed., edited by K. Kempadoo, J. Sanghera, and B. Pattanaik, vii–xlii. Boulder, CO: Paradigm Publishers.

Kivisto, Peter, and Thomas Faist. 2007. *Citizenship: Discourse, Theory, and Transnational Prospects*. Oxford: Blackwell Publishing.

Kothari, Uma. 2001. "Power, Knowledge and Social Control in Participatory Development." In *Participation: The New Tyranny?* ed. B. Cooke and U. Kothari, 139–152. New York: Zed Books.

Kothari, Uma. 2005. "From Colonial Administration to Development Studies: A Post-Colonial Critique of the History of Development Studies." In *A Radical History of Development Studies: Individuals, Institutions and Ideologies*, ed. U. Kothari, 47–66. London: Zed Books.

Krishnmurti, Sailaja. 2013. "Queue Jumpers, Terrorists, Breeders: Representations of Tamil Migrants in Canadian Popular Media." *South Asian Diaspora* 5 (1): 139–57.

Laczko, Frank, and Elzieba Gozdziak, eds. 2005. *Data and Research on Human Trafficking*. Geneva, Switzerland: International Organization for Migration.

Lam, Elena. 2016. "The Birth of Butterfly: Bringing Sex Workers' Voices into the Sex Workers Rights Movement." *Research for Sex Work* 15: 1–4. http://www.nswp.org/sites/nswp.org/files/The%20Birth%20of%20Butterly%2C%20Elene%20Lam%20-%202016.pdf.

Lamont, Michèle, and Virág Molnár. 2002. "The Study of Boundaries in the Social Sciences." *Annual Review of Sociology* 28 (1): 167–95. http://dx.doi.org/10.1146/annurev.soc.28.110601.141107.

Langevin, Louise. 2007. "Trafficking in Women in Canada: A Critical Analysis of the Legal Framework Governing Immigrant Live-In Caregivers."

International Journal of Comparative and Applied Criminal Justice 31 (2): 191–209. http://dx.doi.org/10.1080/01924036.2007.9678768.

Lawrence, Bonita. 2004. *"Real" Indians and Others: Mixed Blood Urban Peoples and Indigenous Nationhood*. Lincoln: University of Nebraska Press.

Lawrence, Bonita, and Enakshi Dua. 2005. "Decolonizing Anitresistance." *Social Justice (San Francisco, Calif.)* 32 (4): 120–47.

Lawrence, Sonia. 2015. "Expert-Tease: Advocacy, Ideology And Experience in Bedford and Bill C-36." *Canadian Journal of Law and Society* 30 (01): 5–7. http://dx.doi.org/10.1017/cls.2015.3.

LeBaron, Genevieve. 2013. "Subcontracting Is Not Illegal, but Is It Unethical: Business Ethics, Forced Labor, and Economic Success." *Brown Journal of World Affairs* 20 (11): 237–49.

Lee, Maggy. 2007. "Introduction: Understanding human trafficking." In *Human Trafficking*, ed. M. Lee, 1–25. Devon: Willan.

Lee, Maggy. 2010. *Trafficking and Global Crime Control*. London: Sage.

Lee, Maggy. 2011. *Trafficking and Global Crime Control*. Thousand Oaks, CA: Sage.

Leidholdt, Dorchen. 2003. "Prostitution and Trafficking in Women: An Intimate Relationship." *Journal of Trauma Practice* 2 (3-4): 167–83. http://dx.doi.org/10.1300/J189v02n03_09.

Lenard, Patti T., and Christine Straehle, eds. 2012. *Legislated Inequality: Temporary Labour Migration in Canada*. Montreal: McGill-Queens University Press.

Lepp, Analee. 2002. "Trafficking in Women and the Feminization of Migration: The Canadian Context." *Canadian Women Studies* 21/22, 4/1: 90–99.

Lepp, Analee. 2003. *Transnational Migration, Trafficking in Women and Human Rights: the Canadian Dimension*. Victoria: GAATW Canada.

Lepp, Analee. 2013. *Do Not Harm: A Human Rights Approach to Anti-Trafficking Policies and Interventions in Canada*. London, ON: Centre for Research and Education on Violence Against Women; http://www.learningtoendabuse .ca/sites/default/files/AnnaLee_Lepp_Human_Trafficking.pdf.

Levine-Rasky, Cynthia, Julianna Beaudoin, and Paul St Clair. 2013. "The Exclusion of Roma Claimants in Canadian Refugee Policy." *Patterns of Prejudice*. 48 (1): 63–93.

Library of Parliament. 2010. "Legislative Summary of Bill C-49." Ottawa: Social Affairs Division. http://www.parl.gc.ca/About/Parliament/ LegislativeSummaries/Bills_ls.asp?Language=E&ls=c49&source=library _prb&Parl=40&Ses=3).

Library of Parliament. 2012. "Legislative of Bill C-10." Ottawa: Parliamentary Information and Research Services. (http://www.parl.gc.ca/Content/ LOP/LegislativeSummaries/41/1/c10-e.pdf).

Lomawaima, Tsianina K. 1994. *They Called It Prairie Light: The Story of Chilocco Indian School*. Lincoln: University of Nebraska Press.

Lucashenko, Melissa. 1994. "No Other Truth? Aboriginal Women and Australian Feminism." *Social Alternatives* 12 (4): 21–4.

Lukes, Steven. 2005. *Power: A Radical View*, 2nd ed. Houndmills: Palgrave.

MacKenzie, Megan. 2012. *Female Soldiers in Sierra Leone: Sex, Security, and Post-Conflict Development*. New York University Press. http://dx.doi.org/10.18574/nyu/9780814761373.001.0001.

Macklin, Audrey. 1992. "Foreign Domestic Worker: Surrogate Housewife or Mail Order Servant?" *McGill Law Journal. Revue de Droit de McGill* 37: 681.

Macklin, Audrey. 2003. "Dancing Across Borders: 'Exotic Dancers', Trafficking and Canadian Immigration Policy." *International Migration Review* 37 (2): 454.

Macklin, Audrey. 2010. "Historicizing Narratives of Arrival: The Other Indian Other." Victoria: University of Victoria. http://law.uvic.ca/demcon/documents/macklin.pdf.

Maggie's Toronto Sex Workers Action Project. 2012, February 14. "Indigenous People in the Sex Trade: Our Life, Our Bodies, Our Realities." News release. http://maggiestoronto.ca/press-releases?news_id=79.

Mancuso, Rebecca J. 2011. "Three Thousand Families: English Canada's Colonizing Vision and British Family Settlement, 1919–39." *Journal of Canadian Studies. Revue d'Etudes Canadiennes* 45 (3): 5–33.

Manitoba Family Services and Housing. 2008. "Tracia's Trust: Front Line Voices: Manitobans Working Together to End Child Sexual Exploitation." Winnipeg: Manitoba Family Services and Housing. http://www.gov.mb.ca/fs/childfam/pubs/tracias_trust_en.pdf.

Maracle, Lee. 1996. *I Am Woman: A Native Perspective on Sociology and Feminism*. Vancouver: Press Gang.

Marshall, Alison R. 2014. *Cultivating Connections: The Making of Chinese Prairie Canada*. Vancouver: UBC Press.

Mason, Jennifer. 2002. *Qualitative Researching*, 2nd ed. London, UK: Sage Publications.

Mawani, Renisa. 2002. "A White World? Whiteness and the Meaning of Modernity in Latin America and Japan." In *Working Through Whiteness: International Perspectives*, ed. C. Levine-Rasky, 69–106. Albany: State University of New York Press.

McCarthy, Bill, Cecilia Benoit, and Mikael Jansson. 2014. "Sex Work: A Comparative Study." *Archives of Sexual Behavior* 43 (7): 1379–90. http://dx.doi.org/10.1007/s10508-014-0281-7.

McCarthy, Bill, Cecilia Benoit, Mikael Jansson, and Kat Kolar. 2012. "Regulating Sex Work: Heterogeneity in Legal Strategies." *Annual Review of Law and Social Science* 8 (1): 255–71. http://dx.doi.org/10.1146/annurev -lawsocsci-102811-173915.

McGrew, Anthony. 2000. "Sustainable Globalization? The Global Politics of Development and Exclusion in the New World Order." In *Poverty and Development into the 21st Century*, ed. T. Allen and A. Thomas, 345–364. Oxford: The Open University in association with Oxford University Press.

McManus, Sheila. 2001. "Mapping the Alberta-Montana Borderlands: Ethnicity and Gender in the Nineteenth Century." *Journal of American Ethnic History* 20 (3): 71–87.

McMaster, Lindsey. 2008. *Working Girls in the West: Representations of Wage-Earning Women*. Vancouver: UBC Press.

McMichael, Philip. 2012. *Development and Social Change: A Global Perspective*, 4th ed. Thousand Oaks and London: Pine Forge Press.

Memmi, Alberto. 1965. *The Colonizer and the Colonized*. New York: Orion Press.

Mensah, Mahia Nengeh. 2006. "Débat feministe sur la prostitution au Québec: Points de vue des travailleuses du sexe." *Canadian Review of Sociology* 43 (3): 345–61.

Merry, Sally E. 2003. "Rights Talk and the Experience of Law: Implementing Women's Human Rights to Protection from Violence." *Human Rights Quarterly* 25 (2): 343–81. http://dx.doi.org/10.1353/hrq.2003.0020.

Merry, Sally E. 2011. "Sex Trafficking and Global Governance in the Context of Pacific Mobility." *Law Text Culture* 15: 187–208.

Mies, Maria. 1998. *Patriarchy and Accumulation on a World Scale: Women in the International Division of Labour*, 6th ed. New York: Zed Books.

Million, Diane. 2013. *Therapeutic Nations: Healing in an Age of Indigenous Human Rights*. Phoenix: University of Arizona Press.

Ministry of Justice and Solicitor General. 1995–2013. "Help for Victims of Crimes." Edmonton: Ministry of Justice and Solicitor General. https://www.solgps.alberta.ca/programs_and_services/victim_services/help _for_victims/Pages/default.aspx#benefits.

Mohanty, Chandra. 1991. "Under Western Eyes: Feminist Scholarship and Colonial Discourses." In *Third World Women and the Politics of Feminism*, ed. C. Mohanty, A. Russo, and L. Torres, 51–80. Bloomington: Indiana University Press.

Monks, Gregory. 1992. "Architectural Symbolism and Non-Verbal Communication at Upper Fort Gary." *Historical Archaeology* 26 (2): 37–57. http://dx.doi.org/10.1007/BF03373532.

Monture, Patricia. 1999. *Journeying Forward: Dreaming First Nations' Independence*. Halifax: Fernwood.

Monture, Patricia. 2007. "Racing and Erasing: Law and Gender in White Settler Societies." In *Race and Racism in 21st Century Canada: Continuity,*

Complexity, and Change, ed. B.S. Bolora and S.P. Hier, 197–216. Peterborough, ON, and Orchard Park, NY: Broadview Press.

Monture-Angus, Patricia. 1995. *Thunder in My Soul.* Halifax: Fernwood Publishing.

Monture-Angus, Patricia. 2005. "Thinking about Change." In *Justice as Healing: Indigenous Ways. Writings on Community Peacemaking and Restorative Justice from the Native Law Centre,* ed. W.D. McCaslin, 275–79. St. Paul: Living Justice Press.

Morrison, Toni. 1997. "The Official Story: Dead Many Golfing." In *Birth of a Nation'hood: Gaze, Script, and Spectacle in the O. J. Simpson Trial,* ed. T. Morrison and C.B. Lacour, vii–xxvii. New York: Pantheon.

Morrison, John, and Beth Crosland. 2001. "The Trafficking and Smuggling of Refugees: The End Game in European Asylum Policy?" Ottawa: UNHCR Canada. http://www.unhcr.org/3af66c9b4.html.

Morriss, Peter. 2006. "Steven Lukes on the Concept of Power." *Political Studies Review* 4 (2): 124–35. http://dx.doi.org/10.1111/j.1478-9299.2006.000104.x.

Mountz, Alison. 2004. "Embodying the Nation-State: Canada's Response to Human Smuggling." *Political Geography* 23 (3): 323–45. http://dx.doi.org/10.1016/j.polgeo.2003.12.017.

Mountz, Alison. 2010. *Seeking Asylum: Human Smuggling and Bureaucracy at the Border.* Minneapolis: University of Minnesota Press.

Nagle, Jill, ed. 1997. *Whores and Other Feminists.* New York: Routledge.

Nakache and Kinoshita. 2010. "The Canadian Temporary Foreign Worker Program: Do Short-Term Economic Needs Prevail over Human Right Concerns?" IRPP Study. Montréal: McGill University. http://oppenheimer.mcgill.ca/IMG/pdf/IRPP_Study_no5.pdf.

National Post. 2006, December 6. "Over 100 Arrested in B.C. Raid on Suspected Brothels." Toronto: Postmedia Network Inc.

National Post. 2012, April 22. "Efforts to Keep Bogus Roma Refugees Out Have Failed Jason Kenney." Toronto: Postmedia Network Inc. http://news.nationalpost.com/news/canada/efforts-to-keep-bogus-roma-refugees-out-have-failed-jason-kenney.

National Post. 2013, January 21. "MV Sun Sea Passenger Loses Refugee Status After Court Denies His Claim That Sri Lanka Could Falsely Link Him to Tamil Rebels." Toronto: Postmedia Network Inc. http://news.nationalpost.com/news/canada/mv-sun-sea-passenger-loses-refugee-status-after-court-denies-his-claim-that-sri-lanka-could-falsey-link-him-to-tamil-rebels.

National Post. 2015, May 13. "Migrant Sex Workers Caught Up in Ottawa Sting Facing Deportation, Further Exploitation: Activists." Toronto: Postmedia

Network Inc. http://news.nationalpost.com/news/canada/migrant-sex-workers-caught-up-in-ottawa-sting-facing-deportation-further-exploitation-activists.

Native Women's Association of Canada (NWAC). 2010. "What Their Stories Tell Us: Research Findings from the Sisters in Spirit Initiative." Ottawa: NWAC. http://www.nwac.ca/sites/default/files/reports/2010_NWAC_SIS_Report_EN.pdf.

Native Women's Association of Canada (NWAC). 2012. "Understanding NWAC's Position on Prostitution: November 2012." Ottawa: NWAC. https://nwac.ca/wp-content/uploads/2015/05/2012_NWACs_Position_on_Prostitution.pdf.

Native Women's Association of Canada (NWAC). 2014. "Sexual Exploitation and Trafficking of Aboriginal Women and Girls." Final Report for the Canadian Women's Foundation Task Force on Trafficking of Women and Girls in Canada. Ottawa: NWAC. http://www.nwac.ca/wp-content/uploads/2015/05/2014_NWAC_Human_Trafficking_and_Sexual_Exploitation_Report.pdf.

O'Connell, Sheilagh. 1988. "The Impact of Bill C-49 on Street Prostitution: "What's Law Got to Do with It." *Journal of Law and Social Policy* 4: 109–45. http://digitalcommons.osgoode.yorku.ca/jlsp/vol4/iss1/4.

O'Connell Davidson, Julia. 2006. "Will the Real Sex Slave Please Stand Up?" *Feminist Review* 83 (S1): 4–22. http://dx.doi.org/10.1057/palgrave.fr.9400278.

O'Connell Davidson, Julia. 2010. "New Slavery, Old Binaries: Human Trafficking and the Borders of 'Freedom.'" *Global Networks* 10 (2): 244–61. http://dx.doi.org/10.1111/j.1471-0374.2010.00284.x.

O'Connell Davidson, Julia. 2013. "Troubling Freedom: Migration, Debt, and Modern Slavery." *Migration Studies* 1 (2): 176–95. http://dx.doi.org/10.1093/migration/mns002.

O'Connell Davidson, Julia. 2015. *Modern Slavery: The Margins of Freedom.* Palgrave Macmillan. http://dx.doi.org/10.1057/9781137297297.

O'Connell Davidson, Julia, and Brigit Anderson. 2006. "The Trouble with 'Trafficking." In *Trafficking and Women's Rights,* ed. C. van den Anker and J. Doomernik, 11–26. Basingstoke: Palgrave Macmillan.

Office of Refugee Resettlement. 2012. "Fact Sheet Human Trafficking." Washington, DC: Administration for Children and Families. http://www.acf.hhs.gov/programs/orr/resource/fact-sheet-human-trafficking.

Ogrodnik, Lucie. 2010. "Towards the Development of a National Data Collection Framework to Measure Trafficking in Persons." In *Crime and*

Justice Research Paper Series. Ottawa: Statistics Canada; http://www.statcan
.gc.ca/pub/85-561-m/85-561-m2010021-eng.pdf.

Oppal, Wally. 2012. "British Columbia Missing Women Commission of
Inquiry." Victoria, BC: Missing Women Commission of Inquiry. http://
www.missingwomeninquiry.ca/obtain-report/).

Organization of American States (OAS). 2008. "1933 International Convention
for the Suppression of the Traffic in Women of Full Age." Washington: OAS.
https://ec.europa.eu/anti-trafficking/sites/antitrafficking/files/1933
_international_convention_en_1.pdf./

Oxman-Martinez, Jacqueline, Andrea Martinez, and Jill Hanley. 2001a. "Human
Trafficking: Canadian Government Policy and Practice." *Refuge: Canada's
Periodical on Refugees* 19 (4): 14–23.

Oxman-Martinez, Jacqueline, Andrea Martinez, and Jill Hanley. 2001b.
"Trafficking Women: Gendered Impacts of Canadian Immigration Policies."
Journal of International Migration and Integration 2 (3): 297–313. http://dx.doi
.org/10.1007/s12134-001-1000-5.

Oxman-Martinez, Jacqueline, Jill Hanley, and Fanny Gomez. 2005. "Canadian
Policy on Human Trafficking: A Four-Year Analysis." *International Migration
(Geneva, Switzerland)* 43 (4): 7–29. http://dx.doi.org/10.1111/j.1468-2435
.2005.00331.x.

Oxman-Martinez, Jacqueline, Marie Lacroix, and Jill Hanley. 2005. *Victims
of Trafficking in Persons: Perspectives from the Canadian Community Sector.*
Ottawa: Department of Justice, Research and Statistics Division. http://
www.justice.gc.ca/eng/rp-pr/cj-jp/tp/rr06_3/rr06_3.pdf.

Parent, Colette, and Chris Bruckert. 2013. "The Current Debate on Sex Work."
In *Sex Work: Rethinking the Job, Respecting the Workers,* ed. C. Parent, C.
Bruckert, P. Corriveau, M.N. Mensah, and L. Toupin, trans. Käthe Roth,
9–30. Vancouver: UBC Press.

Parent, Colette, Chris Bruckert, Patrice Corriveau, Maria N. Mensah, and
Lousie Toupin, eds. 2013. *Sex Work: Rethinking the Job, Respecting the
Workers.* Vancouver: UBC Press.

Parliament of Canada. 2010. "40th Parliament, 3rd Session," Ottawa:
Parliament of Canada. http://www.parl.gc.ca/HousePublications/
Publication.aspx?DocId=4737722&Language=E&Mode=1.

Parliament of Canada. 2012. "Protecting Canada's Immigration System
Act (Bill C-31)." Ottawa: Parliament of Canada. http://www.parl.gc.ca/
HousePublications/Publication.aspx?DocId=5391960.

Parliament of Canada. 2012. "Safe Streets and Communities Act (Bill C-10)."
Ottawa: Parliament of Canada. http://www.parl.gc.ca/HousePublications/
Publication.aspx?DocId=5465759&File=32.

Parrenas, Rhacel S. 2001. *Servants of Globalization: Women, Migration, and Domestic Work*. Palo Alto, CA: Stanford University Press.

Pearce, Diane. 1978. "The Feminization of Poverty: Women, Work, and Welfare." *Urban & Social Change Review* 11: 28–36.

Pearson, Elaine. 2002. *Human Traffic and Human Rights: Redefining Victim Protection*. London: Anti-Slavery International.

Peräkylä, Anssi. 2005. "Analyzing Talk and Text." In *The Sage Handbook of Qualitative Research*, 3rd ed., ed. N. Denzin and Y. Lincoln, 869–86. Thousand Oaks, CA: Sage.

Perreault, Samuel. 2011. "Violent Victimization of Aboriginal People in the Canadian Provinces, 2009." *Juristat* http://www.statcan.gc.ca/.

Perrin, Benjamin. 2010a. *Invisible Chains: Canada's Underground World of Human Trafficking*. Toronto: Penguin Group.

Perrin, Benjamin. 2010b. "Just Passing Through? International Legal Obligations and Policies of Transit Countries in Combating Trafficking in Persons." *European Journal of Criminology* 7 (1): 11–27. http://dx.doi.org/10.1177/1477370809347946.

Peters, Evelyn J., and Oksana M. Starchenko. 2005. "Changes in Aboriginal Settlement Patterns in Two Canadian Cities: A Comparison to Immigrant Settlement Models." *Canadian Journal of Urban Research* 14 (2): 315–37.

Popli, Ushvinder K. 2008. "Contemporary Gender Issue: Feminisation of Trafficking." *Rajagiri Journal of Social Development* 4 (1): 15–32.

Pratt, Anna, and Valverde, Mariana. 2002. "From Deserving Victims to 'Masters of Confusion': Redefining Refugees in the 1990s." *Canadian Journal of Sociology* 27 (2): 135-61.

Preibisch, Kerry. 2012. "Development as Remittances or Development as Freedom? Exploring Canada's Temporary Migration Programs from a Rights-Based Approach." In *Constitutional Labour Rights in Canada: Farm Workers and the Fraser Case*, ed. F. Faraday, J. Fudge, and E. Tucker, 81–108. Toronto: Irwin Law.

Province of British Columbia. 2010. "BC's Office to Combat Trafficking in Persons (OCTIP) Ministry of Public Safety and Solicitor General: 3 Year Status Report July 1, 2007–June 30, 2010." Victoria: Ministry of Justice. http://www.pssg.gov.bc.ca/octip/docs/octip-three-year-status-report.pdf.

Province of British Columbia. 2013. "Mandate of OCTIP." Victoria: Ministry of Justice. http://www.pssg.gov.bc.ca/octip/about.htm.

Provincial Court of Manitoba. 2008. "The Fatality Inquiries Act Report by Provincial Judge on Inquest Respecting the Death of: Tracia Owen." Winnipeg: Manitoba Courts. http://www.manitobacourts.mb.ca/pdf/tracia_owen.pdf.

Public Safety Canada. 2012a. "National Action Plan to Combat Human Trafficking." Ottawa: Public Safety Canada. http://www.publicsafety.gc.ca/prg/le/cmbt-trffkng-eng.aspx.

Public Safety Canada. 2012b. "The Harper Government Launches Canada's National Action Plan to Combat Human Trafficking." Ottawa: Public Safety Canada. http://www.publicsafety.gc.ca/media/nr/2012/nr20120606-eng.aspx.

Public Safety Canada. 2012c. "Marginalized: The Aboriginal Women's Experience in Federal Corrections." Ottawa: Aboriginal Policy Unit, Public Safety Canada. https://www.publicsafety.gc.ca/cnt/rsrcs/pblctns/mrgnlzd/mrgnlzd-eng.pdf.

Quarterman, Lara, Julie Kaye, and John Winterdyk. 2012. "Human Trafficking in Calgary: Informing a Localized Response." Edmonton: ACT Alberta. http://ywcacanada.ca/data/research_docs/00000239.pdf.

Raymond, Janice. 2005. "Sex Trafficking Is Not 'Sex Work.'" *Conscience (Washington, D.C.)* 26: 45.

Razack, Sherene. 1998. *Looking White People in the Eye; Gender, Race, and Culture in Courtrooms and Classrooms*. Toronto: University of Toronto Press.

Razack, Sherene. 2000. "Gendered Racial Violence and Spatialized Justice: The Murder of Pamela George." *Canadian Journal of Law and Society* 15 (2): 91–130.

Razack, Sherene H. 2002. *Race, Space, and the Law*. Toronto: Between the Lines.

Razack, Sherene H. 2004. *Dark Threats and White Knights: The Somalia Affair, Peacekeeping, and the New Imperialism*. Toronto: University of Toronto Press.

Roberts, Nicky. 1992. *Whores in History: Prostitution in Western Society*. London: Harper Collins.

Roots, Katrin. 2013. "Trafficking or Pimping? An Analysis of Canada's Human Trafficking Legislation and Its Implications." *Canadian Journal of Law and Society* 28 (01): 21–41. http://dx.doi.org/10.1017/cls.2012.4.

Ross, Becki. 2003. "Striptease on the Line: Investigating Trends in Erotic Entertainment." In *Making Normal: Social Regulation in Canada*, ed. D. Brock, 146–75. Toronto: Nelson.

Royal Canadian Mounted Police (RCMP). 2004. *"Restricted Information" Project Surrender: A Strategic Intelligence Assessment of the Extent of Human Trafficking to Canada*. Ottawa: Criminal Intelligence Directorate.

Royal Canadian Mounted Police (RCMP). 2010. "Project SECLUSION." Ottawa: RCMP http://publications.gc.ca/collections/collection_2011/grc-rcmp/PS64-78-2010-eng.pdf.

Royal Canadian Mounted Police (RCMP). 2012. "Frequently Asked Questions on Human Trafficking." Ottawa: RCMP. http://www.rcmp-grc.gc.ca/ht -tp/q-a-trafficking-traite-eng.htm#q3.

Royal Canadian Mounted Police (RCMP). 2013. "Domestic Human Trafficking for Sexual Exploitation." Ottawa: RCMP. http://publications .gc.ca/collections/collection_2014/grc-rcmp/PS64-114-2014-eng.pdf.

Rutman, Deborah, and Andrew Armitage. 1993. "Counting on Kids: An Overview of 'State of the Child' Reports." *Canadian Review of Social Policy* 31.

Said, Edward. 1979. *Orientalism*. New York: Vintage Books.

Salt, John. 2000. "Trafficking and Human Smuggling: A European Perspective." *International Migration (Geneva, Switzerland)* 38 (3): 31–56. http://dx.doi.org/10.1111/1468-2435.00114.

Salvation Army. 2008. "Video: The Truth Isn't Sexy – Human Trafficking." Toronto: The Salvationist. http://salvationist.ca/2009/05/video-the-truth -isn't-sexy/.

Sanghera, Jyoti. 2000. "In the Belly of the Beast: Sex Trade, Prostitution and Globalisation." *Quilt* 51–57.

Sanghera, Jyoti. 2005. "Unpacking Trafficking Discourse." In *Trafficking and Prostitution Reconsidered: New Perspectives on Migration, Sex Work, and Human Rights*, ed. K. Kempadoo, J. Sanghera, and B. Pattanaik, 3–24. Boulder, CO: Paradigm Publishers.

Sassen, Saskia. 2002. "Women's Burden: Counter-Geographies of Globalization and the Feminization of Survival." In *Feminist Post-Development Thought: Re-Thinking Modernity, Post-Colonialism, and Representation*, ed. K. Saunders, 89–104. London, UK: Zed Books. http://dx.doi.org/10.1163/157181002761931378.

Sassen, Saskia. 2008. "Neither Global nor National: Novel Assemblages of Territory, Authority and Rights." *Ethics & Global Politics* 1 (1–2): 61–79.

Satzewich, Vic. 1991. *Racism and the Incorporation of Foreign Labour: Farm Labour Migratinon to Canada Since 1945*. London: Routledge.

Satzewich, Vic, and Terry Wotherspoon. 2000. *First Nations: Race, Class, and Gender Relations*. Regina: Canadian Plains Research Center.

Saunders, Kriemild. 2002. "Introduction: Towards a Deconstructive Post-Development Criticism." In *Feminist Post-Development Thought: Re-Thinking Modernity, Post-Colonialism, and Representation*, ed. K. Saunders, 1–38. London: Zed Books.

Scott, John. 2001. *Power*. Cambridge: Polity Press.

Sen, Gita, and Caren A. Grown. 1987. *Development, Crises and Alternative Visions: Third World Woman's Perspectives*. Reading: Cox & Wyman Ltd.

Seshia, Maya. 2010. "Naming Systemic Violence in Winnipeg's Street Sex Trade." *Canadian Journal of Urban Research* 19 (1): 1–17.

Sethi, Anupriya. 2007. "Domestic Sex Trafficking of Aboriginal Girls in Canada: Issues and Implications." *First Peoples Child & Family Review* 3 (3): 57–71.

Sharma, Nandita. 2003. "Travel Agency: A Critique of Anti-Trafficking Campaigns." *Refuge: Canada's Periodical on Refugees* 21 (3): 53–65.

Sharma, Nandita. 2006. *Home Economics: Nationalism and the Making of "Migrant Workers" in Canada.* Toronto University of Toronto Press.

Sharma, Nandita, and Cynthia Wright. 2008. "Decolonizing Resistance, Challenging Colonial States." *Social Justice* 35 (3) 120–38.

Shelley, Louise. 2010. *Human Trafficking: A Global Perspective.* Cambridge: Cambridge University Press. http://dx.doi.org/10.1017/CBO9780511760433.

Sikka, Anette. 2009. "Trafficking of Aboriginal Women and Girls in Canada." Ottawa: Institute on Governance Aboriginal Policy Research Series. http://www.iog.ca/publications/2009_trafficking_of_aboriginal_women.pdf.

Silion v. Canada. 1999. 173 FTR 302 (TD).

Simpson, Audra. 2010. "Under the Sign of Sovereignty: Certainty, Ambivalence and Law in Native North America and Indigenous Australia." *Wicazo Sa Review* 25 (2): 107–24. http://dx.doi.org/10.1353/wic.2010.0000.

Simpson, Audra. 2014a. *Mohawk Interruptus: Political Life Across the Borders of Settler States.* Durham, NC: Duke. University Press. http://dx.doi.org/10.1215/9780822376781.

Simpson, Audra. 2014b. "Race 2014 Keynote 1: 'The Chief's Two Bodies: Theresa Spence and the Gender of Settler Sovereignty." In *Unsettling Conversations.* New York: Vimeo, LLC. https://vimeo.com/110948627.

Smith, Andrea. 2005. *Conquest: Sexual Violence and American Indian Genocide.* New York: South End Press.

Smith, Andrea. 2014, July 13. "Beyond the Pros and Cons of Trigger Warnings: Collectivizing Healing." Blog entry. https://andrea366.wordpress.com/2014/07/13/beyond-the -pros-and-cons-of-trigger-warnings-collectivizing -healing/.

Smith, Andrea, and J. Ke-haulani Kuanaui, eds. 2008. "American Studies without America: Native Feminisms and the Nation-State." *American Quarterly* 60 (2): 309–15. http://dx.doi.org/10.1353/aq.0.0014.

Smith, Andrea. 2014. "Indigenous Feminists Are Too Sexy for Your Heteropatriarchal Settler Colonialism." *African Journal of Criminology and Justice Studies* 8 (1): 89–103

Smith, Cindy, and Kristiina Kangaspunta. 2012. "Defining Human Trafficking and Its Nuances in a Cultural Context." In *Human Trafficking: Exploring the International Nature, Concerns, and Complexities,* ed. J. Winterdyk, B. Perrin, and P. Reichel, 19–38. Boca Raton, FL: Taylor and Francis.

Soderlund, Gretchen. 2005. "Running from the Rescuers: New U.S. Crusades Against Sex Trafficking and the Rhetoric of Abolition." *NSAW Journal* 17 (3): 64–87.

Spivak, Gayatri. 1988. "Can the Subaltern Speak?" In *Marxism and the Interpretation of Culture,* ed. C. Nelson and L. Grossberg, 271–313. Urbana: University of Illinois Press. http://dx.doi.org/10.1007/978-1-349-19059 -1_20.

Stalker, Peter. 2000. *Workers Without Frontiers: The Impact of Globalization on International Migration.* Boulder, CO: Lynne Rienner Publishers.

Standing Committee on the Status of Women Canada. 2007. "Turning Outrage into Action to Address Trafficking for the Purpose of Sexual Exploitation in Canada." 39th Parliament, 1st Session. Ottawa: Parliament of Canada. http://cmte.parl.gc.ca/content/hoc/ committee/391/fewo/reports/rp2738918/feworp12/feworp12-e .pdf.

Stark, Heidi Kiiwetinepinesiik. 2016. "Criminal Empire: The Making of the Savage in a Lawless Land." *Theory and Event* 19 (4).

Statistics Canada. 2011. "Focus on Geography Series, 2011 Census." Ottawa: Analytical Products. https://www12.statcan.gc.ca/census -recensement/2011/as-sa/fogs-spg/Facts-cma-eng.cfm?LANG=Eng&GK =CMA&GC=933.

Status of Women Canada. 2013. "Harper Government Takes Action to Combat Human Trafficking in Edmonton." Ottawa: Status of Women Canada. http://news.gc.ca/web/article-en.do?nid=800359.

Statutes of Canada. 2012. "Bill C-310: An Act to Amend the Criminal Code (Trafficking in Persons)." Ottawa: Parliament of Canada. http://parl.gc.ca/ HousePublications/Publication.aspx?Language=E&Mode=1&DocId =5697415&File=14&Col=1.

Stenvoll, Dag. 2002. "From Russia with Love? Newspaper Coverage of Cross-Border Prostitution in Northern Norway, 1990-2000." *European Journal of Women's Studies* 9 (2): 143–62. http://dx.doi.org/10.1177/1350682 002009002807.

Stoler, Ann Laura. 2002. *Carnal Knowledge and Imperial Power: Race and the Intimate in Colonial Rule.* Berkeley: University of California Press.

Strauss, Anselm, and Juliet Corbin. 1998. *Basics of Qualitative Research: Techniques and Procedures for Developing Grounded Theory*, 2nd ed. Thousand Oaks, CA: Sage.

Suchland, Jennifer. 2015. *Economies of Violence: Transnational Feminism, Postsocialism, and the Politics of Sex Trafficking*. Durham, NC: Duke University Press. http://dx.doi.org/10.1215/9780822375289.

SWAN Vancouver Society. 2015. "Im/migrant Sex Workers, Myths and Misconceptions: Realities of the Anti-Trafficked." Vancouver: Supporting Women's Alternatives Network. http://swanvancouver.ca/wp-content/uploads/2014/01/Realities-of-the-Anti-Trafficked.pdf.

Sweet, Victoria. 2014. "Rising Waters, Rising Threats: The Human Trafficking of Indigenous Women in the Circumpolar Region of the United States and Canada." MSU Legal Studies Research Paper, No. 12-01. https://papers.ssrn.com/sol3/papers.cfm?abstract_id=2399074.

Swift, Karen. 1995. *Manufacturing "Bad Mothers": A Critical Perspective on Child Neglect*. Toronto: University of Toronto Press.

Thobani, Sunera. 2007. *Exalted Subjects: Studies in the Making of Race and Nation in Canada*. Toronto: University of Toronto Press.

Thorbek, Susanne, and Bandana Pattanaik, eds. 2002. *Transnational Prostitution: Changing Patterns in a Global Context*. New York: Zed Books.

Tilly, Charles. 2003. "Political Identities in Changing Polities." *Social Research* 70 (2): 605–20.

Timoshkina, Natalia, and Lynn McDonald. 2011. "Sex Trafficking of Women to Canada: Results from a Qualitative Metasynthesis of Empirical Research." Montréal: Canadian Counsel for Refugees. http://ccrweb.ca/en/sex-trafficking-women-canada-results-qualitative-metasynthesis-empirical-research.

Tocher, Annemarie. 2012. "Domestic Trafficking in Aboriginal Persons: The Legacy of Colonialism and Sexual Exploitation." Ottawa: First People's Group. http://www.firstpeoplesgroup.com/mnsiurban/PDF/reports/Tocher_A-Legacy_of_Colonization_and_Sexual_Exploitation_(2012).pdf.

Totten, M. 2009a. "Preventing Aboriginal Youth Gang Involvement in Canada: A Gendered Approach." Paper prepared for the Aboriginal Policy Research Conference. Ottawa: Elections Canada, March 2009. http://www.turtleisland.org/resources/gangsnwac09.pdf.

Totten M. 2009b. "Aboriginal Youth and Violent Gang Involvement in Canada: Quality Prevention Strategies." *IPC Review* 3: 135–56. www.tottenandassociates.ca/wp-content/uploads/2015/03/Totten-2009-Aboriginal-Youth-and-Violent-Gang-Involvement.pdf.

Trompetter, Sherilyn. 2007. "Trafficking of Women and Girls to Canada."
    Environmental Scan. Edmonton: Changing Together: A Centre for
    Immigrant Women.
Tuck, Eve, and Wayne Yang. 2012. "Decolonization is not a metaphor."
    Decolonization 1(1): 1–40. https://nycstandswithstandingrock.files.
    wordpress.com/2016/10/tuck-yang-2012.pdf
Tucker, Bruce, and Priscilla Walton. 2012. *American Culture Transformed: Dialing
    9/11.* Basingstoke: Palgrave Macmillan. http://dx.doi.org/10.1057/
    9781137002341.
United Nations High Commissioner for Refugees (UNHCR). 2010. "Conference
    Puts Focus on Human Trafficking, Fastest Growing Criminal Industry."
    Geneva: UNHCR. http://www.unhcr.org/4cb315c96.html.
United Nations Office on Drug and Crime (UNODC). 2000. "Protocol to
    Prevent, Suppress and Punish Trafficking in Persons, Especially Women and
    Children." Geneva: UNODC. http://www.unodc.org/unodc/en/treaties/
    CTOC/index.html#Fulltext.
United Nations Office on Drug and Crime (UNODC). 2008. "The Vienna
    Forum Report: A Way Forward to Combat Human Trafficking."
    New York: United Nations. http://www.un.org/ga/president/62/
    ThematicDebates/humantrafficking/ebook.pdf.
United Nations Office on Drug and Crime (UNODC). 2009. "UNODC Global
    Report on Trafficking in Persons." Geneva: UNODC. www.unodc.org/
    documents/Global_Report_on_TIP.pdf.
US State Department. 2002. *Trafficking in Persons Report 2002.* Washington, DC:
    US State Department. http://www.state.gov/j/tip/rls/tiprpt/2002/.
US State Department. 2004. *Trafficking in Persons Report 2004.* Washington, DC:
    US State Department. http://www.state.gov/j/tip/rls/tiprpt/2004/.
US State Department. 2008. *Trafficking in Persons Report 2008.* Washington, DC:
    US State Department. http://www.state.gov/j/tip/rls/tiprpt/2008/.
Valverde, Mariana. 2008. *The Age of Light, Soap, and Water: Moral Reform in
    English Canada.* Toronto: University of Toronto Press.
Vancouver Sun. 2009, October 20. "10 Years After: B.C.'s Chinese Boat Migrants."
    Vancouver: Postmedia Network. http://www.pressreader.com/canada/
    vancouver-sun/20091020/281616711431811.
Vancouver Sun. 2012, June 6. "Pickton Inquiry Ends As It Began, Wrapped
    In Controversy." Vancouver: Postmedia Network. http://www
    .vancouversun.com/mobile/news/vancouver/RCMP+Pickton+serial
    +killer+allowed+file+dormant+months/6741346/story.html.
Van der Meulen, Emily, Elya Durisin, and Victoria Love. 2013. *Selling Sex.*
    Vancouver: UBC Press.

Vanwesenbeeck, Ine. 1994. *Prostitutes' Well-Being and Risk*. Amsterdam, Netherlands: VU Uitgeverij.

Vanwesenbeeck, Ine. 2001. "Another Decade of Social Scientific Work on Sex Work: A Review of Research 1990-2000." *Annual Review of Sex Research* 12: 242–89.

Victim Impact Statement. 2009. "My Name Is TamasMiko." In *Human Trafficking: Victim Impact Statements*, ed. The Hamilton Spectator. San Francisco: Scribd. com. http://www.scribd.com/doc/84688173/Human-Trafficking-Victim -impact-statements.

Vosko, Leah F. 2010. *Managing the Margins*. Oxford: Oxford University Press.

Wade, Robert H. 2004. "Is Globalization Reducing Poverty and Inequality?" *World Development* 32 (4): 567–89. http://dx.doi.org/10.1016/j.worlddev .2003.10.007.

Waltman, Max. 2011. "Sweden's Prohibition of Purchase of Sex: The Law's Reasons, Impact, and Potential." *Women's Studies International Forum* 34 (5): 449–74. http://dx.doi.org/10.1016/j.wsif.2011.06.004.

Ward. 2002. "The Komagata Maru Incident." In *White Canada Forever: Popular Attitudes and Public Policy Toward Orientals in British Columbia*, 3rd ed., ed. W. P. Ward, 79–97. Montreal: McGill-Queens's University Press.

Weinberg, Martin S., Frances M. Shaver, and Colin J. Williams. 1999. "Gendered Sex Work in the San Francisco Tenderloin." *Archives of Sexual Behavior* 28 (6): 503–21. http://dx.doi.org/10.1023/A:1018765132704.

Weitzer, Ronald. 2005. "New Directions in Research on Prostitution." *Crime, Law, and Social Change* 43 (4-5): 211–35. http://dx.doi.org/10.1007/s10611 -005-1735-6.

Weitzer, Ronald. 2007. "The Social Construction of Sex Trafficking: Ideology and Institutionalization of a Moral Crusade." *Politics & Society* 35 (3): 447–75. http://dx.doi.org/10.1177/0032329207304319.

Weitzer, Ronald. 2009. "Sociology of Sex Work." *Annual Review of Sociology* 35 (1): 213–34. http://dx.doi.org/10.1146/annurev-soc-070308-120025.

Weitzer, Ronald. 2010. "The Movement to Criminalize Sex Work in the United States." *Journal of Law and Society. Special Issue* 37 (1): 61–84. http://dx.doi .org/10.1111/j.1467-6478.2010.00495.x.

Weitzer, Ronald. 2012. *Legalizing Prostitution: From Illicit Vice to Lawful Business*. New York: New York University Press.

West Coast Legal Education Action Fund (LEAF). 2009. "Position Paper on Human Trafficking for Sexual Exploitation." Vancouver: LEAF. http:// www.westcoastleaf.org/wp-content/uploads/2014/10/2009-POSITION-STATEMENT-Human-Trafficking-in-Canada.pdf.

Wherry, Aaron. 2009, October 1. "What He Was Talking About When He Was Talking About Colonialism." *Maclean's*. http://www.macleans.ca/politics/ottawa/what-he-was-talking-about-when-he-talked-about-colonialism/.

Williams, Suzanne, and Rachel Masika. 2002. "Editorial." *Gender and Development* 10 (1): 2–9. http://dx.doi.org/10.1080/13552070215894.

Wolfe, Patrick. 1999. *Settler Colonialism and the Transformation of Anthropology: The Politics and Poetics of an Ethnographic Event*. London: Cassell.

Young, Robert. 2001. *Postcolonialism: A Historical Introduction*. Hoboken, NJ: Blackwell.

Yuval-Davis, Nira. 1994. "Women, Ethnicity and Empowerment." *Feminism Psychology* 4 (1): 179–207.

Index